Fly Patterns of British Columbia

Dedicated to Charles, my son and friend

Fly Patterns of British Columbia

Arthur James Lingren

Frank Amato
PUBLICATIONS, INC.

Acknowledgments

In writing a work of this nature, I am indebted to many who gave a helping hand. The thoroughness of this book wouldn't have been possible without their assistance.

Valerie Haig-Brown for allowing me to use written material from her father's records.

Gordon Money for allowing me to use material from his grandfather's game books.

George Brandak, curator of Special Collections at the University of British Columbia, and his staff for their assistance.

Renato Muccillo for permitting the reproduction of his Jock Scott painting.

Bob Taylor for letting me use hooks from his low-water hook collection; supplying some fly-tying material for dressing samples; lending me his Brayshaw originals, gut eyed salmon flies, and Nation's Grey Nymph for photographing; supplying Woolly Worm and Golden Spey samples; reviewing my material and providing comments.

Harry Lemire, Joe Saysell, Denny Boulton, Bob Taylor, Jerry Wintle, Ron Grantham, Dave Winters, Van Egan, Paul Dorrian Smith, Charlie Stroulger, Brian Chan, Jack Shaw, Jim Stewart, Peter Caverhill, Steve Raymond, Barry Thornton, Tom Murray, George C. Reifel, Glen Butler, Rob Brown, Rex Schofield, Alf Davy, and Martin Tolley for providing flies and/or information.

Van and Maxine Egan for providing me with interesting stories and to Van for his other contributions.

Jim Kilburn for sending me his creations and details of their development and answering specific questions about other patterns.

Jay Rowland for allowing me to photograph his Bill Nation Grey Nymph.

Ted Pengelley for allowing me to use and photograph his General Noel Money fishing flies and equipment.

Christopher Brayshaw for allowing me to use material from his father's fishing records.

Stacey Weeks for searching around England and finding me size 5/0 to 10 Limerick hooks so I could dress samples on hooks appropriate to the era.

Ron Schiefke for reviewing the text and providing comments.

Table of Contents

Fly Patterns of British Columbia

Horn

Wing

Cheek

Topping

Tail

Butt

Head

Tag

Rib

Body   Veil   Hackle   Throat

There is an evolutionary process that turns some sport fishers from mere fish catchers to anglers. It is a force from outside that triggers a force deep within; one that helps the individual understand the connections between recreation and creation. It is the phenomenon that brings the fisher to the realization that his hobby is a sport, a craft and, since it is closely bound up with the natural world and its infinite complexities, an art and a science.

Men who have had this epiphany soon make the distinction between quality and quantity. They shed the multiplying reels and fluorescent baits and the competitive aspects of fishing in favour of self discipline of angling with the fly.

Twenty years ago Art Lingren chose the Spartan regime of fly fishing and simultaneously embarked on a thorough study of those who made the pilgrimage before. During that time he has become not only the undisputed historian of angling in British Columbia, but also one of the sport's leading practitioners, and one of its finest fly dressers.

Art was born and raised in Vancouver when the city was relatively small and extraordinarily beautiful; a time, half a century ago, when the Capilano and Seymour were full of wild salmon, when the Coquitlam still had spawning gravel, when Tommy Brayshaw and Bill Cunliffe hooked wild summer steelhead in the Coquihalla River, an age when the powerful summer steelhead of the Thompson River were little more than rumour.

With his wife Beverley and son Charles, Art still makes his home in Vancouver, in the heart of the Lower Mainland. For Art, water is always close at hand. As an administrator for the Greater Vancouver Regional District, Art's vocation helps ensure that the Lower Mainland is properly watered and the wastewater treated, while his avocation has taken him from the streams near his home to those of the Queen Charlotte Islands, the Skeena Valley, as well as to the fabled Dean and Thompson rivers.

The angling roots in the Lingren clan can be traced back to Pinantan where Art's grandfather and uncles homesteaded and where his grandfather ran the Pinantan fishing lodge from 1933 to 1939, while his uncle and father made forays to Hyas and Paul lakes. His interest in angling literature was kindled by Art's mother when she introduced her son to the writings of Roderick Haig-Brown. Since then Art has developed a deep interest and affection for our B. C. angling traditions, which, thankfully, has resulted in the compilation of this keenly researched volume.

It has been said that it is important to understand where you come from in order to see where you are, and to find out where you are going. Art Lingren has filled a much needed gap in this province's history and in the history of angling in general. Just as importantly, he has rescued the achievements and artistry of some notable anglers from obscurity. Admiring the feathered sculptures of Roderick Haig-Brown, Tom Brayshaw, Bill Nation, Jim Kilburn, Denny Boulton, and many other pioneers dating back to John Keast Lord in 1866, and reading interesting anecdotes gleaned from long-neglected letters and fishing diaries, will deepen our appreciation of the contribution made by these men to the history of our sport.

Tapping such sources as General Noel Money's gamebook, Art Lingren provides us with a wealth of entertaining and useful information. Striking patterns like Money's Black, Orange and Jungle Cock and Haig-Brown's Silver Lady will us to our vices to make replicas. With them, Art's clear and meticulous instructions on their use, our fishing will be even more enjoyable and profitable than it is already.

R. H. (Bob) Taylor
Vancouver, B.C.
February 1996

Foreword

In the early days of the colonies of Vancouver Island and British Columbia, many of the British who came to administer the affairs of the colonial governments were fly fishers and, of course, they brought with them sea-trout, trout and salmon flies of British origin. They found the steelhead, cutthroat and rainbows of stream and lake, and coho salmon in the sea fancied their British creations and those flies became staple patterns in the new land. Moreover, as time passed and after the two colonies became one and part of the new Dominion of Canada, many of the colonial administrators left to serve in other spots of the British Empire, scattered throughout the world. However, not all left and those that stayed were joined by more British and other European immigrants who fly fished such as A. Bryan Williams, General Noel Money, William Nation, Thomas Brayshaw, Roderick Haig-Brown and others. It was after those anglers came, saw, fished and realized that although the British favourites worked more suitable patterns depicting local fauna may prove better. In addition, as places like Victoria, Vancouver and Kelowna became more populated and British Columbia's fly fishing became better known and accessible, there was more demand for sporting equipment and that spawned businesses such as Harkley & Haywood in Vancouver, Roger Monteith and Lenfesty & Wilson both of Victoria and J.B. Spurrier of Kelowna to supply the local market with British Columbia-originated patterns. It was during this era—the 1920s, '30s, and '40s—that we saw great strides in fly pattern development with local variations of British favourites and British Columbia-developed flies supplying the market.

The patterns listed in this book are those that detail the development of fly patterns from the first, dressed by John Keast Lord in 1863 after being inspired on the banks of the Moyee River in eastern British Columbia by the trout in that river, to some of the more recent ones developed in the 1970s and '80s. In choosing patterns for inclusion in this work, the pattern must meet some or all of the following criteria:

- **Must be documented in writing**
- **Display some original thought process**
- **Be of some historical importance in British Columbia fly development**
- **Sold commercially or for contemporary patterns, have about 10 years use**
- **Fit the interior trout, coastal trout, steelhead and salmon categories**

The majority of the patterns shown in the book I dressed. However, for many of the more recent inventions, I managed to get originals dressed by the inventor. For the patterns I dressed I tried to match the hook style, materials and follow the dressing as best as I could. For some early patterns, however, where there was no pattern listing, I deduced the pattern make-up from flies shown in colour plates in books such as A. Bryan Williams' *Rod & Creel in British Columbia* (1919), and *Fish and Game in British Columbia* (1935), Roderick Haig-Brown's *The Western Angler* (1939), and W. F. Pochin's *Angling and Hunting in British Columbia* (1946). With some of the early General Money patterns, I followed the tying style using tattered and worn samples dressed by the General which are part of my fly fishing collection.

In the golden years of fly fishing in the province, there were few fishers with many fish, some very large, that were relatively easy to catch and flies dressed on number 6 hooks or larger seemed to be the norm. Many of the early patterns, following their British roots, were over-dressed on too large a hook, and although I did try to maintain dressing style and hook size, I did not over-dress the samples shown in this book. I recommend that fly tiers who intend to dress and sample the patterns, examine and look seriously at reducing hook size to suit local conditions and actual fauna sizes. For example, the original Doc Spratley was dressed on a number 8 hook, however, it is now dressed on hooks as small as 12 and up to 2 for trout fishing. For steelhead fishing, I have dressed it on hooks as large as 5/0.

In dressing the patterns, I followed the convention used in British Atlantic salmon and trout books for wet and dry fly construction. The dry fly is relatively simple to describe as most consist of a tail, body, rib, wing, and hackle while wet flies can be much more complex. The picture on page 6 of a Jock Scott dressed by the author shows all the parts of a complex wet fly. This Jock Scott painting is the work of Renato Muccillo, a Vancouver artist working as a tackle salesclerk at Ruddick's fly shop. With few exceptions, the pattern listings for wet flies in this book use those headings shown in the Jock Scott.

When dressing samples I often used substitutes for some hard-to-obtain or now-illegal materials. However, substituting a small red-orange feather for the specified Indian crow tail in Haig-Brown's Silver Brown pattern makes the fly no less effective. Most fly tiers now use mylar instead of tinsel and, although I say tinsel for all patterns that have a flat, silver body, all Lingren-dressed samples use mylar. It doesn't tarnish or rust, although it is not as tough as tinsel. For most pattern listings, I do not recommend substitutes; I have left that to the fly tier to replace the swan with goose or turkey, silk floss with rayon, seal's and polar bear's fur with synthetics and tinsel with mylar.

It is impossible to list the many variations of specific patterns that came and went over many years and I have tried to determine and list the original dressings in this book. Nevertheless, I have attempted to include some variations and more recently developed patterns with their dressings in supplementary pictures' captions, especially for some of the more contemporary patterns, if I thought they may be useful to fly fishers. Furthermore, some of the feather-winged patterns such as Cowichan Coachman, Brougham's Clowholm and Nicomekl, Lioness and many others in all categories fell into disuse, yet in their day were very effective patterns. Substituting a hairwing of the same colour as the feather-wing, I am sure, would make some of them effective fish-catchers and put them back into the boxes of fly fishers.

The patterns in this book are divided into four sections titled: Interior Trout, Steelhead, Coastal Trout, and Saltwater Salmon. Based on who was the originator, intended use, and location, I segregated the flies into categories. For example, the Alevin (Yolk Sac or Egg 'n' I), the first pattern listed in this book, was developed by Tom Brayshaw; its intended use was a wet fly for rainbow trout and the location was the Adams and Little rivers. Because a fly is in the "Interior Trout" section however does not mean that it shouldn't be used elsewhere in the province and for fish other than rainbows. By way of illustration, the Alevin (Egg 'n' I), although developed in the Interior, is a favoured coastal cutthroat pattern. Many other patterns such as Williams' Grey-Bodied Sedge, Tom Thumb, Doc Spratley, and Carey Special were developed for Interior lakes and streams but have found province-wide use for other fish. The Bucktail which I located in the "Saltwater Salmon" section has seen wide use for rainbows in the Interior, steelhead and cutthroat since its introduction to British Columbia.

Researching past happenings on such a nebulous subject has its difficulties and I have solicited the help of others to fill in many gaps. For some of the information I may not have been able to locate the best sources and some gaps still remain. For instance, in the pattern listings there are a few under the Originator heading that state Unknown. I would like to fill the gaps and ask readers to drop me a line through my publisher if they have documented evidence of those Unknown fly originators or other information.

British Columbia's fly fishers have a rich fly fishing heritage, developed over 1 1/4 centuries, and the flies produced over that time attest to the devotion that British Columbian fly fishers have for their sport and that heritage. If a fly fisher were of the mind to do so, he or she need not go outside the realm of the patterns listed in this book to satisfy all their fly-fishing needs.

Alevin or Yolk Sac

Anderson's Stone Nymph

Big Bertha

*Big Ugly

Black Leech

Black O'Lindsay

Blood Leech

*Bloodworm

*Bottom Walker

Bounder

Brayshaw's Fancy

*Butler's Bug

Carey's Parmachene Bucktail

Carey Special

*Caverhill Nymph

Dexheimer Sedge

Doc Spratley

Edwards' Sedge

*Dressed by the originator

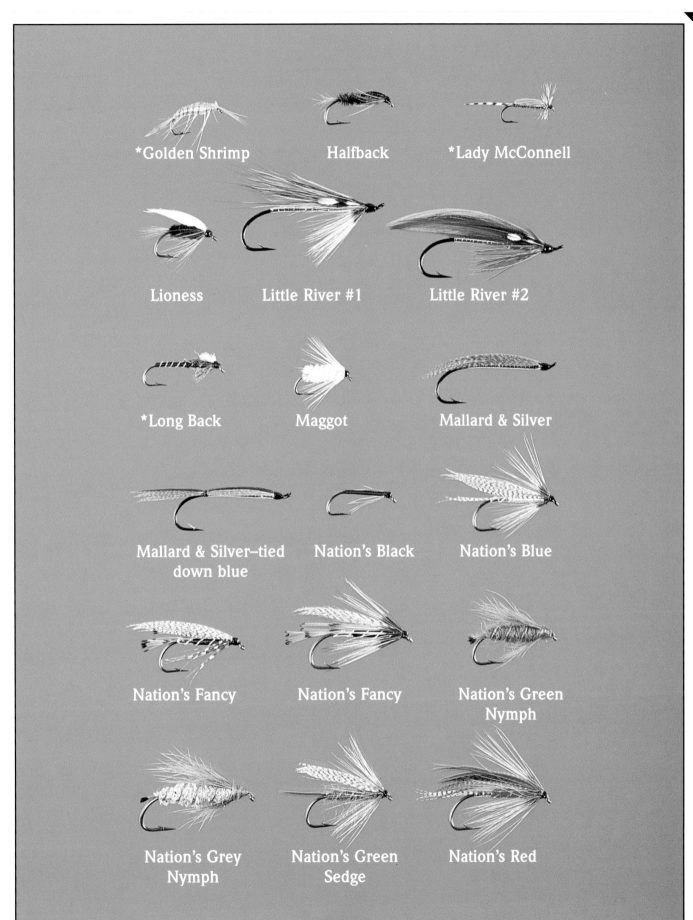

*Golden Shrimp   Halfback   *Lady McConnell

Lioness   Little River #1   Little River #2

*Long Back   Maggot   Mallard & Silver

Mallard & Silver–tied down blue   Nation's Black   Nation's Blue

Nation's Fancy   Nation's Fancy   Nation's Green Nymph

Nation's Grey Nymph   Nation's Green Sedge   Nation's Red

Nation's Silver-tip

Nation's Silver-tip Sedge

Nation's Special

Olive Sedge

Pazooka

*PKCK

*Red Butt Chironomid

Red-shirted Trapper

Red-shouldered Dragonfly Nymph

Stump Lake Damsel

Tom Thumb

Travelling Sedge

*Tunkwanamid

*Vincent's Sedge

*Water Boatman

Werner Shrimp

Williams' Green-bodied Sedge

Williams' Grey-bodied Sedge

After construction of the Canadian Pacific Railway in 1886, travel into British Columbia's Interior became much easier and anglers took the opportunity to explore the lakes and streams in proximity to the rail line. H. W. Seton-Karr was one of the first to record the sport to be obtained in this almost uninhabited land. During an 1890 six-month hunting and fishing expedition to Alaska and British Columbia, he sampled fishing in the interior in places such as the "almost unknown waters of the upper Thompson River," the Adams River, the Coquihalla River and Seton Creek at Lillooet.

In *Bear-Hunting in the White Mountains or Alaska and British Columbia Revisited* (1891), about the fly fishing he encountered at Spences Bridge, Seton-Karr says those railway survey workers fishing with natural fly during every evening of their stay never managed to catch more than one fish apiece. During the only evening he was there Seton-Karr with fly "took eleven, the largest about a pound in weight . . ." (p. 114).

About the Spences Bridge fishing, Seton-Karr concluded:

The result of my visit to Spence's Bridge was to show that fair bags of trout can be caught with fine tackle and small fly . . . . (p. 118)

Next he travelled to and set up a base camp at Shuswap, where he hired a native guide and on July 1st, 1890, trekked up the Adams River to the lake. Being the first non-native fisher and first fly fisher to wet a fly on these waters, with one hour left before darkness set in, he says:

On landing I immediately set to work, with a fine cast and moderate-sized brown flies, and enjoyed the best sport I have met with since I fished the Shellefteo River in North Sweden, the Vuoksa in Finland, or the Sardinian Fluemendosa . . . or other of the best pleasure-grounds of the enthusiastic angler. (p. 126)

Specifically about the quantity and size of fish in the short time he had to fish, he writes:

In half an hour we returned to camp in the canoe with the total of eleven trout and one white fish; the largest trout weighed three and a quarter pounds . . . , while the aggregate weight of the twelve fish was twenty-one and a quarter pounds, being an average weight of a little under two pounds each. (p. 127)

Seton-Karr spent one more day fishing the outlet of Adams Lake, then returned to Vancouver and in September journeyed to Lillooet. As he says in his book, he "enjoyed capital trout fishing" in Seton Creek with trout up to three pounds "taking the fly freely" (p. 154).

A. S. Munro, an associate of Dr. T. W. Lambert, wrote an article published in the *Canadian Medical Journal* and reported a catch of 1,700 trout in four days from Lac Le Jeune in 1897. Lambert wrote about Lac Le Jeune 10 years later in *Fishing in British Columbia* and says that the "true bait for Fish Lake [Lac Le Jeune] is the fly, and, contrary to the usual case, the white man with a fly and modern tackle can make catches which far surpass any that the Indian ever made" (p. 49). He recorded a catch of 1,500 in three days.

Reports of good fly fishing such as those reported by Seton-Karr and Lambert spawned interest in the Interior of the province's angling opportunities. However, some time was to pass before British Columbians produced local fly patterns for interior trout fishing.

A. Bryan Williams left Britain and came to British Columbia in 1888, where he became the Provincial Game Warden in 1905 and held the post for 13 years when he was forced by the "rigid economy" to retire.

He came out of retirement in 1929 to serve as Provincial Game Commissioner until his final retirement in 1934. An avid hunter and fisherman, he travelled and fished every part of British Columbia and it was during those treks into the interior that he noticed the hatches of sedges and the trout's relish for them. From Williams' observations British Columbia's first Interior dry flies were born. Years later in a 26 April 1938 letter to Roderick Haig-Brown about the development of the sedge dry flies, he says:

I have had three different sedges tied, grey, green and yellow bodied. The first two I brought from the Kamloops District. The latter from Vancouver Island.

It is a good many years since I discovered that there were hatches of sedges in the interior and that when a hatch was on trout would hardly look at a wet fly. So I caught some of them, brought them to town and got Harkley & Haywood to make some for me. After several trials they produced a very good imitation.

Haig-Brown in a following letter gives credit by recognizing that Williams "started the sedge fishing . . . the most important dry fly fisherman's insect in B.C." Later a fourth dry fly, Williams' Dark-bodied Sedge, was added to his accomplishments. Furthermore, Williams wrote three hunting and fishing books and I refer to the two—*Rod & Creel in British Columbia* and *Fish and Game in British Columbia*—frequently in this book. However, an excellent example of the quality of the fly fishing that Williams experienced during his expeditions into the interior is described in *Game Trails in British Columbia* (1925). In Chapter XXVIII "Sport with the Rod," he says:

Last summer I fished a lake that had only been stocked a few years. It was probably at its prime as far as size was concerned. The average number of fish per day for ten days' fishing was only twelve, but they averaged over 4 pounds per fish. The heaviest fish taken were of the following weights, 12 1/4, 10 1/2, 9 3/4, and 9 1/2 pounds. (p. 353)

This sounds like the fishing anglers experienced after Knouff Lake was stocked and opened to fishing in 1920. Tommy Brayshaw, who fished Knouff and developed a number of dry sedge patterns for that fishing besides the patterns he developed for Little River, claims that for the five years, 1928 to 1933, that he fished Knouff the fish averaged 5 pounds 2 ounces. In 1933 due to overstocking, the quality fishing was ruined when the size dropped to less than a pound and one half. Brayshaw never returned to Knouff.

British Columbia's fly development took a leap forward when Bill Nation produced his wet-fly patterns. Nation was born in Bristol, England in 1881 and died at Kamloops in 1940. At what age he immigrated I don't know; he apparently fished out of Little River before he headquartered at Echo Lodge, Paul Lake in 1927. On his letterhead Nation says that he guides on "Paul, Knouff, Le Jeune, Hyas Long, Dee, Jewel, Pillar, Hi Hiume, Big Bar, Canim, Mahood, Murtle, and the two Beaver lakes; the Thompson, Adams and Little rivers, with a guarantee of at least 100 trout a week." Besides fishing British Columbian waters, he guided in the "Taupo and Rotorua districts in New Zealand." Also on his letterhead he claims that he is the "originator of the Nation's Special and Silver tip trout flies, the new series of nymphs of the dragonflies and sedges and special flies for large rainbow and steelhead trout, including six original patterns tied personally, $2.00 a dozen."

For years Nation was considered to be the demigod of Interior trout fishing. My grandfather ran the fishing camp at Pinantan Lake for six years from 1933 to 1939 and my uncle Andrew, a teenager during those days, recalls Nation and guests coming and fishing Pinantan numerous times.

Nation was a good observer of the natural world and produced British Columbia's first chironomid and dragonfly nymph imitations besides many more "fancy" flies. During Nation's time there was considerable debate about fish's ability to distinguish colour. Nation thought that they were colour blind and could only see colour as shades of white, black and grey and he put his patterns together with that thought in mind, being very particular about shades of colours and the resulting effects under differing light conditions.

Furthermore, he was very particular about how to fish his wet-fly patterns to get best results. In one of his late 1930s letters to Haig-Brown, he recommended four ways to fish a wet fly; however, he didn't elaborate. From reading his letters and his descriptions of fishing his flies though, they are: 1) trolled with no action, 2) cast and strip while trolling, 3) cast, sunk and slow retrieve while stationary, 4) greased-line, slow or fast retrieve while stationary.

In total, there are about one dozen flies in this book credited to Nation.

After Nation passed away and over the next 20 or so years, anglers relied mostly on the staple patterns, but every now and then some angler would produce a pattern that worked well and was added to the list of locally recommended patterns. Nevertheless, the 1940s, during and after the war and into the late 1950s, were not the years of the fly fisher. The 1960s, '70s and '80s were, however. These years introduced the age of awareness in British Columbia fly development, when anglers looked more closely at the insects fish ate and tried to produce better imitations. This era realized anglers such as Jack Shaw, John Dexheimer, Jim Kilburn, Tom Murray, and Jack Vincent. Those fly tiers laid the foundations for the next generation of fly inventors such as Glenn Butler, Brian Chan, Alf Davy, Wayne Yoshida, Brian Smith and many others who through them the fly-tying heritage of the Interior will continue to expand.

Two Nation-dressed Grey Nymphs
Background letter by Nation to Rod Haig-Brown.

Alevin, Yolk Sac or Egg 'n' I

HOOK: Number 6 or 8 low-water salmon
BODY: Flat, silver tinsel
THROAT: Indian crow feather
WING: Slender strips of light mallard flank feather or white polar bear fur
ORIGINATOR: Tom Brayshaw
INTENDED USE: Wet fly for rainbow trout
LOCATION: Little and Adams rivers

I then got one of 2 pounds 11 ounces followed at intervals by two more of 2 pounds 15 ounces & 2 pounds 1 ounce all on the same fly: grey mallard wing, silver body & badger hackle. In the end I struck a fish & broke, losing my best fly. I had several other rises & played a fish quite a time, later losing it. . . .

The fish we caught were full of nymphs. . . also several alevins, some still showing the sac.

So it was that Brayshaw recorded in his angling diary entry on April 12, 1939, that the Adams River's fry were still showing the yolk sac. The next day he recorded his success with his newly developed pattern:

Bright day with breeze from east. Started on left side of mouth at 9 a.m. I soon was into one, a lovely thick fish which I lost just at the edge of the net. We were very cold & I only got one of 2 1/4 pounds before lunch. After lunch on the right side I got four more [2 pounds 5 ounces, 6 pounds, 2 pounds 15 ounces, 2 pounds 12 ounces] and lost one—the first one was on a size 8 and the others all on size 6 grey mallard & silver with an Indian Crow feather tied in to represent the yolk sac of the alevin.

On the following day he referred to this pattern as the Yolk Sac. But years later on a 1943 day when some of the British Columbian fishing legends of the day—Francis Whitehouse, A. Bryan Williams and Brayshaw—were fishing the Adams River, Brayshaw landed five rainbows totaling 17 pounds 15 ounces on a fly he called "Alevin." The dressing for the Alevin is identical to the Yolk Sac but with the substitution of a white polar bear hair wing for the light mallard of the Yolk Sac. Brayshaw often varied his winging material on his silver-bodied creations.

The fragile and now impossible-to-obtain Indian crow throat feather was later replaced with a tuft of sockeye salmon-red wool. This change made the fly much more durable and, with a name change from the Yolk Sac alias Alevin, the Egg 'n' I was born.

Jim Fisher of Vernon, in a 10 January 1995 letter about the Egg 'n' I, says that for the March fishing on the Adams, "the Egg 'n' I is a tough fly to beat." Jim prefers to dress his flies "with an egg sac of hot orange polypropylyne."

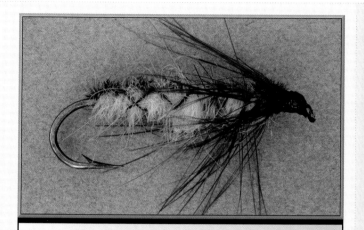

Anderson's Stone Nymph

HOOK: Number 6, 3 extra long
THREAD: Black 00 nylon or monocord
BODY: Full, "dirty" yellow-green wool
BACK: Peacock herl
RIB: Black thread
HACKLE: Dark olive over front one third of body
ORIGINATOR: Earl Anderson
INTENDED USE: Wet fly for rainbow trout
LOCATION: Babine River

Big Bertha

HOOK: Number 2 **TAG:** Flat, silver tinsel
TAIL: Golden pheasant crest feather
BUTT: Red wool **BODY:** Flat, silver or gold tinsel
RIB: Oval, silver tinsel **THROAT:** Light blue cock neck
feather followed with guinea fowl
WING: Narrow strips of red-orange goose enclosed
by light or bronze mallard flank feather
SIDES: Jungle cock **ORIGINATOR:** Roddy Howell
INTENDED USE: Wet fly for rainbow trout
LOCATION: Little River

Fly-fishing expert, professional fly-tier and instructor, fly-casting teacher, sporting goods salesman, and rod and reel repairman Earl Anderson spent most of his long life involved with fishing. The Anderson Stone Nymph is one of his creations.

In 1960, Ces Brown, one of the then owners of Babine-Norlakes Lodge, contacted Anderson in Vancouver and asked him to dress a stone nymph and stone dry fly for Babine River rainbows. From that request the Anderson Stone Nymph was born and it has proved to be a very successful pattern, not only for Babine rainbows, but also for rainbows, steelhead and cutthroat in other waters throughout the province.

Shortly after Earl developed the Anderson Stone Nymph, he recalls a trip into some lakes east of Burns Lake where he and his nephew tested the pattern and caught fish on just about every cast. Nearing the end of another trip to Hefley Lake, Frankie and he wanted to take some fish home. In 3 1/2 hours fishing they hand picked 24 trout, the largest was four pounds, and all were taken on a light green Anderson Stone Nymph.

When Dragon Lake was rehabilitated in the late 1960s, the Anderson Stone Nymph was the pattern to use for its huge rainbows. That event was well documented by an article titled "Anderson's Stone Nymph" by Jim Kilburn in the May, 1971 issue of *Western Fish & Game*. Magazine owner, Jack Grundle, discovered the nymph's attractiveness to those stillwater trout. Kilburn relates how:

He calmly knotted on a nymph and, as only Jack can, hurled it with great finesse in the general direction of the water.
Scant minutes later, he was releasing his third large rainbow of the afternoon.

Like many successful patterns, the Anderson Stone Nymph does not represent a specific species of insect. Earl claims it's a general impressionistic pattern and could represent many aquatic insects. Referred to by many fly-tiers fishers as an untidy creature, Anderson's Stone Nymph's success as a general pattern is reinforced by the fact that this untidy-looking fly has proven itself on many waters for various species of salmonids

On 11 June 1933, Tommy Brayshaw was fishing Little River and noted in his diary that, "Roddy Howell . . . lost one after a long time . . . he was using what he called a 'Big Bertha'—just a silver doctor with jungle cock in wings . . . ." A couple of years later in 1935, A. Bryan Williams' book, *Fish and Game in British Columbia*, was published and he reiterated Brayshaw's comments about the similarity to the Silver Doctor and said that the Big Bertha "can be tied with either a silver or gold body" and was a "very good fly for Steelheads and large *Kamloops* trout." (p. 47) (In 1935 the definition of a steelhead in the fishing regulations was a trout greater than five pounds in weight. It didn't matter whether the larger-than-five-pound fish was caught in coastal or interior rivers or lakes.)

The Silver Doctor Atlantic salmon pattern, with over 13 feathers in its wing alone, is a complex fly to dress and taxed the skills of most local fly dressers of the day. However, there is little doubt that the Big Bertha owes its origin to the Silver Doctor. Nevertheless, it was simplified enough and, with the addition of a different outer throat material, choice of body tinsel, and jungle cock cheeks, I have listed it as a new pattern.

In the 1939 edition of *The Western Angler*, Haig-Brown gives an account on an evening that he and his fishing companion, named Marsh, went out with Bill Nation. Haig-Brown recalls that:

Marsh was after something really big to finish of the day, and had put on a tremendous Big Bertha . . . he . . . wanted to see what it would do. Bill worked the boat gently across the stillwater, and big fish rose all around us. Marsh hooked a good fish and killed him. I was listening to Bill and enjoying the stillness of the evening . . . Marsh hooked another good fish and killed him. . . . Bill told me to change to Nation's Special . . . but Bertha hooked and lost three fish while I was losing one on the Special. She hooked yet another and killed it. (Vol. 1 p. 126)

The name Big Bertha disappeared sometime in the 1940s, but a popular coastal trout fly very similar to this bastardized Silver Doctor—simplified even more without the tip, tag, outer guinea fowl throat, and jungle cock cheeks—referred to as the "local" Silver Doctor remains.

Big Ugly

HOOK: Number 6, three-extra-long
GILLS: Fine black chenille
ABDOMINAL TIP: Orange wool
BODY: Woven of light to medium olive wool; medium to dark brown wool; and light tan thread; alternatively, olive wool with a shellback of dark brown wool, ribbed with a contrasting shade of coloured thread
BEARD: Six fibres from a ring-necked pheasant's rump feather
LEGS: Two brown hackle feathers all but 5 mm stripped and clip the remaining fibres to the shape of a small paddle
WING CASES: Two segments from matching mottled turkey or grey goose primaries
ORIGINATOR: Jim Kilburn
INTENDED USE: Wet fly for rainbow trout
LOCATION: Knouff Lake

Developed by Jim Kilburn in the 1960s as a caddis pupa imitation, this creative but complex pattern is quite difficult to tie but a worthy one to have in the fly box if it is fished correctly. Kilburn was not, however, the first British Columbian fly fisher to realize the value of a sedge pupa imitation. The legendary Bill Nation was one of the first to realize that it was worthwhile for fly fishers to have a sedge pupa imitation in their box. In a May 1938 letter about the sedges and sedge nymphs or pupae, Nation writes:

Curious very large sedge hatches in the higher lakes—nymph is green, long scarab shaped, with surprising jet black legs—hatching fly floats broadside to wind with erect wings for many minutes until the nymph case leaves the body, when the wings come down, the fly walks about three feet, then flies for shore. This is our largest sedge, hatches in July, interests the largest fish, female [insect] 50% larger than male, fish #2 slim body green nymph with black hackle.

Although Kilburn relied on another Nation pattern, Nation Green Sedge, as a pupal imitation, it often failed him. Determined to produce a more exact imitation, he collected sample pupae from Paul, Badger, Knouff, and Lac Le Jeune. Shortly after development, Kilburn's field tests, however, resulted in failure and the pattern was sentenced to the reject box. Years later, while fishing off the Knouff's Sunken Islands Kilburn's son, Rick, rediscovered the "big ugly" reject and the secret of its success. It had to be fished dead drift.

Kilburn in an article called "The Way of the Sedge" in the July 1969 issue of *Western Fish and Game* magazine details the development of the Big Ugly and some of its successes. About the fishing he experienced one evening on Le Jeune's Campsite Shoals he writes:

The take was too gentle to feel. I simply saw the line twitch, then twitch again. I raised the rod tip, felt the pulse of a trout, and struck. The ensuing explosion was just the beginning of a fast and furious sixty-minute session. In that hour, an even dozen rainbows came to the dead-drifted Big Ugly.

Indeed, with such catches, a most worthy pattern to call upon when the sedges are hatching and the fish are taking the pupa. However, because of the dressing's complexity, Jim suggests the amateur fly tier use the alternative body dressing.

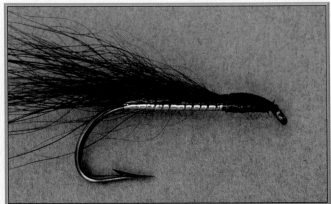

Black Leech

HOOK: Number 6 or 8 **BODY:** Medium, gold tinsel
WING: Black, skunk tail fibres **ORIGINATOR:** Unknown
INTENDED USE: Wet fly for rainbow trout
LOCATION: Peterhope Lake

Leeches, ugh. After my father died in late 1947, I remember my mother sending my younger brother and myself up to Pinantan in the early 1950s for a summer vacation to visit and get to know my grandparents. When we found out that we were going to the lake, we wanted to know if we could go swimming. "Yes," my grandfather replied, "but you will most likely get some leeches on you." "And what are they?" my city-bred brother and I asked. "They're insects that attach to the body and suck your blood," said grandfather, "but they won't hurt you and by sprinkling a little salt on them they come off easily." We didn't swim and leeches still send a chill down my spine when I see them, but fish find them a delectable dish and the fly fisher shouldn't be without a leech pattern when fishing B.C. lakes.

Early Pacific Northwest leech fly patterns were a British Columbian development. However, they were overlooked for a number of years and it wasn't until the later 1950s that anglers started experimenting with leech patterns. Roy Patrick, in the 1958 edition of his *Pacific Northwest Fly Patterns*, in the Canadian fly section, lists this black leech pattern. Patrick says:

The "Black Leech" was first introduced at Peter Hope [sic], B.C. Taken to two other lakes of same elevation and proved very good. Best in August and September. (n.p.)

Many other leech patterns followed this first leech pattern and in Patrick's 1964 edition he lists three and gives Peterhope, Fawn, Glimpse, and Pinantan as places where these patterns were used.

Over ten years ago I developed my own leech pattern. Because I dyed pheasant rump black, used black mohair for the body and dressed it Carey-fashion, I called it the Black Carey. I remember the first day I used the leech pattern. July 1, 1985, I had my eight-year-old son and his friend on Hen Ingram Lake in the Cariboo District. Unskilled fly casters, the boys were content to fish the trolled fly, providing the fish were bit-ing and, with 11 fish hooked and six fish, averaging 15 inches landed, the boys were satisfied. One of the secrets to successful fishing with kids is to try to select the best fishing times in the day and go swimming, hiking or roasting hot dogs on a campfire in the off hours. In looking through my diary for this summer lake fishing trip, many of the trout, with a 17 1/2-incher the tops, that the kids caught were on a leech pattern.

There are many leech patterns available in the stores; two of the more popular are Jack Shaw's Blood Leech and Black Leech.

Black O'Lindsay

HOOK: Number 6 or 8
TAIL: Slender, paired strips of blue goose
BODY: Yellow wool, thick **RIB:** Oval, gold tinsel
THROAT: Beard of blue goose and brown cock neck feather
WING: Underwing of peacock sword with strips of mallard flank feather over
ORIGINATOR: Judge Spencer Black
INTENDED USE: Wet fly for rainbow trout
PLACE: Thompson River

A. Bryan Williams' mention in his book, *Fish and Game in British Columbia*, of the Black O'Lindsay, a comparatively new pattern especially good for interior lakes, dates the fly to before his 1935 publication. However, this pattern originated on the banks of the Thompson River and for it to gain acceptance there and on lakes would require some passage of time. Martin Tolley is most likely correct when he dates the Black O'Lindsay earlier, to the late 1920s.

The fly's originator, Judge Spencer Black, came from a town in California called Lindsay. Thus the name Black of Lindsay or Black O'Lindsay. The judge, because of business connections in the forest industry, was a regular visitor to British Columbia and he combined business with angling pleasure. When concocting the Black O'Lindsay, the judge hoped to produce a suitable grasshopper imitation for Thompson River trout and tied his prototype on size six hooks. With its acceptance in other areas in the interior, the pattern was soon being dressed in a variety of sizes from four to ten.

Martin Tolley, in a 1968 *Northwest Sportsman* article titled "Black O'Lindsay" claims this pattern would be the best all-around choice if you had to limit yourself to a single trout wet fly and says:

If ever there was a versatile fly it is the Black O'Lindsay. The ingredients and form are such that it matches most situations and can everywhere be fished with confidence. In both interior and coastal lakes it will attract trout at every depth from weeds to rippled surface, at all rates of retrieves, and even lying motionless on top. . . . You can have every faith in the Black O'Lindsay when river fishing also. . . .

Be the fish brookies or kamloops trout in small ponds or big lakes, be they dollies and rainbows in the readily waded Skagit or the tortuous Thompson the Black O'Lindsay is the right fly to have. But the pattern is not restricted to fresh water only. Several years ago I mistakenly took my box of interior flies along on a beach excursion for sea-trout. There wasn't a tinsel on the clips so I took pot luck and sent a Black O'Lindsay to sea. My day with the cutthroat is now a memory highlight and, understandably, the fly has touched the tides many times since.

In this day of fast production and simplification of patterns, the Black O'Lindsay, because it's fairly complex to dress, requiring skilled hands, has fallen from vogue.

Blood Leech

HOOK: Number 6 or 8, Mustad 9672
TAIL: Brushed out blended maroon and black wool or seal's fur
BODY: Same as tail **ORIGINATOR:** Jack Shaw
INTENDED USE: Wet fly for rainbow trout
LOCATION: Kamloops area lakes

Leeches have occupied the lakes of British Columbia since the last ice age, about 10,000 years ago. However, in the first 100 years of fly fishing in British Columbia they were thought to be of little interest to the trout. Roderick Haig-Brown in The *Western Angler* (1939) says that leeches are:

Very numerous in Paul and other interior lakes. In Paul Lake, though they represent about 20% of the bottom fauna, they form only about 7% of the food of the trout from May to August. It seems possible that this is because they hide under rocks and stones, and so are not easily available. It is hardly likely that it would be very profitable to imitate them . . . . (Vol. 1, p. 117)

And the fly fishers of the day ignored them. In the late 1950s, however, fly fishers realized their folly and in the late 1950s and early 1960s leech-type fly patterns were being introduced to interior lakes. "The leech is an important invertebrate in the diet of trout and is found in abundance in most ponds and lakes" and "is available to the fish at all seasons of the year," writes the famed *Kamloops* fly fisher, Jack Shaw, in his 1976 book *Fly Fish the Trout Lakes*. Shaw has been taking trophy-sized rainbows from the *Kamloops*' area lakes for years on the Blood Leech.

A couple of years ago, I was invited up to a chum's ranch to spend the July 1 weekend and, if I fancied, some fishing. I have fished my friend's lake on and off since the early 1980s and have had some good fishing. A shallow lake, I decided to row around and cast into the lily pads or close to the reed beds with a floating line and leech pattern. During the day I managed three hours on the water and I hooked 15, landing 10 plump rainbows. And all on a leech pattern.

Brian Chan in his book, *Flyfishing Strategies for Stillwaters* (1991), highly recommends Shaw's Blood Leech.

Bloodworm

HOOK: Number 12 Mustad 79580 (4 extra long)
TAIL: A few strands of black bear fur
BODY: Medium to dark maroon tapestry wool
RIB: Fine copper wire
COLLAR: A ring-necked pheasant red-brown rump feather
ORIGINATOR: Jack Shaw
INTENDED USE: Wet fly for rainbow trout
LOCATION: Kamloops lakes

Fly fishers for years failed to recognize the value of chironomid larvae as a source of trout food. However, they would have been recognized much earlier if Roderick Haig-Brown's advice were followed by Bill Nation.

Nation developed British Columbia's first chironomid imitation, Nation's Black, in the 1920s. During the late 1930s when Haig-Brown was writing The *Western Angler*, he asked Nation for the dressings and samples of his flies and Nation sent along the details of his Black. In following correspondence Haig-Brown questioned Nation about the value of a bloodworm imitation and wrote:

Your chironomid is very much to the point. How about the colour of the bloodworm. A sort of orange-red, more red than orange, in a similarly slender body. I think there's a lot to be done in chironomid imitation . . . .

However, Nation, the Kamloops, lake-fishing guru of the day, in his response to Haig-Brown said that "bloodworm [was] seldom found in stomachs of the rainbow in higher altitudes." And with that he dismissed Haig-Brown's suggestion for an imitation. Over a quarter century elapsed before Jack Shaw realized that bloodworms were an important source of trout food and an imitation was necessary. In about 1965 the first bloodworm imitations came from his tying bench. Further, when developing an imitation he realized that the red bloodworm was a very simple insect and that it would be advantageous to incorporate some moving parts into the fly's design to attract the trout.

In Shaw's second book *Fly Tying for Trophy Trout* (1992), Jack says that "although hackle is usually put on a fly to represent wings or legs, another use is to create the impression of movement" (p. 74). For that reason Shaw dressed his Bloodworm with a collar of ring-necked pheasant rump, a material incorporated in other successful British

Columbian patterns such as the Carey Special, Pazooka or Knouff Lake Special.

To fish bloodworm imitations successfully, the fly fisher should be aware that bloodworms are bottom-dwelling creatures and are more readily available to trout during the spring and late fall. Fly fishers using the Bloodworm need to fish the fly close to the bottom with a slow twitching retrieve or mooched.

Now with about 30 years of fishing success behind them, the Bloodworm is a must pattern for the fly fisher planning a spring or fall trip to British Columbia's interior lakes.

Bottom Walker

HOOK: Number 6 to 10 long shank
BODY: Clipped deer hair with dubbed olive seal's fur over
LEGS: Pheasant tail **BEARD:** Black moose mane
ORIGINATOR: Alf Davy
INTENDED USE: Wet fly for rainbow trout
LOCATION: White Lake

Dragonfly nymphs are a tender morsel for hungry trout, but fishing imitations of those bottom-dwelling creatures can pose problems for the fly fisher. Fishing the fly at the correct depth—just above or in the weeds—and very slow are the main difficulties. Alf Davy, however, designed his Bottom Walker with those problems in mind. Davy wanted a fly that he could fish dead slow on the bottom and says that "the stiff moose mane when tied past the hook point will deflect the weeds from the hook point." Fly fishers will have to match fly line with the presentation so that the pattern can be fished slowly.

Dragonfly nymph imitations catch large fish and Davy can attest to that with a whopping 10 1/4-pounder. He provides the following tidbits of information about the Bottom Walker and its successful use and says:

In the early spring of 1972 I took a 10 1/4 pound rainbow from White Lake. I was fishing [the Bottom Walker] at the drop off with a fast sinking line right on the bottom. The deer hair body permitted a very slow retrieve without bottom hook up. Hence the name Bottom Walker. The fish will even take as the fly is left to sit and move with lake currents.

Davy admits though that because the fish take the Bottom Walker so violently he gets broken-off more frequently with this pattern over any other he uses. He also recommends this pattern for "any interior lake in very early spring through the early summer months."

The Bounder

HOOK: Number 2 low-water salmon
TAIL: A golden pheasant crest feather
BODY: Flat, silver tinsel
THROAT: A badger, cock, neck, hackle feather
WING: A few fronds from a peacock's sword feather followed with strips from a golden pheasant's centre tail feather and strips of blue macaw tail feather and a topping of golden pheasant crest feather
ORIGINATOR: Tom Brayshaw
INTENDED USE: Wet fly for rainbow trout
LOCATION: Adams and Little rivers

Brayshaw's Fancy

HOOK: Number 8 **BODY:** Peacock herl
THROAT: Brown, mottled partridge breast feather
WING: Greyish-coloured deer hair
ORIGINATOR: Tom Brayshaw
INTENDED USE: Wet fly for rainbow trout
LOCATION: Adams River

In the 1930s when Tom Brayshaw fished the Little and Adams rivers regularly, he often used the standard-of-the-day fly patterns such as Jock Scott, Mallard & Silver, Teal & Red, and Bucktail & Silver. His thoughts, however, turned to producing more representative imitations, in both size and colouration, of the migrating sockeye salmon fry which made the Little and Adams rivers' large rainbow trout fly fishing world renowned.

On 10 June 1933, Brayshaw decided to fish Little River with Hugh Mackie. They left Vernon in the early afternoon, arriving on the Little River's fishing grounds about 4 p.m. For the first couple of hours they had no rises, then the fish started taking and Brayshaw says that "we got fish at regular intervals for an hour, he [Mackie] had another of 1 pound 9 ounces and I had four [of] 1 pound 13 ounces, 1 pound 13 ounces, and 15 ounces and 2 pounds 4 ounces." All of Brayshaw's fish were taken on a streamer-type pattern that he detailed with a drawing and notes in his diary.

After landing his first fish of the day, one of 1 pound 9 ounces, and referring to his previous day's catch with this fly, he gave the fly its name and called it "The Bounder." He also commented that he thought that "a variation with Jungle Cock sides might be good."

Brayshaw fished the Little and Adams rivers for nearly two decades and continually altered his patterns to make them better fish catchers. The Bounder and his Golden Pheasant & Silver are the forerunners of Brayshaw's Little River No. 2.

This Brayshaw-originated trout fly was dubbed Brayshaw's Nameless by his good friend and fishing companion Roderick Haig-Brown and is one of the patterns displayed in the frontispiece of Volume 1 of Haig-Brown's *The Western Angler* (1939). How Haig-Brown decided on that name is a mystery because Brayshaw had already given this pattern two different names. Perhaps Haig-Brown was aware of Brayshaw's indecision and decided to give it a name of his own or perhaps he just misstated Brayshaw's Fancy as Brayshaw's Nameless. In any event the naming of the pattern is now history. Nevertheless, it was while fishing the Adams River below the dam for rainbow trout on 27 July 1935 that Brayshaw used his new fly. He recorded in his diary:

I tried all sorts of flies but couldn't rise a fish at the tail of the pool till I put on a new fly. . . .I then got three of 2 pounds 4 ounces, 1 pound 1 ounce & 1 pound 12 ounces the latter forcing me to take to the water & follow downstream about 100 yards. . . Called it the 'Queen Mary' for their Majesties 25th year of reign . . . .

During a trip to Whatshen lakes in May 1939, Brayshaw recorded the name change from Queen Mary to B's Fancy. With his son Kit (Christopher) at the oars and Brayshaw fishing he says, "I picked up a nice 15 ounce rainbow on 'B's Fancy' (old Queen Mary)." And it was this year that *The Western Angler* came out with the fly listed as Brayshaw's Nameless. Brayshaw referred to it as Nameless thereafter. About the Nameless' development and use, in a 2 July 1939 letter to Rod Haig-Brown, Brayshaw writes:

You will see one fly with a peacock-herl body & dark partridge hackle & deer-hair wing. I tied it first in 1935 at Adams River dam and it met with immediate success and since then I have had good sport with it at some of the Kamloops lakes & also in the Thompson from Savona to Macabees' and has definitely taken its place with Jock Scott, Teal & Red, Mallard & Claret and a small silver-bodied fly as one of the best killers for rainbows.

A most impressive statement and a very successful fly it must be for Brayshaw to rank it up there with some of the British greats. Brayshaw used the Nameless primarily for trout fishing on the Adams River when there were no salmon fry migrations. He did, however, use the Nameless with success over twelve years on other waters that he fished such as Whatshen and Pinantan lakes, and the Skagit and Thompson rivers.

After 1947, however, Brayshaw became primarily a steelhead fly fisher and made infrequent trips for trout and his Nameless fly became a victim of no use.

The Nameless is such a simple pattern to dress and, from reading the accounts of its use in Brayshaw's diaries, a very effective fly. It is also one that I have added to my fly box and will call on when I want a sedge-type wet fly for down and across river fishing. I do, though, add a rib of fine silver wire or tinsel because of the fragile peacock herl body.

Butler's Bug

HOOK: Number 6, Mustad 9672
TAIL AND UNDERBODY: Deer hair
BODY: Medium olive seal's fur **RIB:** Medium, gold tinsel
WINGCASE & LEGS: Ring-necked
pheasant tail feather fibres
HEAD: Peacock herl
EYES: Rolled fibres from a ring-necked
pheasant tail feather
ORIGINATOR: Glenn Butler
INTENDED USE: Wet fly for rainbow trout
LOCATION: Plateau Lake

Splash! Some large flies make a big splash when they land on the water and Butler's Bug is a big fly. However, when Butler created this pattern under the light of a Plateau Lake campfire in the spring of 1980, the fly produced a different type of big splash when it caught the attention of fly fishers because of its attraction to large Kamloops trout.

About the fly's development and use, Butler in a March 1995 letter modestly says:

Not a lot to tell you—the fly itself has had widespread success from lakes in Idaho to lakes throughout BC—anywhere dragon flies exist. . . . One of my favourite techniques is to fish it before dusk; to cast it into the shallows, let it sit and wait for a cruising trout; twitch it at the right time and watch the action. It is a very exciting way to fish.

I have also had good luck with smaller sizes and am sure at times it is taken for a large sedge pupa. Brian Chan and I had good success on White Lake, Salmon Arm on a hot July day. We cruised the lake looking for large trout on the drop off. Having located some lunkers, we anchored in the shallows and using 20' sinking tips cast dragons into the fray. I lost several dragons with the ferocity of the hit. They just snapped the leader. But we managed to land some nice trout.

. . . I remember going to Pass Lake with a friend of mine who was somewhat skeptical of the fly's prowess. We had been fishing

without much luck when we decided to head to shore for lunch.

My partner rowed to shore, jumped out of the boat and retrieved the dragon by hand. I heard a shout, turned around to see his rod bent double. It turned out to be a beautiful hen of 6 pounds. My skeptic friend then and there became an avid enthusiast of Butler's Dragon.

Although the original fly was dressed with medium olive seal's fur, "I tie it in various shades of green olive, brown & black," says Butler.

Glenn has many more stories that attest to the effectiveness of this pattern and says that it has lured fish from: "Plateau, Pass, Roche, Lundbom, Peterhope, White, Island, Murphy, Jocko, 6 Mile, Pikes, Courtenay, Divide, Logan" and "several little gems in Clearwater and have heard from other fly fishermen of its widespread success." In other words, "it plain works," says Butler.

Carey's Parmachene Bucktail

HOOK: Number 6 and 8 **TAIL:** Red swan
BODY: Yellow silk **RIB:** Oval, silver tinsel
THROAT: Grizzly
WING: White bucktail with strips of orange swan along side
ORIGINATOR: Colonel Carey
INTENDED USE: Wet fly for rainbow trout
LOCATION: Unknown

The Parmachene series of flies owes its name to Parmachene Lake in Maine and to an eastern brook trout fisherman, H.P. Wells. Wells developed the Parmachene Belle in 1878 as an imitation of a brook trout fin, a common bait used at that time. The fly proved a good fish catcher and its use spread throughout North America. When and who introduced it to British Columbia is difficult to determine, but A. Bryan Williams, in *Rod and Creel in British Columbia* (1919), highly recommends it and says it "is used from one end of the Province to the other" (p. 42).

Sometime in the 1920s bucktails became the fly to use, and Colonel Carey, of Carey Special fame, must have developed the Parmachene Bucktail pattern after bucktails became popular. In later years, after 1935, polar bear replaced bucktail in the wing, but that did not result in a name change.

In the 1930s there was confusion among fishermen about Colonel Carey's patterns and Rod Haig-Brown wrote Harkley & Haywood about this. Haig-Brown was under the impression that the Parmachene Bucktail was referred to by some as Carey's Special and that there was another pattern called Col. Kerry's Special of which he enclosed a sample for Mr. Haywood to verify.

The 12 July 1939 return letter from Haywood says:

Enclosed herewith please find the Col. Carey's Special as known to the Interior of B. C. people. The coast [fly fishers] have always called it the Dredge, and incidentally that is the way it is used. The correct name for the other bright one is Col. Carey's Parmachene Bucktail.

Colonel Carey's Parmachene Bucktail is little used today; however, it provided many years service. Patrick attests to its popularity in *Pacific Northwest Fly Patterns*, 1964 edition, when he says that this fly "has been very good for both interior lake fishing and migratory [trout fishing] on the coast" (p. 73).

Carey Special

HOOK: Number 6
TAIL: A few fibres from a ringed-neck pheasant's rump feather
BODY: Ringed-neck pheasant tail fibres, deer hair or marmot fur
RIB: Black linen thread
COLLAR: Ring-neck pheasant rump feathers extending well past hook bend
ORIGINATOR: Colonel Carey
INTENDED USE: Wet fly for rainbow trout
LOCATION: Arthur Lake

One of the patterns that is a staple in many a British Columbia angler's fly box is the Carey Special. Colonel Carey's Special is listed as a "fancy" fly in Roderick Haig-Brown's classic 1939 book, *The Western Angler*. He says:

This is far from being a complete list of the "fancy" flies . . . it includes at least one fly which, besides being one of the best killers, is as somberly dressed as any natural—Col. Carey's Special. Whether or not it was originally tied as an imitation of some natural insect I do not know, but it has an extremely lifelike action in the water and may well be taken for an imitation of a dragon-fly nymph. (Vol. 1, p. 102)

A sample Carey Special is shown in the frontispiece of Haig-Brown's 1939 classic. The Carey Special's origins, however, date back to the 1920s. Colonel Carey, a retired British soldier, moved from Victoria to the Okanagan in 1925, and, according to Martin Tolley, the development of a sure-fire trout pattern became an obsession.

When you read the words written by Tolley in his "Colonel Carey" article in the October, 1968 issue of *Northwest Sportsman* magazine, a picture is framed in your mind of this old soldier in the wilds of British Columbia dressing flies:

As a prelude to finding the great solution his passion must have overcome the old soldier because he failed to return from one of his spring offensives. Quite naturally, the family became concerned for his safety and search parties were dispatched to recon-

noiter and bring him home. According to legend, the Colonel was wrestling with the issue at Arthur Lake when discovered. He was sitting in his tent experimenting with prototypes for his perfect fly, surrounded by corpses of cock pheasants. He had literally clubbed dozens to death and not let a closed season stay his quest for the prime rump feathers which he deemed the answer to his enigma.

The Colonel produced a number of patterns, but the Carey Special proved the Colonel's most successful. Now it is used all over the province and elsewhere in sizes 2 to 12 in a variety of body colours: green, yellow, olive, black, and red. Tommy Brayshaw, who met Carey one 1934 day while fishing Lac Le Jeune, affirms Carey developed the fly "when he was camped at Arthur Lake and I think dressed it for a dragonfly nymph, at any rate we did the same thing at Knouff with the 'pazooka' and fished it the same way" *(Tommy Brayshaw, The Ardent Angler-Artist, p. 85).*

Brayshaw thought, but was not sure, that the sample Carey gave him at Le Jeune consisted of a tail, body and wing of marmot (groundhog) fur and says Carey's fly was referred to as The Dredge or Monkey Faced Louise. According to Mr. Haywood of Harkley & Haywood, the Dredge was the popular Lower Mainland name for Carey's fly. Brayshaw dressed his Carey with a deer-hair body and ribbed it with black linen thread to protect the fragile hair body.

According to the history of the fly published in Steve Raymond's book, *Kamloops* (1971), the Carey Special, tied on a number 6 hook, was intended to represent a hatching sedge pupa. Whatever the fish take the fly for, it is a very effective pattern, either cast and retrieved, or trolled.

In the spring of 1982 a life-long friend invited me to his 250-acre, interior ranch to fish his small but productive lake. I remember the day well. Large fish were shrimping in the shallows, and I decided to try entice them with a Carey Special. My two largest fish for the weekend were 5 and 6 pounds.

The fly, dressed in its many sizes and variations, is one of British Columbia's most productive patterns.

The Halfback is a most versatile fly and is used in a variety of styles and sizes.

Caverhill Nymph

HOOK: Number 6 to 10, Mustad 9671 or 9672
BODY: Blue-black mohair   **RIB:** Flat or oval, silver tinsel
COLLAR: Blue-black hackle
HEAD: Peacock herl-coloured yarn or peacock herl
ORIGINATOR: Peter Caverhill
INTENDED USE: Wet fly for rainbow trout
LOCATION: Dragon Lake

During the 1960s and '70s Helen Peacock of Kamloops worked as a professional fly tier; one of her creations was called Helen's Heller and the Caverhill Nymph owes its origins to Peacock's creation. In a recent November 1994 letter about the Caverhill Nymph, Peter says that "this fly was simply a case of lazy misidentification and sloppy fly tying . . . I thought that I had been tying a 'Helen's Heller,' however those with greater knowledge and understanding realized this error and had to call it something [and] they decided to give it my moniker."

A fly's reputation is often bolstered when the fishing is slow and what few fish are caught are consistently deceived by that pattern. During an October trip to Dragon Lake, this happened with the Caverhill Nymph and was recorded by Jim Kilburn in the March 1975 issue of *Western Fish & Game*. Skeptical about veteran feather tossers', Jack Vincent and Bob Backus, advice that the fish were targeting only the Caverhill, Kilburn stuck with his favoured Anderson's Stone Nymph for most of that first fishless day and writes:

That night, warmed by campfire and companionship, I calmed down somewhat. I even listened more attentively, and I learned that the few trout that had been taken had been victimized by a strange, black, seedy-looking concoction called the Caverhill nymph. . . .

At daybreak, I was anchored on my favourite shoal, casting with the sink-tip. Early morning came and went. So did 100 casts with a well-chewed Anderson nymph. . . . By late afternoon, I was still fishless. And frustrated. . . .

When I stopped at the Vincent-Backus camper, I was fishless, frigid, and frustrated. There I learned that the majority of the trout hooked that day had taken the Caverhill nymph. . . . I . . . suggested that the cold fishless specimen standing before them required . . . several Caverhill nymphs . . . . Being gentlemen, they took the bait on each cast. . . .

On the following five days, I was able to establish that the trout did indeed favor the Caverhill nymph. And, even though fishing was slow by the standards of previous years, I did manage to hook 16 trout to eight pounds—fishing reasonably hard.

To top Kilburn's trip, Joyce, Kilburn's wife, took a 9 1/2-pounder on a Caverhill Nymph.

When I asked Caverhill for a fish story, he referred me to Kilburn's story partially detailed above and noted that the fly was featured in Alf Davy's book *The Gilly* (1986). "However, the fly must be pretty widely used and appreciated because I'm constantly questioned by new fly fishers that I meet about the Caverhill Nymph," said Peter.

Twenty years has lapsed since Peter made that fly-tying faux pas, but the fly like the ardent fly fisher and fisheries branch biologist, Caverhill, lives on.

Dexheimer Sedge

HOOK: Number 6 or 8   **BODY:** Dark olive wool
RIB: A peacock's herl
THROAT: A brown rooster saddle hackle feather
WING: Brown neck feather from a drake mallard
ORIGINATOR: John Dexheimer
INTENDED USE: Wet fly for rainbow trout
LOCATION: Tunkwa Lake

John Dexheimer, an American born in South Dakota in 1909, moved to British Columbia in 1933. He settled and worked, until his death in 1966, at a sawmill in Savona, a small town located at the south end of Kamloops Lake. One of his favourite lakes was just a few miles south on the Nicola Plateau.

Tunkwa Lake is one of the richest trout-food lakes in the Kamloops area, and with the abundance of food fish grow rapidly. But, because of the vast amounts of food, enticing them with artificial flies can be difficult. According to Don Traeger, son-in-law of the now-deceased Barney Rushton who was an expert Tunkwa Lake fisher of many years, Tunkwa was the haven of trollers until Dexheimer discovered its secrets. One of the wet flies that Dexheimer developed to achieve this task was his sedge pattern, called, according to Steve Raymond in *Kamloops* (1971), by some the Tunkwa Special or Sedge Special. However, the sedge pattern, according to Traeger, was taken as a shrimp imitation by the fish in this shrimp-rich lake.

Dexheimer's secret to success on Tunkwa was a combination of many things: anchoring the boat in the right locations, fishing at the times of day when the fish were actively feeding, using a slow-retrieve presentation, and being persistent. Sounds like a simple solution, however, it wasn't because most fishers were reluctant to abandon the favoured chuck-and-chance wet-fly fishing that provided such good sport on most other waters.

Over the past three decades, Tunkwa fly fishers have honed to perfection the anchoring and slow-retrieve presentation developed by John Dexheimer and the lake which was once a troller's haven is now the haven of the skilled and persistent fly fisher.

Brian Chan, in *Flyfishing Strategies for Stillwaters* (1991), says that the Dexheimer Sedge is "an excellent shrimp" (p. 40) and "in small sizes is also a good boatman imitation" (p. 59).

Doc Spratley

HOOK: Number 6 **TAIL:** Guinea fowl fibres
BODY: Black wool **RIB:** Flat, silver tinsel
THROAT: Guinea fowl
WING: Ring-necked peasant centre tail strips
HEAD: Peacock herl **ORIGINATOR:** Dick Prankard
INTENDED USE: Wet fly for rainbow trout
LOCATION: Unknown

Edwards' Sedge

HOOK: Number 6 to 10 low-water salmon
TAIL: A few fibres of deer hair
BODY: Medium green wool or seal's fur **WING:** Deer hair
HACKLE: Mixed brown and grizzly
ORIGINATORS: Captain Tommy Edwards and Jim Kilburn
INTENDED USE: Dry fly for rainbow trout
LOCATION: Interior lakes

This is my favourite fly for lake fishing. I have so many fond memories associated with the pattern that when I am not sure what to use, the Doc Spratley often ends up on my line. Because I have the utmost confidence in the fly's ability to attract fish and confidence in a fly pattern is paramount to success, I rarely regret that decision.

The Doc Spratley, developed in the late 1940s by Dick Prankard and popularized in the interior lakes of British Columbia by Dr. Donald Spratley, a Mt. Vernon, Washington dentist, is such a consistent fish catcher it is indeed a confidence builder.

Originally, the Doc Spratley was tied on a number 6 hook. Now it is dressed in various sizes, from 12 to 2 with bodies of wool, floss or chenille. The smaller-sized Spratleys should be sparser and have bodies of floss or wool, while the larger may be dressed fuller, with chenille.

The Doc Spratley, in its larger sizes, is similar in size to some dragonfly nymphs, and in size and shape to some minnows; one of the reasons it is excellent trolled, and equal to, if not better than, the Carey Special. In its smaller sizes, say 12 to 8, particularly if tied sparse, it is the same size and representative of a chironomid pupa. Used as a chironomid imitation, the slower the retrieve the better.

The Doc Spratley now sports red, green, olive or brown bodies, and all have proved effective in certain locations at certain times. None, however, can match the fish-catching consistency of the original black-bodied fly.

In 1980, on our way home from the Morice River, Gary Baker and I stopped by Dragon Lake near Quesnel and spent a day and a half throwing number four and six Dark Olive or Black-bodied Spratleys at Dragon Lake rainbows. We had a day and a half of fishing that would be the envy of most fly fishers in North America, if not the world. We boated 49 fish ranging in size from 1 pound to 5 3/4 pounds, of which over 30 were 3 pounds or greater in weight.

I recall nearing the end of the first day taking fish with a dark olive-bodied Spratley fly that had no tinsel rib and with two thirds of the chenille body gone. Yet, the rainbows took it with abandon.

Over the near 50 years since it was introduced to British Columbia, the "Doc," as it is affectionately called by many, has become one of the province's most productive patterns.

This is another British pattern that has been adopted and altered to suit British Columbia's fishing. Jim Kilburn, when he edited the Totem Fly fishers' newsletter the *Totem Topics*, wrote about the Edwards' Sedge and the story was reprinted in the Nov.-Dec. 1968 issue of *Northwest Sportsman* magazine. In the July 1969 issue, of *Western Fish & Game* Kilburn in his article titled "The Way of the Sedge," discusses Edwards' Sedge and the alterations he did to suit local conditions:

When I intend to imitate the scampering stage, I choose a different fly—the Edwards' Sedge . . . fashioned by Captain Tommy Edwards [the then British fly-casting champion] for use on the River Usk in England, is also a deer-hair fly—but with a difference. The deer-hair wing is tied to lie over the back of the fly in the conventional manner, but the hair is fastened by the tip ends. . . .

In an attempt to adapt the Edwards' Sedge to local conditions, I have made a few alterations. One such adaptation is particularly favoured by lake rainbows. Whereas the Edwards' fly calls for bodies of chenille or fully-wrapped pheasant tail, I use medium green wool or seal's fur. I also use low-water hooks of three sizes—6, 8, and 10—and choose the size to imitate the emerging insect. In front of the wings, I use a hackle of mixed brown and grizzly, from the bottom of which I cut a "V" to allow the fly to float closer to the surface film. I also use a short deer-hair tail to increase the fly's floating ability. When twitched or slowly retrieved to create a wake, this modified Edwards' Sedge can produce truly astonishing results.

In Kilburn's *Totem Topics* article reprinted in a 1968 issue of *Northwest Sportsman* magazine, Jim spent an evening with Bill Stephens on Vancouver Island's Cowichan River and says:

And so, late the following Saturday afternoon, I treaded the well worn trail to one of the more beautiful pools on the Cowichan. . . . I tied on an Edwards' Sedge, then eased into the water directly below him.

I cast straight upstream, and he immediately swirled on the fly. But he was too fast and I was too slow. . . . In the ensuing hour, the Edwards' Sedge rose fifteen or twenty good trout. Like Bill Stephens, I lost count after about a dozen. . . . I did manage to beach and release three of about two pounds, and I kept a three-pounder for the pot.

Over 25 years have passed since Kilburn and Stephens used the Edwards' Sedge and it is still in use today. Brian Chan in his 1991 book, *Flyfishing Strategies for Stillwaters*, claims, "An Edward's Sedge is a good emerger pattern" (p. 70).

Golden Shrimp

HOOK: Number 12 **TAIL:** A ginger hackle feather tip
BODY: Light olive floss **RIB:** Fine, gold wire
LEGS & ANTENNAE: A ginger hackle feather
TYING THREAD Tan monocord
ORIGINATOR: Steve Raymond
INTENDED USE: Wet fly for rainbow trout
LOCATION: Hihium Lake

Many years ago, when he was five, Steve Raymond, now a renowned Washingtonian fly fisher and writer, made his first trip with his father into British Columbia to fish stillwater trout. Raymond senior had a love affair with British Columbia's interior stillwaters and their trout. He instilled that love in his son. The Golden Shrimp, a more realistic Gammarus imitation, is the product of much thought and many years' development and it was featured in Raymond's book *Kamloops*, published in 1971. In a letter dated September 22, 1994, Steve recalls the fly's development and says:

As for the Golden Shrimp . . . the pattern was developed over a period of several years in the late '60s, mostly at Hihium Lake where I used to fish in September when scuds were plentiful. It seemed to me that none of the standard patterns in circulation at that time were very good imitations—at least, they rarely brought the results I thought they should. So I began experimenting with my own patterns, using various shades of wool, floss, dyed fur and even raffia for the bodies and different colours and widths of tinsel and thread for ribbing.

One thing I decided early on was that palmered, trimmed hackle wouldn't do; it just didn't appear natural to me. Instead, I began using ginger hackle with one side stripped, laying the quill against the belly of the fly and fastening it on with ribbing material, separating the individual hackle fibers with a dubbing needle so they wouldn't be bound at the ribbing. At first I tried using two hackles, arranged parallel along the belly of the fly, and I think that made the imitation more realistic—at least to me. But it didn't seem to matter to the fish, and it did make the fly more difficult to tie, so eventually I dropped the double hackle and began using only the single one.

When I found a colour-and-ribbing combination that seemed promising, I kept pursuing it and fine-tuning it until finally I ended

up with the pattern published in Kamloops. I recall catching more than 50 trout on it one morning in Hihium Lake and deciding at that point that I had what I wanted, and I have been tying it the same way ever since.

Later, in the letter, Raymond mentions that he uses the Golden Shrimp in May or September and October when scuds seem most plentiful and that he has had good success with this pattern not only at Hihium, but also in the shallows at the south end of Roche, Lundbom, Glimpse, and many of the lakes in the Chataway and Aurora chains. Steve has also found the fly effective for Puget Sound sea-run cutthroat.

In the revised 1981 edition of *Kamloops*, Raymond recommends the Golden Shrimp be dressed on either 10 or 12 hooks and gives a more definite colour for the body: golden olive rayon floss, manufacturer's number 163.

Halfback

HOOK: Number 6 **TAIL:** Ground hog
BODY: Bronze peacock herl with a wing
case of ring-neck pheasant rump feather
THROAT: Ground hog
ORIGINATOR: John Dexheimer
INTENDED USE: Wet fly for rainbow trout
LOCATION: Tunkwa Lake

According to Jack Shaw, famous Kamloops writer and fly fisher, the Halfback was developed in the late 1950s by John Dexheimer of Savona. Totem Fly fisher, Don Traeger, fished Tunkwa with his father-in-law during some of Dexheimer's last Tunkwa years and recalls that Dexheimer dressed the Halfback fly with ground-hog fur and peacock herl.

Some patterns, although the originator intended to develop an imitation of a certain insect, become multi-purpose and their value in the arsenal of a competent fly fisher increases many-fold. The Halfback, one such pattern, is dressed with many variations in sizes from four to twelve. In the smaller sizes, trout take it for a chironomid pupa or the nymph stage of the Callibaetis mayfly and in the larger sizes the nymph stage of the damsel or dragonfly. The Halfback, as a cast fly combined with various retrieves, has been catching fish consistently in British Columbia for over thirty years.

In May, 1991, Bob Taylor and I found ourselves on Leighton Lake a hop, skip and a jump from Tunkwa Lake and near Logan Lake Village. The spring had been exceptionally cold and wet and, in general, the interior lake fishing had been poor.

The conditions we encountered were not unusual for the season, however, we persisted, and rowed around the lake casting into likely spots hoping for a fly hatch to put the fish into a taking mood. The hatch didn't happen and we managed only a couple of fish. Later in the day we discovered a spot where there were numerous fish showing but not taking. Sometimes fish just jump and don't take but we persevered, trying various patterns and sizes of fly. Every now and then we would hook a fish on a Carey or Spratley. Eventually, Bob put on a Halfback and realized instant success. I won't say that we slaughtered the fish, but our catch that evening and the next morning, before we headed home, was impressive compared to others. One regular visitor of the lake, who had put in a good day, had nothing to show for his effort. He came over later, wanting to know what the magic fly was and, although he had numerous Halfbacks in his box, he had neglected to try them. We went home happy, of course. The Halfback had saved the trip.

Originally, the Halfback was dressed on a number 6, 2X long hook but, nowadays, it is dressed on many different hook sizes and styles. Those dressed on 8 and 10 hooks are good general sizes to have. Sometimes a little lead is wrapped on the shank under the dressing. The lead helps sink the fly to a feeding depth, quicker. I prefer to counter-wind a fine, silver wire up the body to protect the fragile peacock herl from unraveling once cut by a fish's sharp teeth.

Like the American Express credit card company's television ad about "don't leave home without it," the fly fisher shouldn't adventure into lake country without a supply of Halfbacks.

In a 1991 article titled "Confessions of a Chironomid Addict" published in British Columbia Federation of Fly fishers' *Fly Lines*, about fishing imitations of the adult insect, he writes:

Trout will often feed on the egg laying adult chironomid. Females typically return to the lake in the evenings when winds are down and darkness approaches. In most situations trout will show a distinct movement pattern which will allow you to anticipate its speed and direction of travel. Cast an adequate distance ahead of the fish with a floating adult pattern. Once the fly hits the water give it a couple of long fast strips so that it forms a wake on the water. This action is a good imitation of a female releasing eggs and will often induce a strike.

Sound advice, Mr. Chan. Fly fishers who use this technique during prime time may experience some very exciting fly fishing indeed.

Lioness

HOOK: Number 6
TAIL: Mixed red and yellow hackle fibres
BODY: Black chenille
THROAT: Mixed red and yellow hackle feathers
WING: White goose
ORIGINATOR: Terry Maunsell
INTENDED USE: Wet fly for rainbow or
cutthroat trout
LOCATION: Unknown

Lady McConnell

HOOK: Number 10 to 16, two extra long
TAIL: A grizzly hackle tip
BODY: Grey sparkle poly with a deer hair shellback
HACKLE: Grizzly
ORIGINATOR: Brian Chan
INTENDED USE: Dry fly for rainbow trout
LOCATION: McConnell Lake

Brian Chan is synonymous with Kamloops lake fishing. Chan, a fishery biologist by profession working for the provincial Ministry of Environment, Fisheries Branch, transferred to Kamloops over twenty years ago. Over those years since he moved to trout-fishing paradise, he has become a master of stillwater, fly-fishing techniques. Chironomid fishing became one of his specialties and loves. About the Lady McConnell, one of his creations, in his 9/7/95 letter he says:

An original pattern that I developed in 1979 to represent an almost completely emerged adult chironomid. I had found that the fish keyed in on the trailing shuck of the adult and the tail of grizzly hackle represents the trailing shuck of the adult.

I first experimented with this pattern on McConnell Lake and thus the name. I have found that certain lakes are better for adult/emerger chironomid fishing. Generally those lakes with the bigger chironomid species and also lakes that are slightly off colour, i.e., slightly tannic acid colouration versus the very clear lakes. Tunkwa, Campbell and Hatheume are good adult chironomid lakes.

Developed in the 1940s or earlier, it was difficult to determine if this fly was developed for interior or coast trout. John Massey, in an article called "British Columbia Trout have world-wide TASTE . . . but Like B.C. Flies Best!," published in the May, 1966 issue of *Northwest Sportsman* magazine, says that the Lioness

...is a very good fly on certain lakes such as Pennask, and is always worth a try when searching for the fly-of-the-moment. Mr. Harkley attributes its dressing to Mr. TERRY MAUNSELL who asked for a fly 'with the body of a Black gnat, the tail and hackle of a Yellow Peril and the wings of a Coachman.' While it is undoubtedly, from its pedigree, a 'fancy' pattern, it is probably taken for a variety of natural nymphs.

Roy Patrick, in his 1964 edition of *Pacific Northwest Fly Patterns*, lists three Lioness flies with slightly different dressings. In the footnotes following the patterns' listings he says the Lioness is "used on the Harrison River and Lake for cuts" and is "a very good Canadian fly, used around Lillooet for rainbow trout" and that it is "best in May and September." (p. 70) However, Pochin, in *Angling and Hunting in British*

Columbia (1946), claims that the "Lyoness (sic) is also a good salmon and jack fly" (p. 43). Steve Raymond in *Kamloops* (1971) says the Lioness has been "used with especially good effect in Peterhope Lake and . . . in some of the lakes around Merritt" (p. 162). Talking about productive cutthroat patterns, Dave Elliott on page 41 of *A Cutthroat Collection* (1984) says "the best has been the Lioness" and, as the following sketch attests, steelhead also fancy it.

During a late 1960s trip to Washington State's Grand Ronde River, Bob Taylor, Art Smith and Ed Weinstein had parked their vehicle and were readying themselves for the fishing when Taylor spotted a fly on the ground. He stooped down and low and behold picked up a Lioness, hundreds of miles away from its birthplace. Intuition often plays a role in fishing, and Taylor replaced his pattern with the newly found fly. The trio walked to the river, Smith and Weinstein waded the Ronde to go fish the far bank, but as Taylor crossed he fancied the streamy water and decided to give it a try. The Lioness swam through the water on the down and across presentation and the eight-pound steelhead Taylor took with the Lioness provided the evening meal for the trio of anglers.

ping the scale at 6 pounds 4 ounces. In two days Brayshaw and friend took 34 trout. "No other boats did anything & we were easily the best both days so were thankful to have such good sport" was one of Brayshaw's final comments recorded in his diary for this two-day trip using tandem-hooked, Brayshaw-dressed patterns.

Haig-Brown in *The Western Angler* noted also that if the migrating smolts were small, Brayshaw preferred a fly dressed on a single, number 2, low-water hook.

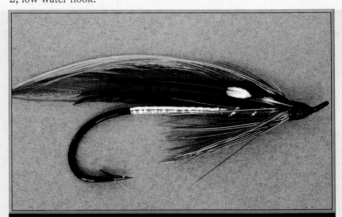

Little River No. 2

HOOK: Number 4 and 5 low-water salmon in tandem or number 2 low-water salmon for single-hooked fly
BODY: First two thirds, flat, silver tinsel; remaining third, red floss
RIB: Oval, silver tinsel over front third
THROAT: Scarlet hackle followed with a blue macaw feather
WING: A few strands of peacock herl, covered with two furnace hackles with a golden pheasant crest feather overall
CHEEKS: Jungle cock
ORIGINATOR: Tom Brayshaw
INTENDED USE: Wet fly for rainbow trout
LOCATION: Little River

Little River No. 1

HOOK: Number 4 and 5 low-water salmon in tandem or number 2 low-water salmon for single-hooked fly
BODY: Flat, silver tinsel
THROAT: Badger hackle
WING: Moose hair, primarily white-tipped
CHEEKS: Jungle cock (optional)
ORIGINATOR: Tom Brayshaw
INTENDED USE: Wet fly for rainbow trout
LOCATION: Adams and Little rivers

Roderick Haig-Brown, in *The Western Angler* (1939), referred to the Little River rainbow trout fishing when the run of fry is on as "something apart, affording a type of fishing that for sheer excitement . . . is almost unequalled," and he goes on to say that "Mr. Brayshaw's patterns are by far the best yet tied for . . . large Kamloops trout . . . feeding on sockeye smolts (V. 1, p. 78)."

Fishing with his friend Eldred, also of Vernon, Brayshaw recorded using his tandem-hooked flies on May 27, 1934 for the first time:

The day was bright & calm & we got up about 5 & started fishing shortly after 8 a.m. I got a fish of 2 pounds 6 ounces immediately & we had five in the first hour; both of us using large double hooked silver bodied flies. . . . I finished up with 9 weighing 18 pounds 2 ounces, Eldred had 7 weighing 14 pounds 14 ounces. Total 16 fish of exactly 2 pounds average.

The next day, Brayshaw outdid his previous day's performance with 10 trout weighing 22 pounds 8 ounces, with the largest fish top-

This is the second tandem-hooked, sockeye smolt, Little River pattern that Tommy Brayshaw standardized on after numerous years experimenting with different combinations of winging materials. However, he did note that other winging material such as badger hackles, strips of teal or golden pheasant centre tail feather can often be substituted for the furnace hackle feathers and a very effective fly the result. And like the Bounder, described earlier in this section, a few strands of blue macaw can also add fish-catching qualities.

Dressing tandem-hooked flies had its difficulties in the 1930s. Fly dressers didn't have the nylon or stainless steel lines that we have today and Brayshaw, in a letter to his friend Roderick Haig-Brown, gives this advice to fly dressers:

Hooks should be joined by double, treble twisted gut—one right twist and one left twist—otherwise, when wet, the tail hook has a tendency to turn round. There should also be a few turns of silk over the tinsel to prevent it breaking when a fish bends the fly up.

Brayshaw was undoubtedly one of the more capable amateur fly dressers of his era, and he was certainly one of the more astute observers

of fish and their habits. The fly patterns that he produced without the aid of a tying vice, as Haig-Brown says, "are attractive to look at, ingeniously worked out and thoroughly practical (*The Western Angler*, Vol.1, p. 120). What better compliment could one master fly fisher give another?

Long Black

HOOK: Number 10 to 12, four extra long
BODY: Black floss tapered to front of hook
RIB: Fine silver tinsel
THORAX: Grouse feather
GILLS: White acrylic yarn
LEGS: Grouse feather fibres
ORIGINATOR: Alf Davy
INTENDED USES: Wet fly for rainbow trout
LOCATION: White and Stump lakes

On my information sheet that I sent many contributors to this book, I have a section titled, "Reason for Development." Davy claims that the reason he developed his Long Black was his need for an "early spring chironomid pattern." About the Long Black's development he says:

When the ice first comes off the interior lakes, I use chironomids. In the early 1970s, I fished mainly the Little Black on 14 to 18 hooks. A cut-back Spratley was used with success at times so I tied a chironomid pattern that was as long as the Spratley but thinner bodied. With a 10 1/2 pound fish from Stump Lake in the early spring of 1974, it proved a winner and takes fish on most interior lakes in early spring.

Most serious fly fishers in this province know that chironomids are a valuable source of food early in the season for interior trout and the black-bodied imitations seem the most productive. However, chironomid pupae, besides black, are found in shades of brown, green, orange and red. In May of this year I spent a few days on Hihium Lake and I managed to do well using a dark olive-bodied fly, however, two Vancouver enthusiasts camped next to me expounded the virtues of a green-bodied Spratley. Their catch proved that that particular colour was producing. Later, as evening drew to a close, I kept a nice fish of about 1 1/2 pound and when I cleaned it I noticed a large bulge in the stomach. Although the mass of food had some other light coloured "blood worms" or chironomid larvae, some darker pupae, the majority was a bright green. I do believe that there are times when fish will target size, shape or colour and in this case I believe that the two Vancouver fly fishers were using a fly of the fishes' targeted colour.

However, black chironomid pupa imitations are usually more productive because they are more common, but not always.

The Maggot

HOOK: Not specified, sample dressed on number 10 hook
BODY: White chenille **COLLAR:** White hackle
ORIGINATOR: Tom Brayshaw
INTENDED USE: Wet fly for rainbow trout
LOCATION: Adams and Little rivers

The trout fishing resulting from the spring hatch and migration of the sockeye salmon fry and smolts drew anglers from far and wide to the banks of the Little and Adams rivers. During May 1943, Tom and Becky Brayshaw spent a week fishing there. Also experiencing the fishing were notable British Columbian fishing personalities of the time, Mr. and Mrs. A. Bryan Williams, Francis Whitehouse, Wallace McMillan, and American, Lee Richardson, who regularly sampled the fishing north of the 49th parallel.

May can be a very pleasant month in British Columbia, but until month-end, winter can return, especially in the Interior. This May trip for the Brayshaws saw the return of cold, windy, winter weather. Brayshaw was catching fish, however, mostly on his Alevin pattern. On May 9, with the weather threatening, all the fishers came in and stayed in camp. When Brayshaw cleaned his catch he noticed that "they were gorged with old dead salmon eggs, dark in colour, together with maggots which must have come from fly-blown sockeyes on the gravel bars and alevins."

Brayshaw, an astute observer and practical angler, believed that although the fish he caught had fed mostly on salmon eggs, they were impossible to imitate with a fly. He did, however, dress a maggot imitation which he used one afternoon and he managed to take two fish of about two pounds each with this new pattern.

Although Brayshaw never recorded another use of "The Maggot," I included this pattern because it shows Brayshaw's ability to observe, analyze and produce solutions that often result in his catching more fish than other less observant anglers.

A nicely coloured, July-caught interior rainbow.

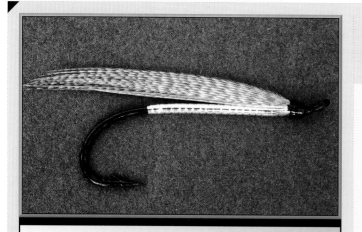

Mallard & Silver

HOOK: Number 2 to 8 low-water salmon
BODY: Flat, silver tinsel
WING: Strips of grey mallard breast feather
ORIGINATOR: Unknown
INTENDED USE: Wet fly for rainbow trout
LOCATION: Adams and Little rivers

In his 1935 book *Fish & Game in British Columbia*, A. Bryan Williams recommended a Mallard & Silver for fishing the Adams and Little rivers when the salmon fry are running. It is the sole pattern listed in his book for which he gives a dressing: number 2 hook, "plain silver body, light grey wing, and no hackle" (p. 48). Mr. Williams, at the time that *Fish & Game . . .* was published had been a regular visitor to this area for almost 20 years. Perhaps he originated the pattern, although that is speculation on my part. I do believe that the Mallard & Silver is an offshoot of the British sea-trout fly, Teal & Silver.

Tommy Brayshaw used the Mallard & Silver pattern quite often when he fished the Adams and Little rivers. He recorded its use on the Adams in 1932 when on May 22 around 11 a.m. he took a fish of "2 1/2 pounds and shortly afterwards another of 2 pound 5 ounces, both on a silver body and grey mallard wing [with] no hackle." Brayshaw dressed the fly on hook sizes 2 to 6 and used it, not only for Little and Adams rivers' trout but for coho salmon in Duncan Bay as well.

For coast fishing, Harkley & Haywood dressed a tied-down-wing version and called it the Silver Minnow. Often they incorporated a blue stripe in the wing which was something that Brayshaw felt enhanced the fish-catching qualities of a fly. Lee Richardson fished the Little and Adams rivers through 19 continuous seasons, starting in 1934, and can attest to the effectiveness of a tied-down, blue-stripped, Silver & Mallard. In his book, *Lee Richardson's B.C.* (1978), he recounts a 1950s Silver & Mallard story and says:

I was using a rather large tied-down Mallard and Silver fly, but with a bright blue narrow feather down the back. We took turns working the rip. About 4:30 in the afternoon a trout hit my fly and headed for the lake, as they invariably did, jumping high in the air. As I pulled anchor Frank [Whitehouse] began to count the leaps aloud, and he continued to count until I was far out on the lake and well beyond earshot. Incredibly this grand trout made eighteen high, distinct leaps before she killed herself, literally, and I slipped the net under her . . . . She weighed five and three-quarters pounds. (p. 6)

Months later Richardson met Whitehouse at Harkley & Haywood and Richardson just happened to have a film of the Little River trip. Whitehouse arranged a showing for some Vancouver anglers at a local country club and when asked about his unusual success (15 trout in

three days from three to eight and a quarter pounds), Richardson told them the fly was a Mallard & Silver but with a blue stripe incorporated in the back. Richardson's show and talk resulted in a run on Harkley & Haywood's Silver and Mallard inventory and aided the fly's reputation as a fish catcher.

Nation's Black

HOOK: Number 7 **BODY:** Black machine silk
THROAT: Four hairs from a brown, coast, bucktail
WING: Six hairs from a brown, coast, bucktail
ORIGINATOR: Bill Nation
INTENDED USE: Wet fly for rainbow trout
LOCATION: Paul Lake

When Rod Haig-Brown was writing *The Western Angler*, he visited Paul Lake and met the then-already-famous William Nation, angler's guide, and through 1938 and in '39 they corresponded, mostly on fly tying and pattern development. In an April 1938 letter to Haig-Brown, Nation, about this plain black fly, says:

I enclose a very simple fly that I have worked out in imitation of the chironomids, slim black silk body, six strands of brown coast bucktail over and four under, #7 best, often take fish up to 8 pounds on it.

When *The Western Angler* was published in 1939, Haig-Brown, when discussing "Some Fauna of Interior Lakes" on the insect "Order Diptera. Two-winged flies," says:

Of this group of aquatic two-winged flies, I believe the chironomids are the most important to the fly fishermen. They . . . come to the surface while the ice is still leaving the lakes, thus making the earliest fishing. They also bring the fish up well at other stages of the season, and are often sufficiently numerous to cause at least a degree of selective feeding. Generally speaking, fish take the emerging pupae rather than the fly. . . . But if there is anything at all to be said for exact imitation in sunk flies for Kamloops trout, it would seem that this is the field that should offer the brightest prospects; success would mean extremely attractive fishing at times when there is now little more than the off chance of picking up the occasional fish. . . . Nation's Black is, so far as I know, the only imitation that has been developed especially for Kamloops waters (Vol. 1, pp. 115-116).

Haig-Brown gave sage advice about this area of fly development when he commented that this field offered "bright prospects." However, even though Nation developed British Columbia's, if not North America's, first chironomid pupa imitation, the development of chironomid fishing progressed slowly in British Columbia and elsewhere in the Pacific Northwest. It wasn't until the more educated, entomology-aware fly fishers of the 1960s and 1970s started developing new patterns and they discovered complementing fly-fishing techniques that chironomid fishing flourished. Now that serious chironomid fly fishers have refined this fly fishing technique to a science, often with subsequent astounding catches, most stillwater enthusiasts depend upon chironomids for much of their early and late season fly-fishing catches.

Nation's Blue

HOOK: Number 6 or 8
TAIL: A solid spear blade of light mallard
BODY: Rear third of flat, silver tinsel; rest of pale blue floss
RIB: Oval, silver tinsel
WING: Strips of light mallard breast feather with a blue overstripe, preferably of blue chatterer colour
COLLAR: A badger hackle **ORIGINATOR:** Bill Nation
INTENDED USE: Wet fly for rainbow trout
LOCATION: Paul Lake

Nation developed this pattern as an imitation of coupled bluets (damselflies) during his guiding career at Paul Lake. Although Roderick Haig-Brown gives credit to Nation as an innovative fly tier and says that most of Nation's flies were "conscientious and highly ingenious attempts to imitate natural insects," Haig-Brown thought that many of Nation's flies, however, fitted the "fancy category." Haig-Brown in an April 1938 letter suggested to Nation that the Blue fitted into the fancy group and not the natural insect group and writes:

> But I am sure you will understand why I am classing these two flies [Nation's Blue & Nation's Red] with the Special and Fancy and Silvertip as "fancy" flies rather than imitations. In doing so I am certainly not suggesting that they are anything but excellent flies to use and very deadly when used properly.

Nation didn't understand and wouldn't concede an inch with Haig-Brown regarding the classification of his Blue and Red as "fancy" flies. To please Nation, Haig-Brown didn't list them directly in the "fancy" fly category in the 1939 edition of *The Western Angler*. He did, however, class the Blue and Red as "suspect" patterns that possibly should be in the "fancy" category.

In the November 1971 issue of *Western Fish and Game*, Jim Kilburn in an article titled "The British Columbia Fly fisher" discusses the fly-fishing possibilities with adult damselfly imitations. He says:

> It's no secret to initiated trout fishermen that adult damselflies are occasionally very easy prey for feeding trout. At one time or another, it's likely that most experienced trouters have seen fish feeding on damselflies . . . .
> Over the years, I've talked with many experienced anglers on the subject of catching trout feeding on adult damselflies. . . . The only British Columbian pattern that I know is the Nation's Blue.

The Blue . . . is a wet fly which represents a pair of in-flight and coupled damselflies. Nation apparently reasoned that the Blue, fished an inch or so beneath the surface, should appear the same to trout as would a natural flying an inch or so above the surface. His reasoning might be debated, but there's no denying that Nation's Blue will often catch trout when damselflies are on the wing . . . .

Nation claims that when the bluets are about you will often find trout so gorged on damsels that most of the stomach contents are "composed practically entirely of adults taken on the wing." He recommends that to obtain success with the Blue, it must be fished about one inch below the surface and with as fast a retrieve as possible.

Nation's Fancy

HOOK: Number 4 or 6
TAIL: Fifteen strands from a golden pheasant tippet feather
BODY: Rear third, flat, silver tinsel; remainder, black floss
RIB: Oval, silver tinsel
THROAT: For number 6: A finely barred speckled guinea feather tied in before wing. For number 4: A light-coloured badger hackle feather tied in after the wing
WING: Strips from mallard's lightly barred breast feather with a few golden pheasant tippet feather strands enclosed
ORIGINATOR: Bill Nation
INTENDED USE: Wet fly for rainbow trout
LOCATION: Paul Lake

This is one of the many flies developed during the 1920s and '30s by Bill Nation for Kamloops trout fishing. Nation, a well-read fly fisher and astute observer of the natural world, attempted to produce flies that represented the natural food of Kamloops trout. About the design of the Fancy, in a 1938 letter to Roderick Haig-Brown, Nation says:

> Note that the reason for the enclosed tippet in the mallard wing of the #6 Fancy, which has a guinea hackle behind the wing, is that the orange of the tippet showing through the centre of mallard wing, when wet, gives the illusion to the trout, of the orange centre of the orange spot gammarus.

Often a fly's success is determined by the designer's confidence in his thought process and that the thought logic is correct. Nation was a very capable fly fisher and, although most of the flies that he designed as imitations would fall far short of present day fly fishers' specifications, he fished his patterns with skill and confidence and was very successful. However, no matter what logic Nation applied to his design, modern fly fishers have no choice but to class the Fancy as a fancy or all-purpose pattern.

During the 1920s and '30s the interior fishing was in its prime with large fish abounding in many lakes and streams and others such as Lac Le Jeune with not so large trout but plenty of them, there was relatively little competition and good catches came regularly to fancy flies. Kamloops trout are often non-selective feeders and if the fly fisher imparts appealing movement and the fly looks lifelike fish often sampled the creations. The combinations of fur, feather, tinsel and floss in varying sizes were numerous. Some were of local design while others were imported from Britain and Eastern North America. Some combinations produced much better than others and Nation's Fancy was one such pattern. Probably not because the fish found it more appealing, but because Nation had confidence in his creations and he fished them effectively. His confidence in his patterns was contagious and he passed that confidence onto those he guided.

The size four Fancy with the mallard wing has often been referred to as Nation's Mallard & Silver. Roderick Haig-Brown, in *The Western Angler* (1939), when recommending a selection of local all-purpose Kamloops trout flies for the visiting angler, included Nation's Fancy in the list.

About his Grey Nymph, Nation, in correspondence to Rod Haig-Brown, mentioned that the nymph dressed on a size seven hook represents the yearling, and on the number four, the mature insect. Regarding sizes, he says that the Grey Nymph dressed on "#4 and #7 are most useful" and the Green Nymph dressed on "#3, #5 & #7 [are] most useful." In his March 1938 letter to Haig-Brown, Nation suggests the fly fisher vary the nymphs' body colours to match light conditions and relates some of the nymphs' successes. He says:

Tying the dragon nymphs as I go, I find that the colouring should vary with the quality of the light. Probably to have them look the same to the fish in different lights this would have to be so. If heavily overcast use a light mottled grey; in bright sunlight use a dull green. The Special and the grey and green dragon nymphs account for the bulk of the larger rainbow. The largest on fly in recent years weighed 17 pounds and took a #4 grey nymph. The two largest last summer went 8 1/4 each, and both took a #4 grey nymph . . . .

When dressing the nymphs, Nation complemented the body colour with gold, olive green, dark grey or off-white tying silks. On the three samples of the Grey Nymph that I examined, Nation omitted the gold rib and instead used off-white tying silk, crisscrossing the body. Haig-Brown in the frontispiece of *The Western Angler* (1939) included four Nation-dressed nymphs: light olive green, emerald green, tan and grey.

When discussing the insect order Odonata which cover both dragonflies and damselflies, Haig-Brown in *The Western Angler* says:

. . .but for the most part Odonata are taken as under-water insects. Nation has developed at least two excellent imitations of the large dragon nymphs—Nation's Green Nymph and Nation's Grey Nymph. Tied on No. 4 or larger hooks, these kill really well, and the only criticism I have to make of them is that they are rather heavy and awkward to cast (Vol. 1, p. 114).

Nation's Green and Grey Nymphs are certainly the first dragonfly nymph imitations developed in British Columbia, if not North America, and possibly, the world.

Nation's Grey and Green Nymphs

GREY NYMPH

HOOK: Number 1 to 7
TAIL: A clump of fibres from a golden pheasant tippet feather
BODY: Emerald green wool built to 3/16 inch and with strips of mallard flank feather wound over
RIB: Oval, gold tinsel
THROAT: Hair from a ground-hog's tail or desert fox's rump
WING: Hair from a ground-hog's tail
ORIGINATOR: Bill Nation
INTENDED USE: Wet fly for rainbow trout
LOCATION: Paul Lake

GREEN NYMPH

HOOK: Number 2 to 7
TAIL: A clump of fibres from a golden pheasant tippet feather
BODY: Green wool, built up to 3/16 inch
RIB: Oval, gold tinsel
THROAT: Hair from a ground-hog's tail
WING: Hair from a ground-hog's tail
ORIGINATOR: Bill Nation
INTENDED USE: Wet fly for rainbow trout
LOCATION: Paul Lake

Nation's Green Sedge

HOOK: Number 6 **TAIL:** Red swan
BODY: Green seal's fur **RIB:** Oval, gold tinsel
WING Mallard or teal flank **COLLAR:** Badger
ORIGINATOR: Bill Nation
INTENDED USE: Wet fly for rainbow trout
LOCATION: Paul Lake

When responding to Rod Haig-Brown's questions on Nation's fly patterns to be included in *The Western Angler*, Nation said that he dressed the Green Sedge on "# 6 only" and that the fly dressers should "vary shade of green to suit season." To alter the shade of store-bought seal's fur, Nation advised Haig-Brown that the fly fisher should "treat bright green with peroxide" when on the water for instant colour changes. But the fly dresser can obtain different shades of green by leaving the seal's fur on the window ledge allowing the rays of the sun to bleach as required.

Nation developed this Grizzly King-like pattern as a wet-fly sedge imitation for Paul Lake rainbows. On its effectiveness, however, he did make the comment that the fly seemed more effective when the hatch was off. That is not untypical of fly patterns that may be dressed too bulky or large and not as representative as could be of the stage of insect life that the fish are targeting. The Green Sedge, dressed on a number 6 hook, is a fly with considerable bulk.

For success with this pattern and others, Nation knew that fly presentation was critical and it must imitate the movement of the natural insect. In correspondence with Haig-Brown about the green sedge nymph, Nation, a well-read and astute observer of fish and the things in fish's natural word, says:

Underwater life movements might be classified into those that flick like a prawn . . .; those that crawl like a snake . . .; those that walk like a sheep, as many of the sedge nymphs. And the working of the fly that imitates these forms should also imitate the action of the particular nymph. Note that the nymph of the green sedge moves in a series of tiny jerks; these seem to be of great intensity, but each fierce, convulsive jerk only manages to move the nymph forward less than an eighth of an inch. This nymph moves on the shoals each evening from 10 o'clock on for a few days before hatching, and are in the chara weed, and the dyed seal's fur body of the sedge fly imitates the case more nearly than it does the actual body of the nymph. The fly is fished quite slowly under these conditions, and a very short, fierce jerk of one inch is sent through the line every ten seconds. This style of fishing works best during the four days preceding the full moon, so does not apply generally. For the Green Sedge it is advisable to carry peroxide of hydrogen to bleach the body to the desired shade of that of the sedge or nymph the fish are feeding on.

In closing this discussion on the green sedge nymph, Nation included sample seal's fur in various stages of bleaching and said that he picked the shade that best suits his own tying. Haig-Brown in The *Western Angler* says that "Nation's Green Sedge is a valuable imitation" and during the early part of the season, May and June, "catches great numbers of fish at Paul Lake" (Vol. 1. p. 113).

Nation's Red

HOOK: Number 4 and 6 **TAIL:** Mallard flank
BODY: Rear third of flat silver tinsel; front two thirds of scarlet wool
RIB: Fine, flat silver **WING:** Bronze mallard
SIDES: Red swan **COLLAR:** Badger
ORIGINATOR: Bill Nation
INTENDED USE: Wet fly for rainbow trout
LOCATION: Paul Lake

In a March 1938 letter to Roderick Haig-Brown, Bill Nation had this to say about the "coupled red dragon flies" which Nation says his Red Dragon imitated:

One rather new fly which I released the fall before last is an imitation of the coupled red dragon flies. I enclose one. You will see that the red front part of the body, with the red stripe on the wing, represents the strongly coloured red female in the lead, the silver end of the body, with the heavy light mallard tail represents the lighter coloured male in tow. This fly I have been working on since the fall on 1927, and find that the final dressing accounts for large numbers of fish when the red dragons are moving.

Haig-Brown, skeptical about Nation's claim that the Red Dragon represented coupled adults, attributed the pattern's success to presentation. When confronted with Haig-Brown's opinion: that because the Red Dragon was a wet fly and that a proper imitation would be a floating fly fished on the surface, Nation, with his commonly held beliefs about fishes' ability to see colours, responded:

Assume the silver end of the body looks white or light grey to a fish, remembering that trout are colour blind, then the objection to the Specials as being fancy disappears. The Red, with its silver end, is continued in a heavy spade tail of light mallard . . . and this imitates the lighter coloured male, carried by the female. . . . The stomachs of the trout are, at certain seasons, literally crammed with adult single dragons and damsels, often up to 20 to a stomach; these were all taken on the wing by the trout jumping out after them. When a damsel or dragon once touches the surface of the water it is unable to rise, and lies there until some fish or bird or bat takes it. These are so few that the enormous gorge of damsels that the trout collect sometimes is composed practically entirely of adults taken on the wing. Therefore it is wrong to fish the Red or Blue as a floating still dry fly. For every natural floating red or blue there are 10,000 winged ones flying an inch or two above the water . . . .

In another letter, Nation says:

I believe that the trout which are cruising some six feet below the surface are unable to tell whether a fly fished submerged 3/4 inch at the end of a greased line and submerged leader is above or below the surface, and believe this is proved when I fish the coupled red dragon at the utmost possible speed with a vertical rod and the fly kept as near the surface as possible.

Most knowledgeable fly fishers in this era know that fish do see colours and Nation's Red does fall into the "fancy" fly category. However, we shouldn't take anything away from Nation's ingenuity: he observed his natural world, formed beliefs and devised fly patterns to suit those beliefs, but most of all he presented the fly in such a way that brought reality to his hypotheses.

Nation's Silver-tip

HOOK: Number 4 to 8
TAIL: Six strands from a golden pheasant tippet feather
BODY: Rear quarter of flat silver tinsel;
remainder of black floss
RIB: Oval silver tinsel
THROAT: Speckled guinea fowl
WING: Very lightly mottled turkey enclosing a few strands
from a golden pheasant tippet feather
ORIGINATOR: Bill Nation
INTENDED USE: Wet fly for rainbow trout
LOCATION: Paul Lake

Nation's Silver-tipped Sedge

HOOK: Number 6 **TAIL:** Red swan
BODY: Rear third of flat, silver tinsel; front
two thirds of green seal's fur
RIB: Oval, gold tinsel
WING: Mottled grey turkey
COLLAR: Badger
ORIGINATOR: Bill Nation
INTENDED USE: Wet fly for rainbow trout
LOCATION: Paul Lake

Originally designed for Paul Lake by Bill Nation sometime in the 1920s, but because of its success, the Silver-tip found devotees throughout the interior and on the coast as well. W.F. Pochin in his 1946 book, *Angling and Hunting in British Columbia*, has this to say about the effectiveness of Bill Nation's Silver-tip for Kamloops and steelhead trout:

> As a game fish the Kamloops trout stands pre-eminent. Its methods of fighting are quite similar to that of the steelhead; both make terrific rushes and both generally jump several times. The Kamloops is taken on the fly . . . and the best fishing is to be had on the streams and smaller lakes, and at the mouths of streams flowing into larger rivers and lakes. Trout up to three or four pounds are commonly taken in such situations, but much larger specimens, up to ten pounds and over, have been taken on the fly. . . .
>
> Best flies in the interior during May and early June are Nation's Special, Nation's Silvertip and Carey's Special. (p. 13)

Later, in his book, Pochin, about the top steelhead pattern for Silver Lake steelhead, says:

> For the angler who insists on taking big fish on the fly, Silver Lake, situated at the eastern end of the lower mainland in the Hope district, is the spot. Here great Steelheads weighing up to 16 pounds rise to feathered lures during September and October. Several patterns will take them but Nation's Silver Tip tied on a number four hook is regarded as tops. (p. 45)

After nearly forty years of use, Roy Patrick in his 1964 edition of *Pacific Northwest Fly Patterns* says that the Silver-tip is "one of the most popular of Bill Nation's patterns" and is "successful in all areas of the interior for whatever fishing is done" (p. 72).

Bill Nation fished many lakes in the Kamloops area, but Paul Lake was home. When Nation first fished Paul, the green sedge was not indigenous to the lake, and Nation thought that the addition of this insect would improve angling opportunities. In a March 1938 letter to Rod Haig-Brown, Nation describes the insect breeding conditions, availability of food for fish, and the green sedge introduction to Paul Lake. He says:

> Paul is much the same, fish in hard silvery condition, and very fat. They will be larger this year than last, as the feed in the lake is on the increase. The lake has been very high for three years, and this has increased the shallow water breeding area of the aquatic insects, and protected the gravid female shrimps from fish and ducks. The green sedge that I introduced in the nymph stage from Knouff to Paul in 1925, 26 and 27 had increased to such numbers by 1928 that it became the principal sedge on the lake, and this is very gratifying, as this sedge was unknown on Paul before the stocking.

In the same letter Nation mentioned to Haig-Brown that "flies are going fine; green sedge pattern fixed now, and find that when the hatch is off the trout take the sedge better if the hind end of the green body is one third replaced by silver tinsel. . . ." When describing to Haig-Brown the dressing for the Silver-tipped Sedge, Nation was very particular that the wing and body colouration match the natural insect and says that the wing should be a "light grey of average correct mottle" and the body: "green seal's fur in various stages of sun bleach."

About the grey turkey wings, Nation was most particular. The next year, 1939, Nation wrote Haig-Brown and mentioned the difficulty he was having in obtaining flies dressed to his specifications and one of the problems was obtaining grey turkey wings. He says that "these grey turkey feathers must have no trace of brown in them, but must be mottled shades of pure grey."

The Silver-tipped Sedge was a staple Kamloops-area pattern for more than a quarter century.

Nation's Special

HOOK: Number 4 to 8
TAIL: Six strands from a golden pheasant tippet feather
BODY: Rear third of flat silver tinsel; front two thirds of black floss
RIB: Oval silver tinsel **THROAT:** Speckled guinea fowl
WING: Mottled grey turkey, enclosing a few strands from a golden pheasant tippet feather
SIDES: Jungle cock **ORIGINATOR:** Bill Nation
INTENDED USE: Wet fly for rainbow trout
LOCATION: Paul Lake

Developed in the 1920s for Paul Lake trout, this is one of Bill Nation's most effective patterns. About the wing on the Special, Nation recommended strips of grey mottled turkey feather be used and that the angler match the Special's wing mottle to that of the sedge or dun hatching. Bruce Hutchison in the chapter titled "For Anglers Only" in his book, *The Fraser* (1950), paid homage to Bill Nation and Nation's Special when he wrote:

> *The Kamloops country was long the undisputed kingdom of Bill Nation. That extraordinary man, who knew trout better than any other British Columbian and had spent his life studying the insect life on which trout feed, chose to call himself a guide. Careless of fame or money, he would row you around Paul Lake, his favourite, or any other lake you fancied for a few dollars a day. After an hour's fishing with him the richest American tycoon was subdued and humble in this shy man's presence. Beside his life of innocence and content, the perfect companionship of man and nature, your own life suddenly appeared for the failure it was. And what could you say for your skill when he could cast a fly and pierce the tail of any fish you pointed out among the autumn salmon horde? . . . .*
>
> *His memorial is the Nation Special, the fly he constructed out of his unequaled knowledge of insect life and the appetite of the Kamloops trout. No fisherman can afford to be without Bill's masterpiece. (pp. 324-325)*

A most glowing tribute indeed. In 1936 Roderick Haig-Brown visited Paul Lake and Echo Lodge, during his research for *The Western Angler*, published in 1939, and in that publication provided additional testimonials to the effectiveness of Nation's Special. In his chapter on tackle and in his discussion of fly patterns for interior use, Haig-Brown examined the Honour Book kept by lodge owner, J. Arthur Scott. Of the 119 large trout between 3 1/2 to 7 3/4 pounds, 46 were deceived by a Nation's Special. There were 13 other patterns in the group, the closest rival to Nation's Special was the Jock Scott. With nine fish, it came in a poor second.

When dressing this fly for September fishing, Nation recommended that along with sides of jungle cock the fly dresser should add strips of red swan for "when the red dragons are around."

Olive Sedge

HOOK: Number 8 or 9 **TAG:** Flat, gold tinsel
BODY: Dark olive-green seal's fur **RIB:** Black floss
BODY HACKLE: An olive hackle feather
WING: Bronze mallard **HACKLE:** An olive hackle feather
ORIGINATOR: Tom Brayshaw
INTENDED USE: Dry fly for rainbow trout
LOCATION: Knouff Lake

Like Bill Nation, the demigod of interior lake fly fishers, Tom Brayshaw, amongst many other talents, was an observer of nature and a master fly dresser. This is a necessary combination if one is to produce flies representative of specific insects that work. Brayshaw produced numerous sedge patterns and he fished the interior lakes in the golden years—the 1920s and 1930s, when fish of 8 to 10 pounds and larger abounded and came to a properly presented dry fly.

A Knouff Lake fly fisher, Brayshaw would often lend a helping hand to anglers he met on the lake. Typical of his generosity and its result was shown when, on July 3, 1932, after examining the fly box of an aspiring Vancouver angler, "who had no suitable flies," Brayshaw gave him one of his Olive Sedges and "he later got a 3 1/2 lb fish on it, the only one he got."

Knouff Lake fishermen such as Tom Brayshaw and Bryan Williams produced numerous dry fly patterns to catch Knouff's large trout. Typical of Brayshaw's sedges is the palmered hackle, the first that I have come across for British Columbian developed dry flies.

One of British Columbia's largest stillwater dry-fly caught trout, a 17 1/4 pound monster, on a dry sedge, came from Knouff Lake. There is some confusion, however, about the date of this feat: Steve Raymond in *Kamloops* (1971) records the year as 1930, Haig-Brown in *The Western Angler* (1939) gives 1930 in his text, but the accompanying photograph shows E.L. Hodgson holding the fish, and the caption states 1932. The day this great event occurred, June 12, 1932, four Hodgsons were at the lake but Brayshaw too was there. About the Sunday afternoon fishing Brayshaw had this to say:

> *Later I got one of 2 pounds 7 ounces on dry sedge and had quite a few rises. Mrs. P[hilips] lost a big one (10 pounds or more) on Pazooka. . . . After lunch I tried Pazooka in almost flat calm and had a fish on at once but lost it after a few jumps. At a quarter to 3 Eldred [Hodgson] had come to Cape Horn . . . Just as the breeze died away he hooked a big one which showed several times and jumped quite a bit. I got up anchor to take him a gaff and stand by. Ten minutes later I netted it—a female 17 1/4 pounds 34 1/4" long 19" in girth. Slight rainbow stripe.*

We do know that this fish took a dry fly and, reference to the capture of this 17 1/4 pounder is given in the text of Williams' Grey-Bodied Sedge found later in this volume. Because Brayshaw was there that day and fishing dry fly with his own sedge patterns and documented the event, I believe this is an appropriate place to record this piece of British Columbia's fly fishing history.

Pazooka

HOOK: Number 6 or 8
TAIL: A few fibres from a golden pheasant's tippet feather
BODY: Green wool **RIB:** Orange floss
COLLAR: A ring-necked pheasant rump feather
WING: A few fibres from a golden pheasant's tippet feather
ORIGINATOR: Len Phillips
INTENDED USE: Wet fly for rainbow trout
LOCATION: Knouff Lake

After European settlers moved into the Kamloops area they discovered that many of the surrounding lakes were devoid of fish, yet many were blessed with prolific aquatic life just waiting for some ingenious soul to stock them with trout. Knouff Lake was one such lake which was stocked with nine ripe trout in May 1917 by local residents, Len Phillips and son.

For three years the fish were left to gorge themselves on the abundant aquatic life and when it was opened for fishing in May, 1920, some monsters in the 15 to 20-pound range were caught. Word of the large fish catches like those experienced at Knouff is difficult to keep secret and Knouff Lake became the destination of many fly fishers. The Pazooka was one of the flies that was developed for the Knouff Lake fishery.

A. Bryan Williams in his *Fish & Game in British Columbia* (1935) says that Knouff "is one of the most beautiful of the interior lakes, and also one of the best for fishing" (p. 107). Williams mentioned that accommodation was available at the farmhouse located at the head of the lake and according to Brayshaw's diary it was the Phillips' who rented rooms in their home at the head of Knouff Lake.

What year the Pazooka was actually invented I have not been able to determine, however, Tom Brayshaw recorded in his diary on Saturday June 11, 1932, that the "Phillips's had fun with the 'Pazooka' but lost a big percentage after hooking but it is very deadly in a breeze." The next day Brayshaw says that "Mrs. P[hillips] lost a big one (10 pounds or more) on Pazooka."

On June 16, 1933, when he arrived at Knouff for a weekend of fishing, Brayshaw learned that prospects didn't look promising as Eldrid, Slee and another "all had a blank day." For the master fly fisher, however, things proved differently and he "got a four pounder . . . from the sunk island nearest shore, and an hour later one of 7 1/4 pounds from the same island—both on 'Pazooka'." About fishing the Pazooka, Brayshaw compared it to the same technique that Colonel Carey used with the Carey Special and says:

At any rate we did the same thing at Knouff with the "pazooka" and fished it the same way. Throw it out, lay the rod down, fill a pipe, light same, half smoke it and then wallop! you had him! (Tommy Brayshaw: The Ardent Angler Artist, p. 85.)

Because the Phillips' introduced fish to the lake and developed the fishery and with their first recorded use of the fly, I have credited them with the Pazooka's development. However, I have no direct evidence to support that assumption and others may prove me wrong.

Over the years the Pazooka somehow lost its unique name. Patrick in an early 1960s printing of *Pacific Northwest Fly Patterns* gave two variations of a fly designed specifically for this lake: Knouff Lake or Knouff Special. Incidentally, earlier editions of Patrick's book didn't list the Knouff Lake patterns. According to Steve Raymond in *Kamloops* (1980), the Knouff Special was intended to be an emerging sedge pupa imitation. Indeed, it is highly impressionistic and, like many flies of that nature, fishers must use their imagination and have faith.

PKCK

HOOK: Number 8 low-water salmon
TAG: Flat, silver tinsel **BODY:** Olive wool
RIB: A stripped eyed peacock quill
WING-CASE: Brown turkey tail feather
THORAX: Olive wool
GILLS: Fronds from a white emu feather
ORIGINATOR: Jim Kilburn & Dave Powell
INTENDED USE: Wet fly for rainbows
LOCATION: Minnie Lake

Many curious Totems' eyes peered through the lantern-and-flashlight lit darkness as Ron Harris' hands performed the delicate autopsy on Jim Stewart's Halfback-taken, five-pound trout. All onlookers—Jim Kilburn, Dave Powell, Jim Stewart, Werner Schmid—were curious to find out what those large, difficult-to-entice Minnie Lake trout were feeding on.

None was surprised at the contents of the fish's stomach. As Jim Kilburn later wrote in the Issue #3, June 1968, *Totems Topics*:

Merely a double handful of chironomid pupae—perhaps ten thousand in all—and a few damselfly nymphs and water boatman. The pupae were large—about 3/4 of an inch long.

That autopsy event took place in May 1968 and that night after the postmortem the PKCK was invented. Unfortunately, because of strong winds the next day, the group of eager anglers was unable to test the pattern. The following weekend Werner Schmid scored and the week after Peter Broomhall, but almost two years lapsed before Kilburn became truly convinced that he had developed a worthwhile and effective fly. In the January 1971 issue of *Western Fish & Game*, Kilburn in his article titled PKCK says:

> So when Werner mentioned an early October conquest (topped by 10 1/4 and 11 3/4 pounders) in a small Kamloops District lake, I was all ears. The top fly was the No. 8 PKCK. I quickly tied a fresh batch, scheduled a week's holiday, and . . . . Thinking back, I believe this was my finest fall. Happily enough, my first single day of sport fell on my birthday. And the best fish that day was as bright and pretty an eight-pound rainbow as I could ever wish. What's more, the fish took a PKCK . . . .
>
> The trout took in inches of water, ran and jumped its way a full 150 yards before stopping for the first time, and proceeded to give me several most anxious moments. It was one of those superbly fat and silver specimens, a female fish as it turned out. I gently weighed her, then released her. Such a fish deserves another life.
>
> That episode was the climax of several memorable days. My catch averaged six pounds, and all had an insatiable appetite for the PKCK.

Although the PKCK was not British Columbia's first chironomid pattern, it was one of the first chironomid imitations where the fly dresser, with a real specimen as a guide, attempted to match with wool, feather and tinsel the structure of the insect.

In a recent letter from Jim Kilburn, about the insect and the fly's name, he says that:

> . . . the pattern was influenced by the pupa of the giant *Chironomus* species at Minnie Lake . . . . The abbreviated name 'PKCK' (short for Powell-Kilburn Chironomid Killer) was influenced by [the American] Dick Thompson's TDC (Thompson's Delectable Chironomid).

Red Butt Chironomid Pupa

HOOK: Number 10 to 16
TAG: Bright red floss or yarn
BODY: Dark brown pheasant tail fibres
RIB: Flat, gold tinsel
THORAX: Peacock herl with pheasant tail shellback
GILLS: White acrylic yarn or ostrich
ORIGINATOR: Brian Chan
INTENDED USE: Wet fly for rainbow trout
LOCATION: Kamloops lakes

A self proclaimed chironomid addict, Brian Chan, the developer of the Red Butt, in a BCFFF *Fly Lines* article titled "Confessions of a Chironomid Addict" claims that as he sees the first chironomids come off the South Thompson River in late February, he starts to get excited about the upcoming "fishing of the rich trout lakes of the Southern Interior."

About this fly fishing passion—chironomid fishing—he says:

> Chironomid or Midge fishing is a pleasant, aesthetically pleasing way to fish. Cast a floating line out with a pupal pattern attached, wait for it to sink to the appropriate depth and begin a slow hand twist retrieve, pausing regularly to take in the scenery around you. Then watch or feel your flyline just move slightly or, take off and another trout is foiled.

Chan makes it sound easy and claims that it is, once you understand the life cycle of the chironomid. This book, however, is not about entomology. To get some insight into that subject, I recommend Chan's book, *Flyfishing Strategies for Stillwaters*, published privately in 1991 by Brian and available in some local fly-fishing shops or through Frank Amato Publications, Inc. in Portland, Oregon. In his book, Chan details the entomology of most trout foods available in British Columbia's stillwater fisheries plus much more on how to catch stillwater trout.

In a recent letter to me about the Red Butt Chironomid Pupa and its development he writes:

> There are literally thousands of species of chironomids in North American waters, both standing and flowing. Fishing chironomids in stillwaters is definitely my favourite form of fly fishing. I began to notice an interesting stage in pupal development the fish seemed to key on. That is the red hemoglobin butt on many chironomid species. I believe these particular species of chironomids have pupa that don't quite completely absorb or metamorphose the hemoglobin of the larval stage. As a result there is often a definite red abdominal tip to them. This pattern is the first one that I put the red butt on. These are the big brown bombers that come off many of our most productive waters.
>
> Since developing this pattern in 1980, I have put red butts on many other chironomid pupae imitations for example black with red butt, green with red butt.

In his closing remarks Chan mentioned that red-butted chironomid pupae appear in all sizes and that trout will target the red-tipped emerging pupae. He recommends two fishing techniques. The floating line with varying lengths of leader from 12 to 24 feet depending on the depth of water to be fished. The pupae should be fished close to the bottom with a dead-slow retrieve or wind drift. However, in the deeper water, often a full sinking line is effective when it is permitted to sink to the vertical and slowly retrieved.

Harold Lohr's intricately dressed damsel.

Red-Shirted Trapper

HOOK: Number 8 or larger blind-eyed trout
BODY: Red wool
THROAT: Ruffed grouse bottle-green neck frill
WING: Ruffed grouse bottle-green neck frill
ORIGINATOR: John Keast Lord
INTENDED USE: Wet fly for cutthroat trout
LOCATION: Moyee River

During many hours of research into the early works about fish and fishing in British Columbia, I found what I believe to be the first fly that was locally tied to catch British Columbia trout. Its inventor was John Keast Lord, the time was the early 1860s, the place was a stream in the Rocky Mountains, and the fish, cutthroat.

Mr. Lord was part of the Boundary Commission, whose job it was to establish, on the ground, through British Columbia, the 49th parallel the boundary between the USA and Canada. Lord was the naturalist attached to the British part of the Boundary Commission. He worked in British Columbia from 1860 to 1863, then returned to England and wrote his now-scarce-and-expensive, two-volume work, *The Naturalist in Vancouver Island and British Columbia*, published in 1866. Amongst his many observations on flora and fauna are a few fishing anecdotes. It is from one of these that an early, if not the very first, trout fly developed in British Columbia is described.

When Lord encountered many rising trout in a stream on the western slopes of the Rocky Mountains, he hastily scraped together some hooks and thread, and red wool from his blanket. He used grouse feathers for the fly's throat-hackle and wing. Then he put all together by hand without the aid of tying tools.

Lord did not name his creation but, later, after he tried to make a more representative imitation of the insect that he saw trout feeding upon, he found that his "poor original was better than a good imitation", and he referred to the original as an old, Red-Shirted Trapper—an appropriate name.

Without a picture and with scant information on the tying procedures, it is hard to determine the fly's style. Because dry-fly fishing was in its infancy at that time, it was most likely a wet fly and Lord did say that he dropped the fly into, not on, the water. From examining woodcut reproductions of flies in some of the books of that era I was able to verify that my tie is fairly representative.

After his creation was complete, Lord related his success with his new fly and wrote:

I tried the pool as a last chance; so, leaning over the rock, I let my tempter drop into the water; it made a splash like throwing in a stone; but imagine my delight, ye lovers of the gentle art, when a tremendous jerk told me I had one hooked and struggling to get free . . . .

Having discovered a secret, I pressed eagerly on to turn it to

my best advantage, and, that day, played havoc amongst the trouts. Some long willow-branches, cut with a crook at the end, served me in lieu of a basket. Passing the sticks under the gill-covers, and out at the mouth, I strung trout after trout until the sticks were filled . . . . (Vol. 1, pp. 80-81)

Red-Shouldered Dragonfly Nymph

HOOK: Number 8 Mustad 9672 (3 extra-long)
BODY: Clipped deer hair with medium light olive seal's fur woven through deer hair
THROAT: Hen pheasant centre tail fibres
ORIGINATOR: Jack Shaw
INTENDED USE: Wet fly for rainbow trout
LOCATION: Kamloops lakes

The red-shouldered dragonfly nymph was one of the insects that Jack Shaw nurtured and studied in his home aquarium and from those observations he devised his Red-Shouldered Dragonfly Nymph pattern in the 1970s.

This pattern is complicated to tie, however. For those that are interested in the tying details Shaw gives explicit instructions in his 1991 book *Tying Flies for Trophy Trout*.

Sometime later, near the end of the 1970s decade, the red-shouldered dragonfly nymph was assumed to be a member of the Gomphidae family and the imitation became affectionately referred to as the Gomphus. However, in the genus Gomphus there are only two species indigenous to British Columbia and they are restricted to the lakeshores and slow rivers in the southern interior, according to a December 1994 article called the "Gomphus that is Not" in the Haig-Brown Fly Fishing Association's newsletter, *The Steelhead Bee*.

The writer of that in-depth article, an enthusiastic angler and amateur entomologist named Loucas Raptis attributes the misnaming of the Gomphus pattern to Alf Davy. In *'The Gilly'* (1985), Chapter IX. "Dragons: The Bottom Predator", Davy writes:

My fishing friend and companion . . . took this weed-crawling pattern, shaped it to look like Jack Shaw's seal fur Gomphus mud-dwelling nymph pattern, added some pheasant tail legs on either side . . . and it became the "Gomphus" . . . . (p. 78)

After considerable delving into the fly fishing literature associated with the misidentification and naming of the red-shouldered dragonfly nymph Gomphus, Loucas Raptis writes:

The evidence was unequivocal: all the accounts, descriptions, illustrations, and photographs of the dragonfly adult and nymph carrying the name "Gomphus" in all contemporary fly-fishing pub-

lications in British Columbia are in fact those of the genus *Sympetrum*. This discovery was particularly striking when one considers that some authors treat the subject with apparent entomological clout and assumed air of authority, yet in fact their search has been utterly superficial. (p.3)

However, it is not really important that the pattern developed to imitate the red-shouldered dragonfly nymph was misnamed. The pet insects from which Shaw produced the red-shouldered dragonfly nymph frequent lakes throughout the province and smart fly fishers will have the Red-Shouldered Dragonfly Nymph in their fly box. Fish find them a delectable dish.

Stump Lake Damsel

HOOK: Number 12 Mustad 9672 (3 extra-long)
or 79580 (4 extra-long)
BODY: Pale, muddy, yellowish-green wool
RIB: Fine, gold wire for flies fished on dull days and fine, silver wire for bright days
THROAT: Pale or medium yellow hackle
WING: Light mallard or polar bear fur
HEAD: Fine, light yellow chenille
ORIGINATOR: Jack Shaw
INTENDED USE: Dry fly for rainbow trout
LOCATION: Stump Lake

In Jack Shaw's 1976 book *Fly Fish the Trout Lakes*, about fishing the adult damselfly, he says:

The floating line is used to best present imitations of this terrestrial insect. Fish close to the sedge grass and rushes, presenting the fly in such a manner as to represent insects fallen to the water. Let the floating imitation lie for a moment, twitching occasionally to represent a struggling insect. (p. 83)

Later in his discussion he recommends some available commercial patterns such as Nation's Blue, Teal & Blue and Teal & Silver. However, Shaw, a secretive, man does not give details about his own pattern. In the early 1990s, *BC Outdoors* magazine ran a series of articles on Shaw-developed patterns. In the January/February 1990 issue, Shaw gives the damselfly particulars in an article called "The Stump Lake Damsel." About the fly's effectiveness, he writes:

A gust of wind came up and lasted several minutes. A few fish moved in close to the weeds, the wind died and the trout no longer moved. Thinking the wind blowing the weeds against each other was knocking newly-emerged insects into the water, I thought it was wise to try something that looked like a newly-emerged damsel fly. . . .

The off-shore wind made casting a bit troublesome as we were now facing into the wind; however, as long as we cast in the right-hand quarter, there was no problem. Fred got the first take on a fish that ran wildly for open water . . . . About the time Fred was going into his second with the trout my line tightened . . . and run it did well into the backing. . . . Finally in the net, we saw that it was a prime silver trout of about 1 1/2 kg.

More often than not, however, Shaw advises that the fly fisher should rely on the nymphal form. Fish relish them and when emergence time approaches, the nymphs swim in the top foot of the water towards shore-side reeds. Hungry trout ambush them as they swim to shore. In his book *Tying Flies for Trophy Trout* (1991), Shaw recommends a damselfly nymph dressed on a size 12, four-extra-long hook, with a grizzly hackle tail, a golden olive, light yellow, or medium olive-green body, a medium yellow or golden olive hackle throat, a light olive-green goose feather wing case, and a golden olive or light yellow head.

Tom Thumb

HOOK: Number 8 to 14 Mustad 94840
TAIL: Deer hair **BODY:** Deer hair
HACKLE: Deer hair **WING:** Deer hair
ORIGINATOR: Unknown but named by Collie Peacock
INTENDED USE: Dry fly for trout **LOCATION:** Jasper

In the early days of fly fishing in the province, it was not uncommon for fish of 10 pounds and larger to be taken on dry flies. There is only one insect that brings large fish up to the surface to feed and that is the medium to large sedge, or caddisflies as they are called elsewhere, that inhabit many Interior lakes. These medium to large flies pop to the surface when hatching and scamper over the surface causing quite a disturbance. The fish find them irresistible. Every fisherman should have something in his arsenal just in case he finds himself on a lake and the sedges are coming off. Famed Kamloops fly fisher Jack Shaw in his 1976 book, *Fly Fish the Trout Lakes*, says that:

one of the most successful representations is not identified as a sedge pattern and is not especially representative of it. This is the Tom Thumb, and in various sizes is a most productive pattern when this fly is active. (p. 102)

Jim Kilburn, noted 1960s and '70s fly fishing author, also thought much of the Tom Thumb as a sedge imitation, but claims it also doubled as a mayfly imitation. Kilburn writes in an article titled 'Mayflies and the Armchair Angler' in the May, 1969 issue of *Western Fish & Game* that:

My first cast with the little deerhair floater dropped amid the naturals, and slightly upwind of the rising trout. I let it drift over the feeding post, and it was quickly and confidently accepted. During the next hour and a half, I concluded that there is simply no fly better suited to the emergence of lake Mayflies than is the Tom Thumb.

According to Martin Tolley, in a 1968 'Tom Thumb' article written for *Northwest Sportsman* magazine, the Tom Thumb was found to be in use in Jasper during the 1950s. Earlier datings have been supposed but the Tom Thumb was not listed in Patrick's 1958 or 1962 editions of *Pacific Northwest Fly Patterns*, but it did appear in the 1964 edition. The late Collie Peacock, long-time guide, tackle store operator and salesman, is credited with popularizing it in British Columbia and providing its name—Tom Thumb. Peacock recalled meeting a California dentist who was using the fly in Jasper, but he could not recall the origins of the fly, its name, or that of the dentist fishing it, so he pulled the name "Tom Thumb" out of his hat.

No other dry fly has the fame of and is more widely used in British Columbia than the Tom Thumb.

Travelling Sedge

HOOK: Number 8 and 9 **TAG:** Flat, gold tinsel
BODY: Dark olive seal's fur **RIB:** Black floss
BODY HACKLE: A badger hackle
WING: Hen pheasant's tail feather
HACKLE: A furnace-coloured hackle
ORIGINATOR: Tom Brayshaw
INTENDED USE: Dry fly for rainbow trout
LOCATION: Knouff Lake

Knouff Lake during the 1920s and '30s produced some fine catches of large trout to the dry fly. The insects that drew fish to the surface were the sedges and in particular the travelling sedge. Tom Brayshaw fished Knouff often during its hey day and on July 1, 1932, about the travelling sedge, he writes:

This sedge was much larger than the one up in June and hatches sparsely and is more olive in colour. For a time on the water it resembles the green drake and then [it] folds its wings and runs on the water but seldom gets far before a feeding trout has it.

Fishing dry-sedge patterns was often very rewarding and on June 30, 1933, Brayshaw recorded in his diary a day's catch of seven large trout taken on a sedge fly by a fishing friend. About that friend's sedge catch and his own dry fly sedge catch, he says:

Everybody gone but Slee who is in the cabin so I joined him. He had 7 fish weighing 43 pounds this day all on sedge. Got afloat about 7:30 . . . as the breeze got stronger we tried the big island—nothing rising so I went to the brown saucer to be out of the wind. I got 4 there—2 1/2 pounds, 1 1/2 pounds, 5 3/4 pounds, & 3/4 all on a dry sedge; then I pottered back to No. 2 Island fishing the

big island en route. I got an 8 pound on No. 2 . . . Wind very strong . . . came in at 3 p.m. Slee had a 9 pounder & a 1 pound fish.

Including the two smaller fish of 3/4 and one pound and Slee's day-before catch, Brayshaw and Slee's 14 fish averaged over five pounds apiece. A most envious catch indeed.

Tunkwanamid

HOOK: Mustad 9671, size 4 to 12
TAG: Fine, oval tinsel **BODY:** Peacock herl
RIB: Fine, oval tinsel
COLLAR: Ostrich herl: white or black
ORIGINATOR: Tom Murray
INTENDED USE: Wet fly for rainbow trout
LOCATION: Tunkwa Lake

Originally called the Tunkwa Lake Chironomid but later christened the Tunkwanamid by Dave Elliott, this pattern was developed by Tom Murray for the lake bearing the fly's name in the early 1970s. In his "Popular Flies" column in the January 1977 issue of *Northwest Sportsman* magazine, Murray, in a story about a large trout he took with the Tunkwanamid says:

The fly was a No. 12 Tunkwanamid, the leader my own 16-foot, hand-tied; the line a No. 6 and the rod my favourite nine-foot "graphite." A decent cast, 60 feet or perhaps a little more. Let the leader sink. Wait—wait, until the tip of the line is being pulled under by the fly. Now, retrieve enough line to get the big loops out of the cast and carefully give the line enough "twitch" just to pull the last kinks out of the line (About 3 or 4 inches). Let the kinks settle into the line again and twitch it again.

This time, the line suddenly tightened. All I remember was the line being torn at right angles through the water. It was as though there was a hole in the water that the line disappeared into, and then the sight of the line under the water getting longer by the second, at right angles. . . . This is a BIG one. . . .

The first time I landed the fish it was for myself. Lucky as I was that day, a fishing partner came by just in time to see the final result. Did I want a picture? he asked as I was admiring the fine bright cock fish in the net. I sure did, because I knew I was going to release it. I weighed the fish in the net and subtracted the net weight.

"About 8 1/4," I said, shaking. I eased the fish out of the net and at the same time tried to pass my camera to my buddy. That is when I had to land the monster the second time. Pictures taken, I carefully revived my prize by supporting it underneath and holding the tail, then drawing it slowly back and forth through the water. The fish revived, gave a swish of its huge tail and slowly swam off. . . .

As readers may know, it [the Tunkwanamid pattern] is sup- posed to be an imitation of the larger chironomid larva . . . .

In a recent October 1994 letter to me where he included a sample pattern, Murray said that "the Tunkwanamid was so successful every- where in the world" he fished it—New Zealand, Japan, USA, Italy and at home—that he relies totally on the Tunkwanamid for his chironomid fishing.

Vincent's Sedge

HOOK: Number 8, 3 extra long
TAIL: A substantial clump of deer hair
BODY: Kelly green seal's fur **RIB:** Light green floss
WING: Underwing: A substantial amount of deer body hair
OVERWING: Grey turkey primary from the inside (or off-side) of the quill that has been lacquered with head cement
HACKLE: Brown hackle
HEAD: Green tying thread, lacquered
ORIGINATOR: Jack Vincent
INTENDED USE: Dry fly for rainbow trout
LOCATION: Roche Lake

Fly fishers have flocked to the lakes of the interior for the past 75 years in pursuit of sedge-taking rainbow trout and, during that time, numerous fly patterns have been developed to take those surface-feed- ing fish. Long-time fly fisher, commercial fly tier, and sporting goods salesman Jack Vincent was often found pursuing those surface-feeding, stillwater trout. The Vincent Sedge is one of his creations and he details the fly's development in Issue number 38, August, 1975 of the *Totem Topics*. He writes:

If compliments from expert fly fishers and the fact that a fish was taken on its maiden cast mean anything, then perhaps a fly I dreamed up may have some merit . . . .
Fishing as best I could, which couldn't have been good enough, I failed to connect that weekend or for the best part of the subsequent weekend, 'til in desperation I dressed the fly. . . .
Anyhow, sitting by myself in the tent trailer, I retrieved what came out of the jaws of the vise and proceeded towards the lake. On the way I met Boyd Aigner of the Washington F.F. Club and Art Micheluk of the Hook and Hackle Club of Calgary, showed them the fly and they seemed very impressed with what they saw. Frankly, they both opined it was one of the best sedge imitations they had seen. Being a sucker for any form of flattery I acknowl- edged they were obviously anglers of impeccable taste and it was only a matter of time before I showed those Roche Lake rainbows a thing or two.
I don't know how it happened*probably when Boyd and I were swapping tales *Art got on the lake, and by the time I arrived

at the far end he was already swinging at anchor casting away, as were Karl Hauffler and Harold Baker.
"Got that good fly on?" asked Art. "What good fly?" the oth- ers asked. Art replied telling them what a great-looking sedge imi- tation it was. I came close to blushing at all this praise for a com- pletely untried pattern.
Assuring them that I did, indeed, have the newest Vincent pattern on, I flicked the fly out about ten feet, saw that it was rid- ing as it should and fired out about a 55 foot cast.
The fly no sooner hit the water than there was a good splash and a rainbow of about 1 and a half pounds was dancing over the top of the water. Talk about being gratified. Unfortunately, it was the only fish I took on that pattern, but I found solace in the fact that the fish appeared to be leaving the naturals on the surface alone, too. The Roche Lake experts have since told me that although Roche has good sedge hatches in some years, the fish are known more for feeding on the emerging pupa rather than the adult fully-developed fly. Be that as it may, it was a small triumph that I savoured.
I used this fly off and on for a day and a half and was unable to sink it. So, if nothing else, it is a good floater. Also, I found that after the fly was in use for several hours, the turkey wing started to split at the fold line. This in no way detracted from its appearance as the deer hair underneath filled in any void formed. Indeed, it then looked for all the world like a newly hatched adult sedge test- ing its wings.

Vincent's fly is a fairly complicated pattern but is a much more real- istic impression of the adult sedge than many other simpler dressed pat- terns. Over the past 20 years, it has found homes in many interior fly fishers' boxes.

Water Boatman

HOOK: Number 8 sproat bend **BODY:** Silver tinsel
BACK: Dark ring-necked pheasant centre tail
PADDLES: Small diameter rubber strips
ORIGINATOR: Jim Stewart, Ken Coker, Mickey Caldwell
INTENDED USE: Wet fly for rainbow trout
LOCATION: Roche Lake

The water boatman, a water-dwelling, air-breathing, diving insect, is found in lakes and streams throughout the world. However, it wasn't until the 1970s that British Columbian fly fishers realized their impor- tance as trout food. In the spring just after ice-off and again in the fall trout search out the boatman and fishing a good water boatman pattern is worthwhile.

Brian Chan in *Flyfishing Strategies for Stillwaters* (1991) recom- mends during the times of water boatman activity that the fisher "cast a boatman pattern right into the tulle beds, then retrieve in quick 5 to 10 cm strips" (p. 57). Chan also advises that the strike to this fast-moving fly can be very hard and counsels the fisher not to overreact and break off the fly.

According to Totem Fly fisher, The late General Sir Charles F. Loewen in his 1978 book *Fly Fishing Flies*, the water boatman pattern he described originated with a fellow Totem Fly fisher, Mr. Jim Stewart.

In a recent telephone conversation with Stewart, he provided me with the particulars on the Water Boatman's development. During a 1974 fall stay at Roche Lake Lodge, Stewart one day noticed a considerable amount of fish and boatman activity and, of course, he had no pattern in his fly box that imitated the fishes' prey, the water boatman. When he returned from his day's fishing he mentioned what he saw to the then lodge owners, Ken Coker and Mickey Caldwell, and they set to work, each at their own tying vices, creating water boatman patterns.

Dressed on a number 8 hook with a silver body, black back and rubber legs or paddles, their boatman imitation is a relatively simple pattern, but does it work!

Relying on memory Stewart doesn't remember all the details about that long-ago fall day's next morning fishing with the Water Boatman, but he referred to it as "tremendously good fishing with fish up to 5 and 6 pounds" Jimmy said that he has been catching fish with this boatman pattern ever since.

Werner Shrimp

HOOK: Number 6 to 12 Mustad 3906 or 3906B
TAIL: Deer hair **BODY:** Olive seal's fur or chenille
HACKLE: Brown, cock neck feather, palmered up the body
SHELLBACK: Deer hair **ORIGINATOR:** Mary Stewart
INTENDED USE: Wet fly for rainbow trout
LOCATION: Interior lakes

British Columbia's most notable fly fisherman, author and conservationist, Roderick Haig-Brown, in his book *The Western Angler* (1939), was among the first British Columbian fly fishermen to note the importance of the fresh water shrimp, Gammarus, as a trout food and, therefore, the need for the fly fisherman to develop effective imitations. Haig-Brown found that his Gammarus imitation caught fish just about everywhere in the province that he tried it, but he also commented that his pattern was probably not so good as what might be produced.

Much later, sometime in the 1960s, the Werner Shrimp, a Gammarus imitation developed by professional fly-dresser Mary Stewart and popularized by Werner Schmid, both of Vancouver, became "the shrimp pattern." Like many British Columbia flies, the original Werner was dressed on number 6 or 8 hook, but now the pattern is dressed on smaller hooks to better represent the natural crustacean's size.

Often when a pattern is developed by a commercial tier, it is a skiiled angler who takes a fancy to the pattern and proves its worth.

That happened with the Werner Shrimp. In the early 1960s when Werner Schmid was pursuing stillwater trout with a vengeance, he was always in search of flies that better represented the fish's natural food. With the intensity that he pursued that passion, he fished the patterns he chose with confidence and his catches on Mary Stewart's shrimp pattern are testimonial to that devotion and confidence.

Williams' Green-bodied Sedge

HOOK: Number 6 **BODY:** Apple green seal's fur
HACKLE: Two badger hackles **WING:** Light mallard
ORIGINATOR: A. Bryan Williams
INTENDED USE: Dry fly for rainbow trout
LOCATION: Hyas Lake

During the years of discovery and abundance in the 1920s, '30s, and '40s, British Columbia's interior lakes became known as a fly fisher's paradise, particularly so because of the dry-fly fishing. When the sedges were hatching some very large fish rose and took the dry fly and those catches drew anglers to British Columbia from many places in the world. The insect that enticed the fish to the surface were the large sedges. While some Interior lakes had tremendous populations of the grey-bodied travelling sedges, others boasted a green-bodied variety. A. Bryan Williams is credited with the discovery of the sedges: the grey on Knouff and green on Hyas and their first imitations. In a April 1938 letter to Rod Haig-Brown about the sedges and their imitations, Williams had this to say:

It is a good many years since I discovered that there were hatches of sedges in the interior and that when a hatch was on trout would hardly look at a wet fly. So I caught some of them, brought them to town and got Harkley & Haywood to make some for me. . . . I may also say that I believe that dry fly fishing in this country was hardly ever practiced, at any rate to any extent, until I started it with the grey sedge. Later on I originated the green bodied which is also even more deadly on the waters where they hatch.

About the interior sedges and their respective sizes, in *Fish & Game in British Columbia* Williams writes:

In the interior there are at least five species, and when there is a good hatch of the large varieties the trout feed on them voraciously, so much so that nothing but that fly is of much use. Of these large Sedges, one has very light fawn-coloured wings with a dark body, the other two are light grey winged with bright apple green bodies which change to a brown by degrees.

Of the green-bodied Sedges, one is larger than the other, and both larger than the light fawn-coloured one. (p. 41)

To match the size, Williams recommended that the green-bodied sedge be dressed on a number 6 hook.

That the fish found the green-bodied sedge appealing to the appetite is attested to by Williams' recommendation: on Fish, Hyas Long, and Paul lakes "For dry fly fishing, use the Green-Bodied Sedge . . ." (*Fish & Game in British Columbia*, p. 93). Hyas Long Lake, at the writing of Williams' book, had some impressive catches of dry fly-caught fish. Williams writes:

This lake is about the same size as Knouff Lake and the fishing is very similar, except that the Sedges there are of the green-bodied kind, and the trout average somewhat larger. The best fish caught on a dry fly that I know of weighed 15 1/2 pounds. (p. 99)

The photo accompanying the Hyas write up showed three dry-fly caught Kamloops trout of 8 1/2, 8 1/4, and 8 pounds, quite impressive indeed. Williams' largest dry fly-caught trout from Hyas was a whopping 15 1/4 pounds.

Williams' Grey-bodied Sedge

HOOK: Number 8 **BODY:** Medium grey wool or seal's fur
RIB: A thin strand of black floss **HACKLE:** Ginger hackle
WING: Hen pheasant centre tail
ORIGINATOR: A. Bryan Williams
INTENDED USE: Dry fly for rainbow trout
LOCATION Knouff Lake

In Williams' 1935 book *Fish & Game in British Columbia* on pages 46 and 47 he lists the recommended fly patterns of the day. Most are British or American imports but he does list a smattering of locally developed ones. For dry flies Williams modestly mentions that "the Sedges are the most important. The principal ones for the interior are Williams' Sedges, the grey-bodied to be tied on a No. 8 hook . . ." (p. 47). He goes on to mention the remaining three Williams-developed sedges. Nowhere in his writings does he refer to them as his patterns and, unfortunately, he doesn't give the dressings for most patterns, including the sedges. The dressing given here is one that Rod Haig-Brown gleaned from a Harkley & Haywood sample, dressed to Williams' specifications by Harkley & Haywood's lady fly tier. In a May 1938 letter to Williams, Haig-Brown wrote that he was most interested to hear that Williams started the sedge fishing in British Columbia and about the Grey-bodied dressing he writes:

Very many thanks for your extremely interesting letter on the sedges. I had not realized that the girl at Harkley & Haywood's had

actually done the work on matching the naturals . . . both wing and body of the more recent grey sedges are extremely clever and well-worked out. The way I dress the fly myself is as follows:

Body: Medium grey wool or seal's fur.
Ribbed: Black floss.
Wing: Hen pheasant centre tail.
Hackle: Ginger.

Which is so close to her tying . . . .

In the 1920s and 30s Knouff Lake, northeast of Kamloops, became renowned for its large fish and in Williams' opinion when the sedges were hatching a good imitation was a must and it was for these fish that the Grey-bodied was devised. In *Fish & Game in British Columbia*, Williams writes:

. . .but for fly fishing, it is best to wait until the first week of June, when the Sedges begin to hatch. This lake is noted for its enormous number of Grey-Bodied Sedges. When they are in the water you need to be a dry fly fisherman or your chances of hooking a fish on the wet fly are not good . . . .
The weight of the fish in this lake vary considerably from year to year. Some years they average about 3 pounds, another year they will go 6 or 7. You never can tell what sized fish you will hook; but the best fish I know of was a magnificent specimen of 17 1/4 pounds, caught on a dry fly (Sedge) . . . . For dry fly fishing, use the Grey-bodied Sedge . . . . (p. 107)

Bill Nation believed that the sedges afforded some of the finest dry fly fishing each spring for about ten days and recommended Williams' Grey-bodied Sedge. Nation was at Knouff on the day that the 17 1/4 pound fish was taken and confirms that:

Hodgson, of Vernon took one of 17 1/4 pounds in Knouff while I was with B. H. Smith, who had one of 16 pounds, both on Bryan Williams' dark dry sedge.

Although Williams' developed this pattern for Knouff Lake rainbows, Roderick Haig-Brown found it a very effective fly for coast trout fishing and in *The Western Angler* (1939), he gave the fly an unequivocal recommendation:

The deadliest dry fly, and the deadliest fly of any sort, wet or dry, in the mountain streams is the William's (sic) Grey-bodied Sedge. The fish will rise to it in midsummer at any time of day . . . (Vol. 1, p. 194)

Williams' Grey-bodied Sedge was often referred to on the coast as Williams' Brown Sedge because of the brown wing. When Haig-Brown questioned Mr. Haywood about the correct name, Haywood said that Haig-Brown was absolutely correct and the fly's proper name was Williams' Grey-bodied Sedge.

This nice rainbow took the author's Black Carey leech pattern.

Steelhead Patterns

Section Two:

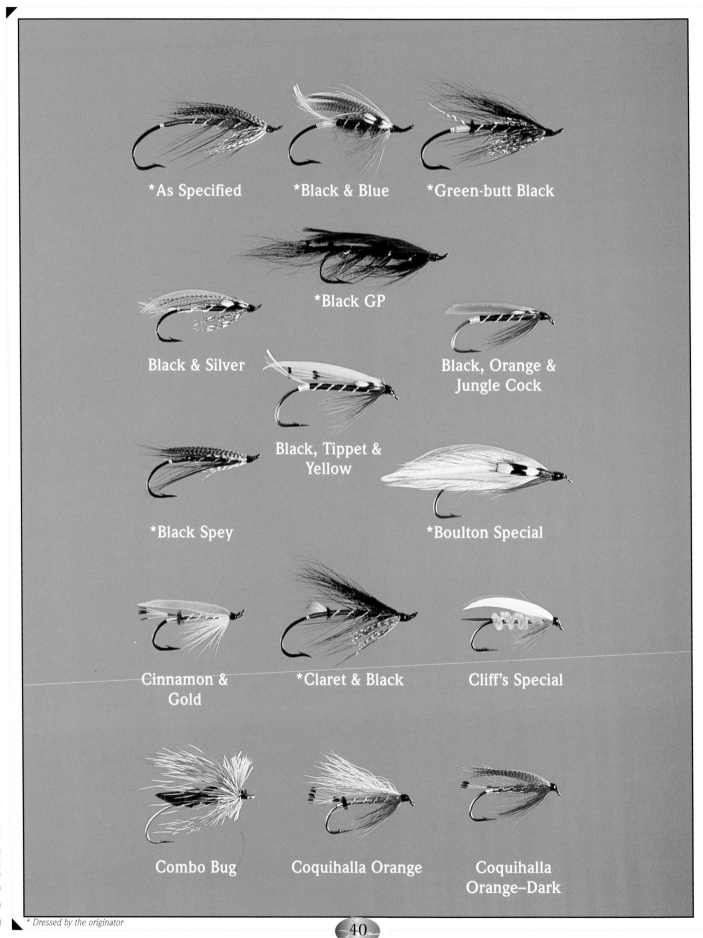

*As Specified   *Black & Blue   *Green-butt Black

*Black GP

Black & Silver

Black, Orange &
Jungle Cock

Black, Tippet &
Yellow

*Black Spey   *Boulton Special

Cinnamon &
Gold   *Claret & Black   Cliff's Special

Combo Bug   Coquihalla Orange   Coquihalla
Orange–Dark

Coquihalla
Orange–Light

Coquihalla Red

Coquihalla Silver

•Cowichan Special
(Dressed by Joe Saysell)

Dick's Fly

*Doc Spratley

Dusk

General Money #1

General Money #2

General Practitioner

Golden Girl

Golden Red

Grey Fly

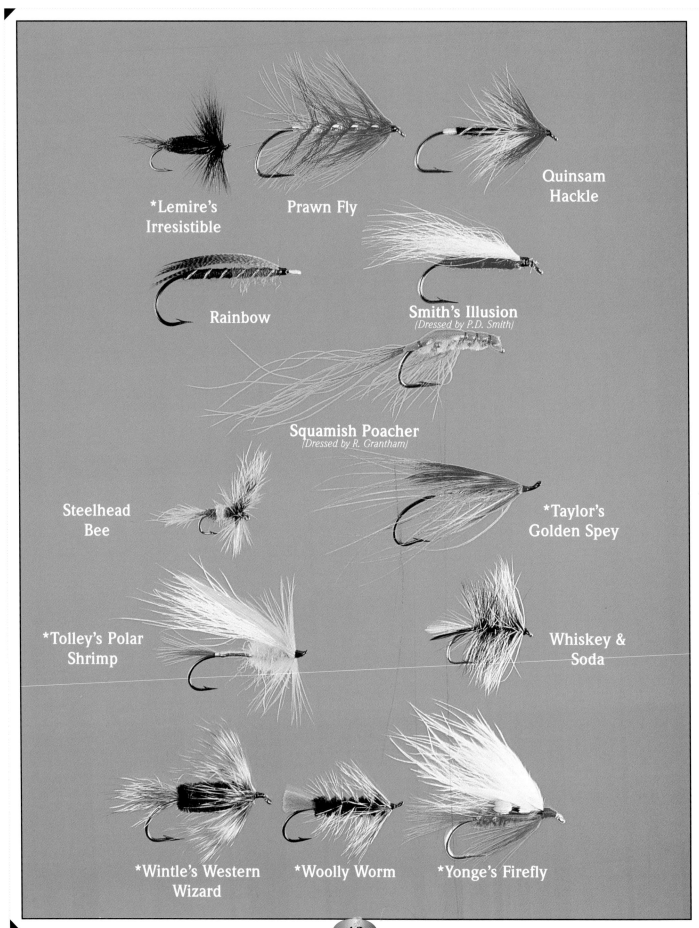

*Lemire's Irresistible

Prawn Fly

Quinsam Hackle

Rainbow

Smith's Illusion
(Dressed by P.D. Smith)

Squamish Poacher
(Dressed by R. Grantham)

Steelhead Bee

*Taylor's Golden Spey

*Tolley's Polar Shrimp

Whiskey & Soda

*Wintle's Western Wizard

*Woolly Worm

*Yonge's Firefly

Colonialists in the early days of British Columbia's development noticed in coastal rivers large trout and were tempted into angling for them. One of the earliest large catches of these trout was recorded in *Vancouver Island and British Columbia* (1865) by Matthew MacFie. About the trout, he writes:

> *A superior kind of trout abound in the lower Fraser, weighing 7 pounds or 8 pounds . . . and . . . that twenty mountain-trout were recently caught in a stream near Hope, whose aggregate weight was 146 pounds, and two of them weighed 11 pounds each. (p. 167)*

What form of angling the fisherman used to catch these trout MacFie did not state. However, reports about large trout drew other anglers such as John Keast Lord, H. W. Seton-Karr and Dr. T. W. Lambert to the Coquihalla River in pursuit of its trout and it is probably fair to say that the Coquihalla was the birth-place of steelhead fishing in British Columbia. Lord in his 1866 book, *The Naturalist in British Columbia*, Seton-Karr in his 1891 book, *Bear-Hunting in the White Mountains or Alaska and British Columbia Revisited*, and Lambert in his 1907 book, *Fishing in British Columbia*, record fishing this river with the fly. However, none records catching a steelhead with a fly.

Fly fishing for steelhead from the earliest of colonial days was considered to be more difficult than spinning. However, fly fishing was practiced by the dedicated and the stories in this book on Smith's Illusion and the Whiskey and Soda attest to that usage. A. Bryan Williams in *Rod and Creel in British Columbia* (1919) says that "whenever the water is in proper condition and there are steelheads in the river, they can be taken on the fly and there is no fish that swims that will give better sport" (p. 48). However, he recommends the standard British Atlantic salmon flies for success.

General Noel Money moved to British Columbia in 1913 and fished some of the east coast of Vancouver Island streams. However, because of the First World War, the fish in river, lake, and sea would have to wait his return from overseas service. After his return he fished the Stamp River for the first time on September 15, 1920, and took six steelhead the largest, 10 1/2 pound and smallest, 4 pound on a Dusty Miller. The next year he returned and from the descriptions in his game book, it was apparent that he used flies designed and dressed by himself. I have listed nine patterns that are of General Money origin. Unfortunately, most have lost favour with the passage of time and it's regretable that the patterns developed by the father of British Columbia steelhead fly fishing met that fate. It is my hope that this book may revive some.

Money's success as a steelhead fly fisher had a strong influence on the young Roderick Haig-Brown and through that influence Haig-Brown persevered, particularly with winter fish, and developed other patterns. The master craftsman and fisherman, Tommy Brayshaw, after he moved to Hope and learned the secrets of our steelheading birthplace river—the Coquihalla—developed specific patterns for that river's steelhead.

Money, Haig-Brown, Brayshaw and others such as Paul Moody Smith, Frank Darling and Bill Cunliffe kept fly fishing alive during the 1920s through to the 1960s and provided the roots for future generations of steelhead fly-fishing and fly-tying aficionados to perpetuate our fly-fishing and fly-tying heritage.

Men like Denny Boulton, of Boulton's Special fame, and others and the flies they developed, such as Jerry Wintle—Wintle's Western Wizard, Bob Taylor—Taylor's Golden Spey, Martin Tolley—Tolley's Polar Shrimp and Bill Yonge—Yonge's Firefly, all provided additional roots for anglers of my era. In turn, my generation—if the steelhead survive the onslaught of the 1990s northwest development, population explosion, commercial and native interception, and poaching—will add to those roots from which future generations of fly fishers will continue to build our steelhead fly-fishing and fly-tying heritage.

Over the past 75 years our steelhead fly fishers have produced many fly patterns and those listed in this book provide a good selection and will cover most steelhead fly fishing presentations. There are large flies such as Money's Prawn, Squamish Poacher, Black or Orange GP for cold or coloured water; slim-bodied ones such as the As Specified, Black & Silver, Dick's Fly, Black Spey for the floating line; flies designed for skating such as the Combo Bug and Lemire's Irresistible; others designed for the dry fly presentation such as the Whiskey & Soda and Steelhead Bee; and flies such as the Woolly Worm or Quinsam Hackle that could be used for the deeply sunk upstream presentation.

As Specified No. 1 & 2

HOOK: Number 2 to 10 low-water salmon
TIP: Two or three turns of fine, gold, oval tinsel
TAG: Purple floss
TAIL: A few sprigs from a purple hackle feather
BODY: In two sections: first third of purple floss with the remainder purple seal's fur
RIB: Medium gold, oval tinsel
HACKLE: From the second turn of tinsel, a black hackle feather with one side stripped to maintain sparseness
THROAT: One or two turns of teal or widgeon flank feather with one side stripped
WING: No. 1: Bronze mallard; No. 2 black squirrel
HEAD: Black Cellire varnish **ORIGINATOR:** Art Lingren
INTENDED USE: Floating-line fly for steelhead
LOCATION: Morice River

This is one of my favourite floating-line flies which I developed in early 1982. Originally, I christened it Purple Lady. Lee Straight caught the first steelhead on it at the Dean River in 1982. I didn't get to use it for steelhead until September of '82. The details of that trip, and the subsequent renaming of the fly to the "As Specified" are detailed below.

In 1982, I had planned, with a long-time steelheading chum a trip to the Morice River in the latter part of September. For some reason or other at the last minute, he wasn't able to go. The unappealing, lonesome, 700-mile, one-way trip done with, I could now get absorbed into the world of steelhead fishing.

I found a high and somewhat coloured river when I arrived, and the first two mid-September days were slow. By the third day, however, the river had dropped and cleared considerably. On my first time through the Billy Goat Run, using a number one Green-Butted Spratley on a floating line—just before I was going to lift my fly for another cast—I had a beautiful head and tail rise. Overeager, I pulled the fly from the fish's mouth.

I decided to go through the run again and thought a change of fly was necessary. The water temperature was up in the mid-fifties so I reasoned a smaller fly should do and a newly developed, size six Purple Lady caught my fancy. After a couple of casts I heard the noise that a steelhead makes displacing the water as it turns quickly to take a subsurface fly and before I knew it a good fish had taken all my fly line and most of the backing from my St. John reel. The only time I saw the fish was as it jumped on the other side of the river and in the process broke my 9-pound test leader. After flogging the water for a while, I climbed into my boat and started exploring up river. In a small pocket upriver, I came across another good fish which I successfully hooked, landed and released.

In the next three days I had six more offers for a total of nine and eight of them came to the Purple Lady. One fish came after the fly and

made one heck of a noise doing so but missed it totally. I went back to this spot the next day and picked up a 34-inch male fish. Of the six fish hooked well, one broke me, two threw the hook after really good runs and jumps and three were landed. Of all the fish hooked only one was small—approximately six-pounds. The remaining were in the 8 to 15-pound class which made them good fish for the Morice. Although it was not a great trip, I was very satisfied with the success of my new fly.

I knew when I saw my chum he would ask what fly did they take? So on the way down I devised a new name for the fly and wrote the dressing down on a piece of paper and listed, after all the dressing materials, the two words: as specified.

Sure enough the questions were asked and out came the piece of paper with the fly's new name and dressing. All he said after reading it was, "aha the As Specified fly," and that is what we called it from then on.

This is a summer-run pattern to be used on a floating line and since that trip to the Morice I have used it with success on the Dean, Campbell, and Thompson rivers. In 1987, I used the As Specified No. 1 almost exclusively on the Thompson and during seven days on the river 9 out of 10 of my fish took that pattern.

The fly I call As Specified No. 2 is tied identically to No. 1 but, instead of a bronze mallard wing, I use black squirrel tail. Also, I use the As Specified in sizes 8 and 6 for cutthroat when conditions warrant a dark-bodied fly.

Black & Blue

HOOK: Number 1/0 to 6 low-water salmon
TIP: Fine oval, gold tinsel
TAG: Yellow floss or blue seal's fur
TAIL: Golden pheasant crest feather
BODY: Black floss or black seal's fur
RIB: Oval, silver tinsel
THROAT: Bright blue cock neck feather
WING: Married strips of blue, yellow and red goose with bronze mallard alongside and a golden pheasant crest feather overall or hairwing as described in the text
CHEEKS: Jungle cock **ORIGINATOR:** Van Egan
INTENDED USE: Sunk-line fly for steelhead
LOCATION: Campbell River

Over the years many steelhead fly fishers realized that dark-bodied, low-water style flies suited the light and water conditions encountered with summer-run steelhead. Once the winter runs started arriving, however, fly fishers reverted to the tried and proven bright-coloured patterns. Seldom did you find an adventurous soul that ventured from the norm. Van Egan did that in the early 1970s and about the development of his Black & Blue says:

...llowing the ...ase Line on ...sents a case ...of the year, ...t flies he was ...k and includ- ...ething along

...flies like the ...es for winter- ...Blue from the ...x. On its first ...d in the Main ...s sent the fly ...ease my stock.

...he fly, particu- ...es, to assuage

...fly of slim pro- ...inter fishing in ...To obtain this ...e wing consist- ...ear with brown

...ake include the ...and yellow floss ...e butt of seal's ...rly effective on the Gold River the year I made these changes, but since then it seems to be no better than a hair-wing without the blue butt. Still, I like to have both when on the river.

Egan's sample pattern, dressed on a Partridge Bartleet hook, has the body he recommends for the winter fly and the wing of his original design. Over the years Steelhead from the Campbell, Gold, Nimpkish, and Dean rivers have felt the sting of Egan's Black & Blue.

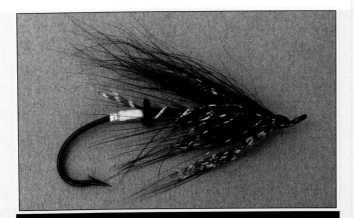

Black and Green-Butt Black

HOOK: Number 2 to 12 low-water salmon or Wilson dry-fly
TIP: Two or three turns of fine oval, silver tinsel
TAG: Black floss for Black and fluorescent green floss for Green-Butt Black
TAIL: Guinea fowl **BUTT:** Black ostrich herl
BODY: In two sections: rear third of black floss with remainder black seal's fur
(body is all floss on sizes 8 and smaller)
RIB: Oval, silver tinsel

HACKLE: From the second turn of tinsel a black hackle with one side stripped to maintain sparseness
THROAT: A couple of turns of guinea fowl
WING: Black squirrel **HEAD:** Black Cellire varnish
ORIGINATOR: Art Lingren
INTENDED USE: Floating-line fly for summer steelhead
LOCATION: Dean River

This fly was developed in the spring of 1983 by combining some of the characteristics of the Doc Spratley and the British Stoat's Tail. It was an instant success. Even though this fly was first tied in the spring of 1983, I didn't get to try it out until I went to the Dean River, later that summer.

As I completed the trek over to the Totem Flyfishers' camp on this hot August day, I saw the Dean for the first time. It was low and clear and, in my opinion, good floating-line water and that is what I strung on my rod—a floating line. Exploring a new river is exciting and on that first-ever Dean River evening I ended up at the Fir Pool and, after putting on a size 2 Black dressed on a Wilson dry-fly hook, I proceeded to cast into the top part of the pool. I can't recall if it was my first cast but it wasn't long before I was into a fish. The fish was running out my line and then to my surprise my line went slack. I watched in horror as my line slithered through the rod guides. Away went fish, fly and a brand-new, double taper, floating fly-line.

I strung up my spare sink-tip line and fished my way down river to camp. Arriving back at camp, I was asked the usual questions about what sport I had. These brought forth my story about losing fish, fly and fly line.

Peter Broomhall questioned me a little further and asked what size did I think the fish was, the colour of fly line and fly, and the time I lost my fish. I don't think I am prone to exaggeration and estimated the fish to be a good one, around 10 pounds. But, in the preliminary excitement at the moment a fish is hooked, misjudgments regarding size are not uncommon. I told Peter the colour of my fly line was pink, the fly black and I lost the fish just after 6 p.m.

Peter had good reason for asking his questions because Jerry Wintle had found a fly line just before I got back into camp. Jerry had been sitting in front of his camp with his wife Jean when she noticed a fly line floating down river. Jerry quickly waded into the river and managed to grab the line and, to his surprise, found that there was still a fish attached. He hand-played the fish and was successful in getting the line, fly and fish, which was released.

The line was a pink, double taper floater and the fly, a sparsely tied black pattern but Pete, toying with me, wasn't so sure they belonged to me because I was sure the fish I had hooked was around 10 pounds or so and the fish Jerry had landed was a small fish of 5 pounds or so.

It amazed me that a fish would back down approximately 1/2-mile or so of river in 1 1/2 hours and not get the 90 feet of line hung up on the numerous rocks and stump obstacles and that the barbless hook did not come away.

How did my line come undone from the line-backing? I thought about that for a long time and all I can recall is buying this double taper fly line and trying to get it on one of my reels. After trying many reels, eventually, after stripping some backing off my St. John, I got it to fit. Delighted it fitted one of my reels, I forgot to take it off and fix it to the backing.

That trip to the Dean was slow but half of my fish came to the Black and Green-Butt Black. I find no difference as to whether the fluorescent green butt is there or not: both flies work equally well. The big thing with sparsely dressed patterns is matching them to light and water conditions.

Besides the Dean, I have used this pattern regularly on other summer-run rivers when clear, low-water conditions prevail and a dark, sparsely dressed enticer is required. It is another pattern that I use in sizes 8 and 6 for cutthroat when water conditions warrant a dark-bodied cutthroat fly.

Black & Silver

HOOK: Number 4 to 8 low-water salmon
TAIL: A golden pheasant crest feather
BODY: Rear half of flat silver tinsel followed by black floss
RIB: Oval, silver tinsel
THROAT: A couple turns of a speckled guinea fowl
WING: Strips of bronze mallard flank feather and strips of
red golden pheasant breast feather and topped with
a golden pheasant crest feather
CHEEKS: Jungle cock
ORIGINATOR: Tom Brayshaw
INTENDED USE: Wet fly for summer steelhead
LOCATION: Coquihalla River

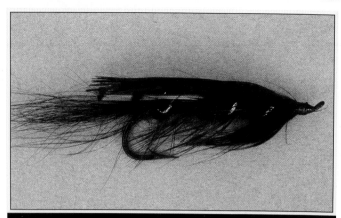

Black General Practitioner

HOOK: Number 5/0 to 2 low-water salmon
TAIL: Black squirrel tail a little longer than the hook
shank and a small, red, golden pheasant breast feather
BODY: Wrap hook shank with lead then black mohair or
wool, set tippet eyes in about 1/3 up body
(often I omit the tippet eyes)
RIB: Medium oval, silver tinsel
HACKLE: Black cock neck feather wound up the body. Cut
the fibres off on top so the back can lie flat along body
BACK: Two layers of black spade hackles, large black
wood duck, or black hen neck feathers, if narrow enough
HEAD: Black Cellire varnish **ORIGINATOR:** Art Lingren
LOCATION: Campbell River

Replying to a request for information on steelhead flies from a Dr. Webster of Cornell University, in Ithaca, New York, Brayshaw in his November 1959 response says that "if I fish a pool down a second time or if I rise a steelhead and it misses or refuses the fly, I put on a No. 6 'Black & Silver' and that usually does the trick."

An offshoot of the Mar Lodge fly that he simplified for rainbows when he fished Little and Adams rivers, Brayshaw first used the Black & Silver for steelhead in 1946 when he moved to the small town of Hope and started fly fishing the Coquihalla River summer-run steelhead. In the afternoon of July 9 of '46, Brayshaw decided to leave his Hardy Silex-equipped spinning rod and Devon minnow-type lures at home and, armed only with his fly rod and flies, walked up to the Coquihalla Bridge to fish the Rock Pool. He records that he:

fished the stream down with a #4 L[ow] W[ater] hook and a 'black & silver' & then tried it again. I saw a steelhead rise, cast over it & rose it at once: it made a fine long run & jump & then worked back to almost where I hooked it & there it sulked.

Having on a light nylon cast I had to go easy & for three or four minutes things were more or less at a stand still when the fly came away.

That was Brayshaw's first encounter with a Coquihalla summer-run on the fly and after supper that evening he returned with his wife, Becky, and he hooked two more steelhead. The first came to the Black & Silver but the knot attaching fly to the nylon leader slipped and the fish was away with his fly. He rose one more fish that evening to a number 4 Jock Scott, but the hook failed to get a good hold and that fish too escaped. Brayshaw, however, was not disappointed with this, his first afternoon with a fly rod after summer-runs. Indeed, the opposite is the truth as witnessed by his closing journal entry comment: "I think it was a successful afternoon & evening—rising 3 fish even if I didn't land any."

I think if I had to limit myself to one fly for the rest of my days the Black GP would be the fly. Ever since its inception in January of 1984, I have been catching steelhead and many other types of fish: cutthroat, browns, rainbows, Chinooks, cohoes, pinks, Dolly Varden quite regularly in various water conditions with both sunk or floating-line presentations.

The idea for the fly came from reading some British Atlantic salmon books. In January, 1984, I had just finished reading John Ashley-Cooper's *A Salmon Fisher's Odyssey* (1982), and was in the process of reading Arthur Oglesby's *Salmon* (1971), and was greatly influenced by both the above gentlemen's thoughts on dark fly patterns.

At that time I was looking for a dark pattern for sunk-line winter steelhead fishing. My main pattern at the time for winter fish was Colonel Esmond Drury's orange General Practitioner; but I did not like offering this bright fly to steelhead in low, clear, cold water conditions as I did not feel that I was getting the offers I should. Therefore, I tied up some Black GPs and stuck them in my fly box to try the next time I went out.

On the afternoon of February 13 that year, I found myself in the Campbell River's Lower Island Pool playing a 30 3/4-inch female steelhead. My first steelhead on my new fly.

Since that first-ever Campbell River fish, I have used the Black GP successfully on many steelhead streams in the province. I have used it with sunk and floating lines, river temperatures varying from 39 to 60 degrees Fahrenheit, in big and small rivers during sunny and overcast days, and in clear and dirty water conditions. I have had numerous double-digit days fishing steelhead with the Black GP but one of the real bonuses is its appeal to fish other than steelhead.

The following are some personal Black GP statistics:

- Used successfully on 27 different British Columbian rivers
- Methods of presentation: sunk and floating line
- Number of different types of fish caught equals 10: summer- and

winter-run steelhead to 20 pounds, cutthroat to 18 inches, rainbows to 16 inches, browns to 23 1/2 inches, Dollies to 23 1/2 inches, pinks to 5 pounds, cohoes to 10 pounds, chums to 15 pounds, and Chinooks to 35 pounds
- My two best days for numbers of fish hooked are 16 steelhead and 15 salmon, mostly coho

The Black GP is truly a fly for all seasons, methods and fish.

Black, Orange & Jungle Cock

HOOK: Number 1/0 to 3 **TAG:** Oval, silver tinsel
BODY: Black, silk floss **RIB:** Oval, silver tinsel
THROAT: Purple hackle **WING:** Orange
SIDES: Jungle cock **ORIGINATOR:** General Noel Money
INTENDED USE: Wet fly for steelhead
LOCATION: Stamp River

Black Spey

HOOK: Number 2 to 6 Wilson dry-fly salmon
TIP: Fine oval, gold tinsel **BUTT:** Black floss
TAIL: Red-orange Indian crow type feather
BODY: Black floss **WING:** Bronze mallard
RIB: Medium or fine, gold twist to match hook size
HACKLE: Black heron or substitute
THROAT: A couple of turns of teal flank feather
SIDES: Black Cellire varnish **ORIGINATOR:** Art Lingren
INTENDED USE: Floating-line fly for summer steelhead
LOCATION: Thompson River

As I started to write this article I noticed the variations in dressing of Money's flies in the two of his fly boxes I have open sitting next to my computer. One of the boxes the General gave to his gilly, Ted Pengelley, of Campbell River and the other was given to Rod Haig-Brown by Mrs. Money after the General's death in 1941. Later, when Haig-Brown passed away the box was given to Van Egan, Rod's friend of many years, by Valerie Haig-Brown. Included among the Money-dressed flies are many commercially-dressed salmon flies, an original Preston Jennings' Muddy Iris and a Haig-Brown Silver Lady and some Van Egan ties. Because there are original Haig-Brown, Jennings and Egan patterns in the box, it is obvious to me that Haig-Brown used the Money box of flies.

However, a close examination of the patterns dressed by Money shows many variations of the black floss-bodied flies: one with bronze mallard and orange swan wings, one with just orange wings, some with tails and others without, some with jungle cock cheeks, some with orange, yellow or red throat hackles, and others with body hackles. Yet others of a similar style to the black-bodied flies had bodies of yellow, silver or burgundy. Most, however, are not described in great detail in Money's game books. A simple note like this from an August 1924 entry—"Stamp alone, 2 fish, 8 and 7 pounds, red body, yellow hackle, & grey wing has done well this season"—is all there is.

Late September was one of the General's favoured time to fish the Stamp and in 1924 he spent five days—September 23 to 27—on the river. They took 59 steelhead. On September 24, he had a great day's sport with 10 fish killed. His note in the game book read: "River high—all on Black body, ribbed with silver, orange & jungle cock wing, purple hackle."

The Black, Orange & Jungle Cock sports a most striking colour combination, indeed, and with the "catch of the day" on September 24th, one the fish found irresistible.

Spey flies date back into the last century and originated in the River Spey valley for Scottish Atlantic salmon. Arthur Knox in his 1872 book *Autumns of the Spey*, was the first to record in writing old Spey patterns, and he gives the dressing for 16 patterns. Because of the problem of obtaining specific materials such as Spey cock hackles, Berlin wool, and heron feathers, steelheaders have simplified the dressings and adopted more readily available materials for their dressings. There are, however, a few characteristics that steelhead flies must possess to be true to the Spey style and they are: thin bodies, flowing body hackle, and a wing, usually of bronze mallard, that envelops the upper body. Following those characteristics, my Black Spey fly owes its origin to the Black Spey listed in Knox.

The long heron hackle fibres fluctuate and provide life to the Black Spey even in the slowest of currents. Throughout most of their life, to steelhead, movement meant something good to eat and even though returning fish are non-feeders there is still, in some fish, that urge to test life-like things. Steelhead are attracted to the Black Spey, and it complements the floating-line technique in suitable water and light conditions.

I remember my first steelhead taken on the Thompson with this pattern. I was on Martel Island with Bob Taylor, and we were fishing during an early November extreme cold spell. The water temperature was 45 degrees Fahrenheit, and the river height at 1.0 metres. The water we were fishing was about one metre deep—important to note because Thompson fish will come and take flies presented on or just under the surface in cold water if the water is not too deep. On the Thompson the rule of thumb is: if you can wade it you have a good chance of moving fish to the surface even with temperatures in the 30s.

Shortly after I started fishing on the main island, I hooked and landed a prized 35-inch male fish. Indeed, I remember this fish well, because it was my first steelhead on the Black Spey and in a season where there were few fish and, that combined with the cold weather, takes were few and far between. This was our only fish that day. Another fish later in the trip also took the Black Spey. Unfortunately, the hook I dressed this fly on was over tempered and it snapped in half as the steelhead thrust itself from the water in one of its breath-taking, heart-thumping jumps.

With certain water and light conditions, cutthroats and Dollies also find the Black Spey appealing.

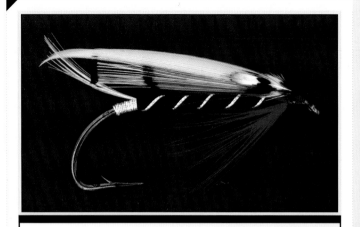

Black, Tippet & Yellow

HOOK: Number 2/0 to 4
TAG: Oval, silver tinsel
BODY: Black floss
RIB: Oval, silver tinsel
THROAT: Red hackle
WING: Strips of fibres from a golden pheasant's orange tippet feather
ORIGINATOR: General Noel Money
INTENDED USE: Wet fly for winter steelhead
LOCATION: Somass River

Boulton's Special

HOOK: Number 2 or 4, 6 extra-long
TAIL: Small, whole, golden pheasant, red breast feather
BODY: Flat, silver tinsel
THROAT: Golden pheasant red breast feather
WING: Two badger hackles extending to the tip of the tail, veiled with white hackles, and with a golden pheasant crest feather overall
CHEEKS: Jungle cock **ORIGINATOR:** Denny Boulton
INTENDED USE: Wet fly for summer steelhead
LOCATION: Capilano River

From that September 15th day in 1920 when General Money fished the Stamp River system for the first time up to the end of 1925, he often jotted down in his game book some particulars about the flies he used. Often those particulars were, however, not sufficient to dress the patterns. But by examining the many samples in two of his fly boxes that have survived these many years for style and composition I was able to put together a reasonable composite for some of these unknown-until-this-time Money flies.

Sometimes the General made a specific reference to the fly he used and names such as his Rainbow, Golden Red, Prawn and Grey flies can be found in his game book. However, many times he listed the general composition and didn't give a reference name: such is the case with the Black, Tippet & Yellow. I dressed and named this pattern after reading about the fly in two of Money's diary entries.

On December 29, 1924, General Money fished Swanson's Run on the Somass River and took an 11 1/2 pound winter steelhead. About the fish and fly he says it was "A grand fish very short & thick, fresh from the sea; blk. silk body, silver ribbing, red hackle, tippet & yellow wing, jungle cock cheeks."

On March 2, 1925, the General slipped over to Swanson's again. This time an 8 3/4 pound winter steelhead was lured to his black-bodied fly. About the fly the General noted it was dressed on a 1/0 hook and that it consisted of a "Blk. silk body, ribbed silver, red hackle, tippet & jungle cock wing."

In one of his fly boxes, I found a tippet-winged pattern similar, although not exact to the one I have dressed, instead of a yellow wing the sample has bronze mallard—the General dressed many patterns with this winging material—and he used a blue jay throat instead of red.

The Black, Tippet & Yellow is just another sample of General Noel Money's striking colour combinations: attractive to the eyes of the fishermen as well as the fish. It is the first British Columbian steelhead pattern to incorporate golden pheasant tippet in the wing.

The Boulton Special, inspired by the magnificent summer-run steelhead of the Capilano River, is the brainchild of Denny Boulton. Vancouver-bred-and born, Boulton moved to West Vancouver in 1941 and with that move to the North Shore, the Capilano added another fisherman to her long list of admirers.

Boulton saw the last of the Capilano hey days. With the completion of the Cleveland Dam in 1954 and, after one cycle of returning spawners, the river forever lost its majestic run of summer steelhead. Real fish don't eat pellets and all Capilano fish are now hatchery-bred, wind-up ones.

In his early fly-fishing days, Denny favoured the Golden Demon and Optics, but later, his thoughts turned, as many fly fishermen and fly tiers do when they have a theory that they want tested, to developing his own steelhead pattern. Denny Boulton's creation came from the vise in about 1955.

Many years later in the Totem Fly fisher's newsletter the *Totem Topics*, Boulton related the fly's development:

Originally tied for the lower Capilano River, this streamer was conceived at one of the Boulton, Moir, and Traeger fly-tying sessions.

It would be nice to say that a steelhead dashed away with it immediately, however, that was not the case. But, as time passed summer steelhead started to impale themselves on it with reasonable regularity. Don Traeger made a valiant effort at conservation by wagers against said streamer but found himself quickly paying for several steak dinners which were greatly appreciated.

I was asked to tie some for Harkley & Haywood but declined because of lack of time. However, I wrote the pattern on a piece of paper and told them to do with it as they saw fit.

Years later I was amazed to find out that the fly had been given a name and was still being used. The origins of the tandem hooked Boulton Special that appears in some of the books remains a mystery.

Jerry Wintle is responsible for the tandem setup. Wintle had some Boultons tied up on the long singles Boulton preferred, but the hooks straightened out on him when he was into a good fish. Losing fish on the Boulton happened often enough that Jerry complained to Bob Taylor about it. Taylor suggested that the Boulton would be better if they were tied with a tandem setup similar to the English terrors and demons. Thus, the tandem hook-up evolved and that is why many editions of *Flies of the Northwest* showed the tandem-dressed Boulton.

Although developed as a summer-run steelhead pattern, local fly fishers found the Boulton an excellent pattern for spring steelhead and Dolly Varden on the Squamish and some anglers have found the fly appeals to large interior trophy trout as well.

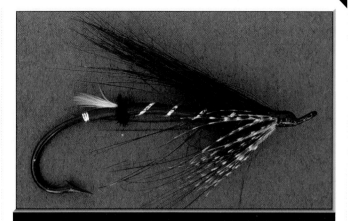

Claret & Black

HOOK: Number 2 to 6 low-water salmon
TIP: Fine oval, gold tinsel **TAG:** Claret floss
TAIL: A small, red-orange, hen, neck feather
BUTT: Black ostrich herl
BODY: In two sections: rear third of claret floss with the remainder of dark claret seal's fur
RIB: Medium gold, oval tinsel
HACKLE: From second turn of tinsel a black hackle with one half stripped off to maintain sparseness
THROAT: Two turns of widgeon or pintail flank
WING: Black squirrel **HEAD:** Black Cellire varnish
ORIGINATOR: Art Lingren
INTENDED USE: Floating-line fly for summer steelhead
LOCATION: Coquihalla River

Cinnamon & Gold

HOOK: Number 4 salmon
TAG: Orange silk floss
TAIL: A few fibres from a golden pheasant tippet feather
BUTT: Black ostrich
BODY: Flat, gold tinsel
RIB: Oval, gold tinsel **THROAT:** Yellow hackle
WING: Slender strips of cinnamon turkey
ORIGINATOR: Bill Cunliffe
INTENDED USE: Wet fly for steelhead
LOCATION: Lower mainland

Bill Cunliffe fished lower mainland rivers—the Capilano, Seymour, Vedder and Coquihalla—from the 1930s to his death in March 1964. Way back in the late 1950s while wandering the Seymour and searching the steelhead holts, Cunliffe gave Bob Taylor one of his Cinnamon & Gold flies and it was from that Cunliffe-dressed sample that I gleaned the dressing.

Cunliffe, an industrial arts teacher, would pack his bags and leave his North Vancouver home and spend a good part of the summer break fishing the Coquihalla River, using a rented cabin on the banks of the Camp Pool just above Othello railway station as his base. It was during one of these summer vacations that he met and became friends with the master craftsman and fly fisher, Tommy Brayshaw.

In an 8/10/49 letter to Brayshaw, besides talking about his preference for two-handed rods for steelhead, Cunliffe mentions catches of steelhead on North Shore streams: "I have heard of three people who claim to have caught over a hundred each, one man told me that he had 128 so far." With such numbers of fish it's no wonder that Lower Mainland steelhead fly fishing was birthed on the Capilano.

Cunliffe in his letter to Brayshaw also mentioned his ventures into the interior with a 12 pound, dry sedge-caught rainbow from Knouff Lake in the early 1930s being one of his better fish, and pleasant trips to Devick and Le Jeune lakes. But he is best remembered as a dedicated steelhead fly fisher, who disdained the use of other methods. His Cinnamon & Gold is his tribute to this grand sport fish.

It was on a 1983 September day on the Coquihalla that my thoughts jelled regarding this pattern. After returning home, I scribbled down the pattern listing on a piece of paper and after picking up all the ingredients I dressed the first specimen.

I liked the finished product, dressed on a number 2 Wilson dry-fly salmon hook. I tied up a half dozen more for my next trip to the Coquihalla, named it Claret & Black as I taped the first fly and wrote its details into my pattern book. Then my thoughts turned to how this fly came into being.

One day in late August, 1983, up on the Dean River, Peter Broomhall and I were talking fly fishing. I recall making the statement that there had been about eight minds of notable anglers and fly tiers who had influenced my thoughts on the development of a fly that I call Black and its variation Green-Butt Black. Later, I wondered about my statement so with this new fly—Claret & Black—I decided to write down the names of the anglers/fly tiers. I was surprised by the number—George Kelson, Captain J. W. Hale, Dr. T. E. Pryce-Tannatt, A. Bryan Williams, Arthur Woods, Rod Haig-Brown, Clark Van Fleet, R. V. Righyni and John Ashley-Cooper—nine in total.

The old tiers—Hale, Kelson, and Pryce-Tannatt—through studying their books taught me the mechanics involved in tying a classic fly, which complements the classy fish I angle for—the steelhead. On many of my floating-line flies, I incorporate tips, tags, butts and body hackles in the traditional Atlantic salmon tying style. Although the fish could care less about such things, it pleases me to catch fish on well-dressed flies.

Because I prefer to fish for summer steelhead, if the river conditions are suitable, with a floating line I wanted the style of fly to match the sparsely dressed ties of A. E. H. Wood.

I decided on a claret body because of a statement made by A. Bryan Williams in his book *Rod and Creel in British Columbia* (1919), where he stated that a Claret and Grouse fly was better for steelhead than a Jock Scott or a Silver Doctor.

Rainbow trout.

T. Brayshaw.

I chose a gold tip and rib because they complemented the body colour. Oval tinsel over flat for two reasons. First, the fabric core of oval tinsel was not as easily severed by the fish's teeth. Second, by nestling the hackle stem next to the oval tinsel, it provided good protection from the fish's teeth. The orange tail because Rod Haig-Brown wrote many times that winter steelhead seemed to have a preference for orange. In reverence to The Man, I gave the fly an orange tail.

I wanted a body hackle to give the fly extra movement, which better represents a living thing, as described by Kelson in *The Salmon Fly* (1895) and reiterated by Clark Van Fleet in his book *Steelhead to a Fly* (1951). A black hackle was chosen because it too complemented the body colour. To keep the tie sparse, one side of the hackle was stripped.

For the throat I decided on the barred flank feather from either the pintail or widgeon duck. I believe that as water flows through and fluctuates the fibres of barred feathers, a better illusion of movement and thus a more lifelike appearance is achieved.

There was only one choice of colour for the wing—black. During the summer prior to tying this fly, I bought John Ashley-Cooper's book, *A Salmon Fisher's Odyssey* (1982), and when it first arrived I thumbed through it and read the section on flies. In one of his statements on fly winging he said that if he had to choose just one colour for the wing of the fly it would be black. That pleased me because it confirmed my thoughts on the subject and black it was for my new fly. I wanted a fine hair that fluctuates well even in the slightest of currents for the wing and chose squirrel tail.

A black Cellire varnished head adds the last touch of class. The product was a dark-toned fly that will give a good silhouette when observed from below with the sky as a background, similar in appearance to those flies that suit R.V. Righyni's silhouette pattern description in his book *Advanced Salmon Fishing* (1973).

The first day I used the fly—September 15, 1983—up on the Coquihalla, I managed to hook and land one 24-inch steelhead and six rainbows from 10 to 16 inches. This was on my original tie which I retired and mounted. I have been using the Claret & Black on and off for the past 12 years and am pleased with its performance.

The above passage written by W. F. Pochin in his book, *Angling & Hunting in British Columbia* (1946), is the earliest reference to the Cliff's Special that I have been able to locate. However, I suspect that because Pochin referred to the Cliff's Special as one of the "standard patterns" (p.32) that for the fly to become a standard it must have been developed earlier.

Welch spent most, if not all, of his working life as a salesclerk at Harkley & Haywood sporting goods store in Vancouver until his retirement in about 1965. Besides working at Harkley & Haywood, he and his wife dressed flies commercially and they also made bamboo rods. A keen outdoor enthusiast, he saw the hey days of the Capilano River and was instrumental as a Vancouver Angling & Game member in introducing Vancouver's first fly casting classes at Lost Lagoon in Stanley Park.

According to sales records kept by Harkley & Haywood, for many years Cliff's Special was amongst the four most popular steelhead patterns in the province. In Roy Patrick's *Pacific Northwest Fly Patterns* (1958), he says that this "standard throughout B.C." pattern is a "Canadian coastal fly for Sea-Run Cutthroat" and that it is "also good for Summer-run Steelhead." However, like most other British Columbian and North American feather-winged patterns, the Cliff's Special has been replaced by patterns of similar colour schemes but with hair wings.

Combo Bug

HOOK: Number 4 or 6 Tiemco TMC 200
TAIL: Deer hair or none **BODY:** Black foam
RIB: Black rod-binding thread
WING & THROAT: Deer hair **COLLAR:** Deer hair ends
ORIGINATORS: Robert Brown and Bob Taylor
INTENDED USE: Waked-fly for summer steelhead
LOCATION: Dean River

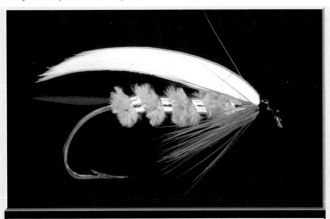

Cliff's Special

HOOK: Number 2/0 to 8 **TAIL:** Red swan or goose
BODY: Orange chenille **RIB:** Flat, gold tinsel
THROAT: Hot orange hackle **WING:** White swan or goose
ORIGINATOR: Cliff Welch
INTENDED USE: Wet fly for steelhead
LOCATION: Capilano River

Lower mainland Steelheads will average better than ten pounds and specimens up to nineteen pounds have been taken on the fly from the Capilano and Coquihalla rivers.

In wet flies silver-bodied bucktails, the General Money, Cliff's Special and Royal Coachman tied on number two to four hooks have been killers. (p. 11)

In the early 1990s, Pete Soverel, well known Washingtonian steelhead fly fisher, showed Robert Brown, alias The Skeena Angler, a fly designed for the waked-fly surface presentation, an exciting method to take summer-run steelhead. The fly, simple in design, consisted of a piece of green foam strapped to a hook with the front end cut at a 45 degree angle to improve its waking ability. Brown grabbed the concept and added a moose hair tail and body hackle, named the fly the Riffle Cricket, and found the pattern produced well for the summer-run steelhead in the streams around his Terrace home.

Taylor, however, steeped in the tradition of proper fly design years ago, wanted Nature to pass a law which wouldn't permit any steelhead to take non-classic looking flies. Unfortunately, even with all his connections and persuasion, Taylor was unsuccessful and that is the reason you often see steelhead taken on god-awful looking flies. A man of principle, he set about to re-engineer the foam-bodied fly improved by Brown and added a deer hair tail and wing.

During our 1993 Dean River trip, I noticed the foam-bodied lures now transformed into flies in Taylor's box and hinted that he should let me have a couple to try. On an overcast July 28th afternoon, I tested the pattern I had nicknamed Bob's Fly and christened it with a 35-inch female from the Lower Camp Run. On the last day of the trip I hooked two more steelhead using Bob's Fly, landing a 28-inch female and losing another. The fly, quite tattered, I slipped into my box.

When I replenished my box of steelhead flies in the off-season, I noticed the bedraggled fly and thought that I could possibly make it wake better if I added more to the deer hair wing, a deer hair throat, and forced back the deer hair stubs forming a collar.

In 1994, I returned to the Dean and during that trip took three more fish, giving me a total of six fish hooked and five landed, on the same sample pattern. I renamed it the Combo Bug because it was a combination of efforts that resulted in the pattern described here. The initial concept came from Pete Soverel, the pattern was enhanced by Robert Brown and Bob Taylor, and I added the finishing touches with the addition of the thicker deer hair wing, the throat, and the deer hair collar.

This contemporary pattern is a rather simple one to dress yet it is effective whenever a waked-fly presentation is required.

Coquihalla Orange

HOOK: Number 2 to 6 **TIP:** Fine gold, oval tinsel
TAIL: A few strands from a golden pheasant tippet feather
BUTT: Black ostrich herl
BODY: Rear half orange floss followed
by orange polar bear underfur
RIB: Medium oval, silver tinsel **THROAT:** Red hackle
WING: White over orange polar bear fur
ORIGINATOR: Tom Brayshaw
INTENDED USE: Wet fly for steelhead
LOCATION: Coquihalla River

This pattern is another of Tom Brayshaw's creations, mostly used for Coquihalla River steelhead. In the 1930s, however, when Brayshaw was a regular visitor to the Adams and Little rivers east of Kamloops near Chase, he used an orange-bodied, white polar bear hair wing fly which he dubbed "Mother." Although Brayshaw did not record it, perhaps "Mother" was the forerunner of the Coquihalla Orange.

Brayshaw's first-ever hook-up with a Coquihalla steelhead was on his Black & Silver. On that day with the Black & Silver, he lost two steelhead. The account of that evening is detailed in this book under the pattern with that heading. The next day, 9 August 1946, Brayshaw took his first fly-caught Coquihalla steelhead on the British sea-trout fly Teal & Red. The next week, on August 14, he took his first Coquihalla steelhead on one of his original patterns—the Coquihalla Orange:

Darc Means, the Indian, told me there were 8 to 10 fish lying half-way down so I waded the pool . . . I saw one steelhead rise where he said they were lying but though I could cover it I got no response. Changed to a #6 Orange & White polar bear with orange body & tried again. At first cast I was into a wild fish which put up a short but violent fight before I beached her—a hen of 8 pounds in beautiful condition.

This orange pattern became the first of Brayshaw's Coquihalla series of flies, and from an examination of steelhead fly-use recorded in his diary from 1946 to 1959, one of his favourites.

Coquihalla Orange — Dark

HOOK: Number 2 to 6
TAIL: A few strands from a golden pheasant tippet feather
TIP: Fine oval, silver tinsel
BODY: Rear half of orange floss followed
by orange polar bear underfur
RIB: Flat, silver tinsel **THROAT:** Scarlet hackle
WING: A few hairs of orange polar bear
under bronze mallard
ORIGINATOR: Tom Brayshaw
INTENDED USE: Wet fly for steelhead
LOCATION: Coquihalla River

On a grey, showery, September 30, 1949 day, Brayshaw spent a good part of the day working his way down river from the Lear railway station bridge pool on the Coquihalla River, and after breaking the point off on his Coquihalla Silver "changed to a #4 dark mallard & orange." In a run next to the railway tracks that Brayshaw had previously "always passed up," he "had a pull several feet above the big rock." The next cast he found himself securely fixed to a "good jumping," and "most obliging" summer-run steelhead which he landed. His first fish on the new pattern.

Brayshaw had a rule that he followed: before he would detail in his diary the components of a new pattern, the fly must be christened. On October 7, 1949, he was fishing the pool marked by the telegraph pole 83/16, and after having three fish come to his Coquihalla Silver with no solid hook up, he put on a number 4 Coquihalla Orange—Dark, which was the same fly he "caught the 5 1/4-pounder on a week ago," and with his subsequent 6 1/2-pounder, decided that the pattern needed recording.

The dressing details for the Coquihalla Orange—Dark, as listed above, are those that he wrote in his diary on October 7, 1949. Brayshaw, however, preferring to catch his steelhead on classic-looking flies, often varied his dressings and incorporated many of the characteristics of traditional Atlantic salmon patterns. In Trey Combs' book *Steelhead Fly Fishing and Flies* (1976), the dressing given for the Coquihalla Orange—Dark lists many of those additions and has a golden pheasant crest feather tail veiled with red hackle tips; a black ostrich butt; a silver, oval tinsel rib following the flat; a golden pheasant topping over the bronze mallard and polar bear wing; and jungle cock cheeks.

The Coquihalla Orange—Dark dressed in all its finery is a most beautiful example of the fly-tier's craft and by dressing the fly so elaborately, I believe, shows the high regard that some anglers such as Brayshaw have for the steelhead as a game fish.

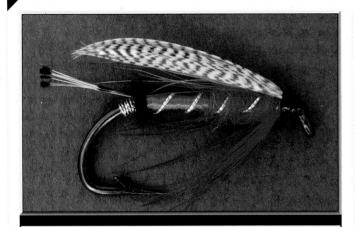

Coquihalla Orange — Light

HOOK: Number 2 Mustad 5X strong
TIP: Fine oval, gold tinsel
TAIL: A few strands from a golden pheasant tippet feather
BUTT: Black ostrich herl
BODY: Rear half orange floss followed
by orange polar bear underfur for front half
RIB: Medium oval, silver tinsel
THROAT: Red hackle
WING: A few strands of orange polar bear
under light mallard
ORIGINATOR: Tom Brayshaw
INTENDED USE: Cold-water steelhead
LOCATION: Coquihalla River

Tommy Brayshaw with a nice Coquihalla steelhead.

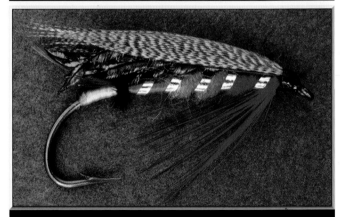

Coquihalla Red

HOOK: Number 2 to 6 **TAG:** Yellow floss
TAIL: Collarette magnifique
BODY: Orange floss, orange and then red
mohair in equal sections
RIB: Flat, silver tinsel **HACKLE:** Red neck hackle feather
WING: A few peacock swords enveloped
with strips of grey mallard
ORIGINATOR: Tom Brayshaw
INTENDED USE: Wet fly for summer steelhead
LOCATION: Coquihalla River

For years after Brayshaw moved to Hope, once the water became cold, he turned to the Silex with Devon minnow for his winter-run steelhead fishing. In a 2 November 1959 letter to Dr. Dwight A. Webster of Cornell University in Ithaca, New York, in a discussion about fly-use for summer and winter runs, he says:

> The most usual sizes seem to be 2, 4, & 6, though for winter fish I have seen 1/0 and even 2/0 flies used, however most of us spin for the winter runs, deep fly fishing is rather a bore. Personally I use much the same sizes as for summer fish but dress them on 4x or 5x strong hooks. I have struck with a variant of a "Light Coquihalla Orange" . . . tied on one of these heavy hooks which takes the fly down deeper to winter fish.

The variant Coquihalla Orange had an over wing of light mallard flank feather and it was with one of those heavy-wired hooks that Brayshaw lured the first fly-caught Thompson River steelhead on 13 November 1953.

During that historic event, Brayshaw had teamed up with his long-time and famous fisherman friend Roderick Haig-Brown of Campbell River for this Thompson River trip. In the afternoon Brayshaw fished the Y Run and just about opposite where the Y railway spur ends at the river, he had two pulls on a 1/0 Light Coquihalla Orange. With a change to a fly dressed on a 5X strong heavy wired-hook, he was soon into a lively fish that threw the hook after three or four jumps. He resumed fishing, rising two more, and just before dark connected solidly with another and, with Haig-Brown's help, Brayshaw landed a 12 1/2 pound male steelhead.

Although this fly is not significantly different from Brayshaw's fly of similar design that he used for summer-run steelhead, it is the concept of using heavy-wired hooks to give that little extra sinking bonus that needs to be documented.

On October 25, 1951, Brayshaw wrote in his diary about a fly that he had designed almost to the day but one year earlier and referred to the pattern as his "latest." On that October day one year earlier, Brayshaw took a 5 pound 2 ounce poor fighting female fish from the "long stream" near Gold Pan Pool and then "went to Bailey's pool and pool above" to finish the afternoon. In the pool just above the bridge he got another poor fighting female fish of 6 pounds 6 ounces and he "got both on a size 2" pattern dressed with a tag of yellow floss, a tail of collarette magnifique, a body of orange floss shading through orange mohair to red ribbed with flat silver tinsel, red throat hackle, and a wing of grey mallard enveloping peacock sword.

For years he referred to this pattern as Brayshaw's Latest. However, sometime between 1951 and 1959 his "latest" became the last of his Coquihalla series when he renamed it Coquihalla Red.

In 1959 Brayshaw mentioned in a letter to a Dr. Webster that most of the dressings for his patterns could be gleaned from examining the patterns he sent with the exception of the tail feather in his Coquihalla Red. He says that if "you hold it up to the light you will see a most beautiful translucent red. The feather is called 'Collarette magnifique' and I got them from Paris over 50 years ago and I guess I shall never be able to replenish my stock." For those wishing to dress the Coquihalla Red, substitute a scarlet hackle tip for the "Collarette magnifique."

The Coquihalla Red was not only Brayshaw's "latest" pattern, it was the last that he developed for steelhead and it culminated a long career as an innovative fly tier.

This 12-pounder was Brayshaw's second largest ever steelhead from the Coquihalla, a 13 1/4-pounder taken on 17 July 1952 tops the list. The Coquihalla is noted for its small-sized, summer-run steelhead: over a 14-year period from 1946 to 1959, Brayshaw's fish from the Coquihalla River averaged just over six pounds. A whale-sized fish of 12 pounds from this small river is very impressive and a suitable topping to their thought-to-be wedding anniversary which was actually the next day.

Cowichan Special

HOOK: Number 4 to 10
TAIL: A few sprigs from a white hackle
BODY: Red or orange chenille
COLLAR: Soft, white hackle **ORIGINATOR:** Ron Saysell
INTENDED USE: Wet fly for steelhead, brown
and rainbow trout
LOCATION: Cowichan River

Coquihalla Silver

HOOK: Number 4 and 6
TAIL: A few sprigs of golden pheasant tippet feather
TAG: Red floss **BODY:** Flat, silver tinsel
RIB: Oval, silver tinsel **THROAT:** Red hackle
WING: A few fibres of orange followed by
a few fibres of white polar bear fur
ORIGINATOR: Tom Brayshaw
INTENDED USE: Wet fly for steelhead
LOCATION: Coquihalla River

After years of fishing silver-bodied flies for Little and Adams rivers' rainbows and cohoes in Vancouver Island's Duncan Bay with great success, Brayshaw devised this silver-bodied steelhead fly in 1947. On that July 4 afternoon, Brayshaw accompanied by his wife Becky and, thinking it was their 31st wedding anniversary, celebrated the day on the river. They started fishing at the Coquihalla's famous Steelhead Pool and after lunch moved upriver to the Rock Pool. Brayshaw says that:

I went up to the Rock Pool—water on low side and very clear so I tried it down with a #4 Orange & white polar bear - silver body, red hackle.

A steelhead took savagely and ran down & across and then turned up and broke water about 40 yards above where my line cut the water; it worked steadily upstream to where some children were bathing on the far side and then came back accompanied by another fish. I gaffed it—a nice male 12 pound bright fish.

In the annals of British Columbia river fly-fishing, the Cowichan River has few rivals. Fly fishers have been travelling to this prolific Vancouver Island river for more than 110 years. Vancouver Island's first trout pattern, the Cowichan Coachman, was devised to deceive the cutthroat and rainbows of that famous river. The Cowichan Special was developed in the 1940s by Ron Saysell and dressed by his wife-to-be. Saysell's son, Joe, in a recent letter to me relates the fly's development:

The Cowichan Special was tied by my mother as my dad did not tie, he only fished and would borrow (use) other people's flies. Because he took a lot of people out fishing, he seemed to have an endless supply of flies coming into the house.

My mother tied before they were married (maybe part of the reason for the attraction) and they were married in 1947. . . . she probably first tied the Cowichan Special in 1945 or 1946. The original fly was dressed with wool body (mostly oranges and reds) and later with the new chenilles, therefore the salmon egg look.

. . . Some of the originals had a white polar bear wing (optional) . . . and more an attractor type of fly. . . .

The salmon-egg-type pattern is dressed in sizes 10 to 4 with the larger sizes to be used during higher coloured water. Saysell recommends a leaded body to help get the fly quickly down to a proper fishing depth.

Joe has lived on the river all his life and can tell numerous stories of large fish taken on the Cowichan Special. One recent fish that Saysell told me about was a five-pound brown taken by General Paul Smith of Parksville in the spring of 1994. Besides the introduced-brown trout, the fly is readily taken by Cowichan steelhead, rainbows and cutthroat.

General Noel Money at Qualicum Beach.

When the General passed on in 1941, Mrs. Money passed his fly box on to Haig-Brown and Haig-Brown filled empty clips with some of his own or flies given him. Haig-Brown valued the contributions of those that came before him and, although he did use some of the Money patterns, he preserved this Money treasure and it is now part of our fly-fishing heritage.

Fly fishermen often abandon the flies developed by our predecessors because they believe their new sure-fire patterns are better. The old often are just as good as the new was my thought as I slipped some General Money patterns into my fly box. On August 28, 1994, I decided to give one of Money's patterns a try and knotted on a size 2 Dick's Fly. As I worked my way through the Cottonwood Run a 17 1/2-inch cutthroat took the fly, which was a bonus. In 12 years of fishing the Dean, this was my second cutthroat. I returned the fish to the river and carried on down the run and was soon taken by a small 24-inch-long but lively summer-run steelhead, my first steelhead on a General Money pattern. In the early afternoon on this 80-degree day in the bright sunlight, I decided to test Dick's Fly under those trying conditions and wasn't surprised that I took another 29-inch-long summer-run. Slimly dressed patterns like Dick's Fly fished on a floater are often the only technique that works under trying weather, similar to that experienced on this bright sunlit August afternoon.

Yes, with three fish landed the first day I used a Money pattern, I mused, the old is certainly just as good as the new.

Dick's Fly

HOOK: Number 2/0 to 4 **TAG:** Oval, gold tinsel
TAIL: A golden pheasant crest feather
BODY: Black floss **RIB:** Oval, gold tinsel
HACKLE: Yellow or cock-y-bondhu
WING: Bronze mallard **CHEEKS:** Jungle cock
ORIGINATOR: General Noel Money
INTENDED USE: Wet fly for steelhead
LOCATION: Stamp River

Doc Spratley

HOOK: Number 1 to 4 low-water salmon
TAIL: A few sprigs of guinea fowl
BODY: Chenille, wool, floss or seal's fur
RIB: Silver tinsel, flat or oval **THROAT:** Guinea fowl
WING: Slender strips of centre tail feather
from the ring-necked pheasant
HEAD: Peacock herl (optional)
ORIGINATOR: Dave Winters
INTENDED USE: Floating-line fly for summer-run steelhead
LOCATION: Thompson River

General Noel Money of Qualicum Beach fished the Stamp regularly with a fellow named Billy Dick from Alberta and this was Dick's favourite Money pattern.

The General, after coming to British Columbia in 1913, fished extensively on the east coast of Vancouver Island, but his favourite stream was the Stamp River, near Port Alberni located at the head of Alberni Inlet on the west coast of Vancouver Island. In a note written in his game book on October 14, 1922, the general commented on the fishing he experienced in this uncrowded land: "A grand season 77 fish, averaging just under 7 pounds—all rainbows [steelhead] but 2, which were cutthroat trout. . . . " The General, one of British Columbia's first steelhead fly fishermen, had a profound influence on the young Roderick Haig-Brown and what he was to later write about steelhead fly fishing.

This old lake pattern is one of my favourites for the Thompson River. For lake fishing it is usually dressed short and stubby—more buggy-looking—but for river fishing it needs to be streamlined.

Others claim that they used the Doc Spratley on the Thompson River and undoubtedly many did use it for trout fishing. However, the confidence necessary to take a rainbow trout lake fly to a steelhead river and use it successfully for a much harder-to-catch fish is something that most anglers shy away from. Even the most liberal-minded become extremely conservative when it comes to adopting a new or novel idea in fly selection. Most fly fishers prefer to rely on proven favourites.

The streamlined Spratley was successfully introduced to Thompson River steelhead by Washingtonian Dave Winters in the late 1960s. Dave dressed his Spratleys on long-shanked hooks with a thin chenille body. Jerry Wintle preferred them even sparser and, with the tying skills of fly dresser Ron Grantham, made the fly very sparse which suited the clear, warm-water, early-season conditions.

During the 1979 season, Peter Blain, one of my chums, spoke with Wintle and Winters after seeing them catch some fish from the Y Corner and when he returned back to camp he mentioned to me the "skinny Spratley" they were using. Next season, a poor one, I had some thinly dressed ones in my fly box and on a November morning I went across to Martel Islands with Pete Peterson and took two Thompson steelhead on my "skinny" Spratleys.

Because of the success that Winters, Wintle, and others have had with the Spratley, it has become a staple Thompson River steelhead pattern.

Dusk

HOOK: Number 4 and 6 sproat
TAG: Silver thread **TAIL:** Collarette magnifique
BODY: Scarlet and pale olive chenille wrapped together with the finished effect of light, dark, light, dark all up the body
THROAT: Mixed scarlet and white hackles
WING: Polar bear **ORIGINATOR:** Tom Brayshaw
INTENDED USE: Wet fly for steelhead
LOCATION: Coquihalla River

In Brayshaw's earlier years as a young fly tier he corresponded with George Kelson, the famous British Atlantic salmon fisherman and author of *The Salmon Fly* (1895). One of the patterns that Kelson described in detail is one with a variegated body. Possibly Kelson's multi-colour-bodied fly influenced Brayshaw in his design of this evening steelhead pattern.

It was on an evening in September 1947 that Brayshaw tested this new pattern. He says that "at 7 I rose one, a good bulging rise but didn't touch on a new fly size #6 Sproat." A couple of evenings later, on September 26, he went back to the Rock Pool and after taking two fish on a Coquihalla Silver in the low, clear water he gave the pool a rest and on returning switched to his variegated-bodied fly. He says:

I fished the rough water at the top but rose nothing so went back to upper Rock pool; getting dark now 7:10 p.m. but I could see two fish in position.

I changed to a heavier cast and a size 4, white polar bear with red & pale olive chenille body—same as one I [rose] fish on Sept. 23. but two sizes larger. Rose one immediately & landed my third and limit fish, a nice 6 1/2 pounder.

All three were bright and in excellent condition. I left the water after killing it at 7:20—a thoroughly good evening, fished within 50 feet of the road, sat down to fish & caught all three switching from behind the boulder.

On August 1, 1950, Brayshaw revised the dressing by replacing the collarette magnifique tail with a few sprigs from a golden pheasant tippet feather and the pale olive chenille with white. Although Brayshaw used this pattern for three years, he didn't bother to give it a name. However, his friends in the Washington Fly Fishing Club named it Dusk for him. On September 20 of that year on a "bright cloudless, windless day," Brayshaw recorded the name of the fly: "In the stream at the head of the School House pool I got a small female of 2 1/4 pounds on 'Dusk' size # 6 . . . ."

Although Brayshaw maintained the general configuration of the pattern, he would sometimes add an oval, silver tinsel rib and sometimes he would leave the white or red hackle from the throat, but never both. Later in the 1950s he made the last change by replacing the polar bear wing with strips of light mallard.

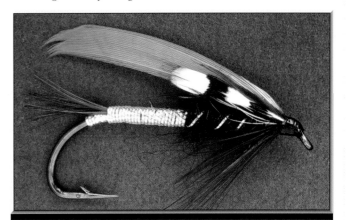

General Money No. 1

HOOK: Number 2/0 to 4 **TAG:** Oval, silver tinsel
TAIL: A small clump of golden pheasant breast feather fibres
BODY: Rear 2/5s of oval, silver tinsel; front 3/5s black polar bear underfur or black wool
RIB: Oval, silver tinsel **THROAT:** Burgundy hackle
WING: Orange swan **CHEEKS:** Jungle cock
ORIGINATOR: General Noel Money
INTENDED USE: Wet fly for summer steelhead
LOCATION: Stamp River

Examining the steelhead patterns in this and other books, you will see a myriad of colours deployed in the dressings of an almost infinite number of patterns. One can only speculate on the fly tier's thought processes that produce these unique combinations of fur, feather and tinsel. General Money's flies were some of the first patterns developed for British Columbia's summer-run steelhead. Money's No. 1 & 2 patterns were a result of many years' experimentation with different colour schemes and fly tying material combinations.

General Money's No. 1 fly with its colour combination of silver, black, orange, and burgundy is quite unique. In 1989 I interviewed Ted Pengelley of Campbell River, who in his younger years gillied for the General from the early 1930s to the General's death in 1941. Pengelley had many interesting stories to tell about the General and his family. But one of the things that Pengelley recalled was the General's fondness for burgundy-coloured things. That fondness was the reason he chose a burgundy hackle for this particular pattern.

For decades, until it went out of business in April 1982 after 63 years, Harkley & Haywood sporting goods store in Vancouver was the emporium of choice for many sportsmen. They kept a record of yearly fly sales and into the 1970s General Money's patterns topped the sales list for steelhead patterns.

General Money No. 2

HOOK: Number 2/0 to 4 **TAG:** Oval, gold tinsel
TAIL: A golden pheasant crest feather
BODY: Black floss **RIB:** Oval, gold tinsel
HACKLE: Yellow
WING: Red swan, with optional golden
pheasant crest feather over
ORIGINATOR: General Noel Money
INTENDED USE: Wet fly for summer-run steelhead
LOCATION: Stamp River

Developed for Stamp River steelhead by General Noel Money of Qualicum Beach in the 1930s after experimenting with different colour schemes for 10 years, this became one of the General's standard patterns. Roderick Haig-Brown, who was introduced to and mentored by Money on steelhead fly-fishing techniques, in *The Western Angler* says that the general's flies "may be tied on any size of hook from 2/0 to No. 4" but "the best sizes for summer fishing are usually Nos. 1/0-3" (Vol. II, p. 177). The colour frontispiece in Volume II shows this red and black General Money's Fly along with two other Money creations: Dick's Fly and the Prawn Fly.

The 1/0-3 recommended by Money to Haig-Brown for summer-run fish seem large by today's standards. The clear-flowing Stamp River and fishing conditions encountered during the summer months combined with the greased-line, a British Atlantic salmon fly-fishing technique which was introduced to British Columbia by Haig-Brown and Money on the Stamp, is usually more successful with flies in the size 4 to 8 range. About the introduction of this technique to the Stamp and its effectiveness, Haig-Brown in an August 20, 1939 letter to Bill Nation says:

> *Have had some splendid steelhead fishing on the Stamp with General Money in the last month or two. Grand fish, mostly 6-10 pounds. Using the greased line method almost entirely and they respond to it well, though I'm not so good on that strike. Very attractive method.*

However, when a new technique is introduced it requires some experimentation with fly size, colour and shape and Money, advanced in age when he switched to this method, only used the greased-line method during the last two years of his angling life. Given more time, he may have developed the niceties and refined the technique. Money did realize the importance of size and shape and thought that fish responded possibly a little better to a red fly but he did use large-sized patterns. In examining two of Money's fly boxes there were no flies smaller than number 4 and no flies dressed on the traditional low-water style of hooks recommended for the greased-line technique.

Whether fished using the greased-line-or, more traditional, sunk-line techniques, there is little doubt that his patterns were successful.

His 1933 Christmas and New Year greeting card is a testimonial to their effectiveness. The card shows General Money fishing the Stamp with a hand-written caption: "The last day of the season 5 rainbows [steelhead] 6 1/2 to 9 pounds. Many tight lines to you in 1934." Signed, "Noel Money."

The black, gold, yellow, and red is a striking colour combination that appeals to both fish and fishers. Dress some, you'll like them. However, you will have to substitute goose or turkey for the swan.

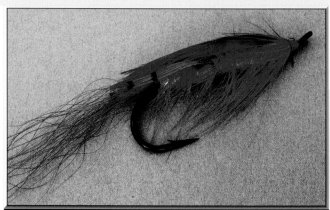

General Practitioner

HOOK: Number 2 to 5/0 low-water salmon
TAIL: Orange polar bear hair a little longer
than the hook shank and a small, red, golden
pheasant breast feather
BODY: Orange wool or seal's fur
EYES: Golden pheasant V'd tippet feather
RIB: Medium, oval, gold tinsel
HACKLE: Orange cock neck feather wound up the
body. Cut the fibres off on top so the wing can
lie flat along body
WING: Two layers of golden pheasant breast feathers
with an overwing of orange-red hen neck feather
extending to bend of hook
HEAD: Black Cellire varnish
ORIGINATOR: Colonel Esmond Drury with Bob Taylor
introducing the fly to North America
LOCATION: Vedder River

One March 1983 morning I was working the right bank of the Vedder River above Peach Road. The morning was getting on as I approached one of the last spots I could fish before the river swept into an impassable rock bluff. I drifted the fly into a small pocket, it stopped, I struck, and away went the fish. In the hope of stopping the fish from going over the rapid's lip to where I couldn't follow, I threw some slack into the line. The fish turned and slowly came back into the pool. Heart thumping, I slid my largest ever Vedder River fish—a 37 1/2-inch male—onto the beach. It took a number two Orange General Practitioner.

I can tell, as I am sure other Practitioner lovers can tell, many other stories about fish caught on General Practitioners.

The original General Practitioner fly was developed as a prawn imitation by Colonel Esmond Drury for British Atlantic salmon in 1953. Its successes in Britain and elsewhere quickly enhanced its reputation and in 1960 Colonel Drury's account of the fly's development appeared in *The Fishing Gazette*.

The dressing given by Colonel Drury is lengthy and extremely complicated. The dressing given here is a simplified version, however, it has all the important features of the original.

In Colonel Drury's own words, "I christened the fly 'General Practitioner' because it is almost all made of golden pheasant (G.P.)."

In the early 1960s there were few steelhead fly fishermen and Bob Taylor obtained much of his more useful information about fly fishing from British sporting journals. Taylor decided, after reading Drury's article in *The Fishing Gazette*, that he should tie some General Practitioners. He writes about his early GP experiences:

I first became aware of the General Practitioner Salmon fly after reading about it in two British publications during 1960. The first was A Fly fisher's Life *(1959), by Charles Ritz. In "Part V, Reminiscences—Sweden," Ritz, on page 208, mentions using a #2 General Practitioner prawn fly for his sea-trout fishing on the Em River, but unfortunately gave no clues as to the dressing. . . .*

The other publication was The Fishing Gazette, *January 1960 issue, which contained the article written by Esmond Drury and titled "The General Practitioner" gave particulars on the origin and the pattern dressing. As a former float fisherman who had enjoyed much success with shrimp as a bait I was keenly interested in a good prawn fly imitation for steelhead fly fishing. . . .*

My first attempt to dress a General Practitioner was not a great success so I decided to order some flies from Hardy's which I could use as models. . . .

My next attempt at tying the G.P. met with more success and I tied up a half dozen or more and waited for an opportunity to try them. I can't recall having too much happening with these flies, but somewhere along the way I gave a few to friends for them to try. A couple of these ended up in the fly box of Peter Broomhall.

During one of the summers of 1965 or 66, I am not sure which one, when I was a regular on the Stilliguamish River in Washington State, I showed some of my G.P.'s to Jerry Wintle and said something to the effect "they should be good steelhead flies." Jerry replied, "They are Atlantic salmon flies and won't be any good for steelhead." Later, when talking about this with my wife Karin, I told her that many steelhead had been caught on other Atlantic salmon patterns and I was going to prove Jerry wrong. A day or so later when I was fishing 'The Flat' below Deer Creek, I put on a General Practitioner . . .after a short while and part way through the run, I had a take from a nice bright fish which was duly landed—my first steelhead on the G.P.

Later, when I told Jerry the story about my Atlantic salmon fly—General Practitioner—taking a steelhead, the accomplish-ment which I described with considerable detail and pride, Jerry remained as usual unimpressed and said something like, "It just goes to show you that steelhead will bite on anything."

The General Practitioner remained dormant in Taylor's fly box, but the pattern caught the attention of another fly fisher, Bruce Gerhart, of Campbell River. He too attempted to dress some and managed to hook a west-coast steelhead on it in 1970, but again it fell into the unused section of his fly box but his interest was rekindled when Jack Vincent wrote about Bill Yonge's Vedder River successes with his newly found fly. Eventually, enough fly fishers used the fly and with the continued use, combined with the better sinking fly lines that came along, the fly chalked up some impressive results and it became a staple British Columbian pattern with a big fish reputation.

Peter Broomhall has the honor of taking the first very large steelhead with the G.P. and he writes:

My memories of the General Practitioner are vivid for several reasons. . . the double-hook pattern produced a steelhead the first time I tried it, and the steelhead it produced was the largest I had beached up to that time. The event occurred on September 25, 1973 on the Sustat River. . . .It was a strong but not spectacular fish. It took an Atlantic salmon pattern (the General Practitioner) tied for me several years ago by Bob Taylor. I hooked the fish under some fast water at the head of the pool, and landed it at the tail of the pool 25 minutes later. The fish did not jump, but made several very strong and speedy runs. I did not see the fish for 15 minutes, and when I did I was more than somewhat surprised by his size. The fish, a male, was 39 inches long and 23 1/4 inches in girth; it weighed 26 pounds.

That is the General Practitioner's story. Introduced by and first fish caught on a Pacific coast river by Bob Taylor, first fish hooked in British Columbia by Bruce Gerhart, first British Columbian fish landed by Bill Yonge, first big fish by Peter Broomhall, and popularized locally by Jack Vincent. I tied the black version in early 1984 and caught my first fish on it in the Campbell on my first attempt using it in February 1984. The General Practitioner became well known in the Pacific Northwest as "the fly" after my group returned home from our 1984 Dean River trip. With 175 hookups, most of them on General Practitioners, word spread of this amazing fly and it has become one of the Pacific Northwest's most productive steelhead patterns.

Red, Black, Orange, and Purple G.P.s.

Golden Girl

HOOK: Number 2/0 to 8 **TAIL:** A small Indian crow feather
BODY: Flat, gold tinsel **THROAT:** Yellow hackle
WING: Two large golden pheasant tippet feathers back
to back, enclosing orange polar bear fur with a golden
pheasant topping overall
ORIGINATOR: Roderick Haig-Brown
INTENDED USE: Wet fly for winter steelhead
LOCATION: Campbell River

Golden Red

HOOK: 1 to 2 inch blind-eyed salmon
TAG: Silver tinsel and yellow floss
TAIL: Red woodpecker and a golden pheasant crest feather
BODY: Oval, gold tinsel **RIB:** None
THROAT: Red hackle
WING: Bronze mallard with a golden pheasant
crest feather topping
ORIGINATOR: General Noel Money
INTENDED USE: Wet fly for summer steelhead
LOCATION: Stamp and Ash rivers

During World War II, while Haig-Brown was away from steelhead fishing, his thoughts repeatedly turned to what he considered to be the make-up of the ideal winter steelhead fly pattern. Believing that winter fish had a preference for reds and oranges, he envisioned a fur, feather and tinsel combination much simpler than, but similar to, the more elaborately dressed full-feather winged Atlantic salmon flies such as the celebrated Durham Ranger, Red Ranger, William Rufus, President, and the Red Sandy. All of these patterns, with the exception of the Red Sandy, utilized large golden pheasant tippet feathers for wings. The Red Sandy too had whole-feather wings, but not golden pheasant tippet, instead its brilliant red-orange winging consisted mainly of large Indian crow feathers.

The pattern Haig-Brown developed was a combination of the slim-bodied Red Sandy and the golden pheasant tippet-winged Durham Ranger without many of the frills. In an 18 May 1949 letter to Al McClane of *Field & Stream* magazine, Haig-Brown says that "the Golden Girl—the one with tippets—is a final dressing and has proved itself many times for winter steelhead." And later he gives the dressing for the Golden Girl:

Tag:	Orange silk
Tail:	Indian Crow
Body:	Flat gold tinsel
Hackle:	Yellow
Wing:	Two large tippets, back to back, enclosing orange bear fur. Topping over.

Haig-Brown remained loyal to this dressing but with one slight alteration: he substituted a golden pheasant crest feather, often referred to as a topping, for the Indian crow tail.

Almost two years later, in a January 1951 letter to a Seattle fisherman, Haig-Brown says that the Golden Girl "is primarily a winter steelhead fly, in sizes 2/0 to 2" and that he has "also taken cutthroats and summer steelhead on it in sizes down to No. 8."

The Golden Girl is an attractive pattern that catches the eye of both the fly fisher and the fish. It is one of the oldies that has survived the passage of time and can be found in fly shops, particularly in the Campbell River area.

On July 20, 1922, Money bought a property, located high above the river but on a pool just downstream of the junction of the Stamp and Ash rivers, described legally as Lot 10, Block 262, Alberni and owned by a Mr. Butler. It became his Stamp River home for many seasons to come and the pool at the base of the hill he named House Pool. This pool, with the famous white kidney stone shaped rocks described by Roderick Haig-Brown in his writings, in later years became known to fishermen as Money's Pool.

During the 1922 and 1923 seasons, the General often put short notes in his game book about gold-bodied flies and it is obvious from those notes that he found the gold-bodied flies effective. Moreover, he liked to experiment with colour combinations and varied the makeup of his gold-bodied flies. Some examples of these references to the Stamp River fishing and gold-bodied flies are: August 24, 1922, 3 fish, thin gold body, dark mallard wing; September 9, 1922, 3 fish all on 1 1/4" fly with gold twist body, cock-y-bondhu and fiery brown hackles; and on October 8, 1923, 6 fish to 8 pounds, all on gold, red & purple. However, on November 1, 1923, with six fish of 11 1/2, 6, 10 1/2, 8, 7, and 8 pounds killed, and in spite of the heavy rain that day, Money says that he had

*A great day's sport. 2 in One Log. 2 above. 1 in House Pool
& 1 in Junction. Lost 4 other. All on my *Golden Red Fly.*

After summarizing the total for the 1923 season: "Rainbows 109 fish averaging over 7 pounds", General Money gives the dressing for his "*Golden Red Fly. Tag - S. Tsl, Y floss. Tail - Red woodpecker & topping. Body - oval gold tsl. Body [Wing] - Brown mallard & topping over. Red hackle."

Early in the new year he used a variation of this fly with an orange hackle and took three "grand fish, deep and silvery," winter steelhead of 8 pounds, 7 pounds and 6 pounds from Swanson's on the Somass River.

This pattern is almost identical to the Golden Demon, introduced to California summer-runs by Zane Grey. However, Money's introduction of his Golden Red Fly to Vancouver Island summer-run steelhead preceded Grey's introduction of the Golden Demon to California summer-runs by at least 10 years.

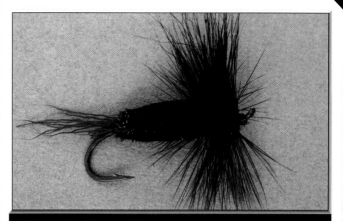

Grey Fly

K: Number 2/0 to 4 **TAG:** Oval, silver tinsel
ODY: Grey wool **RIB:** Oval, silver tinsel
AT: Orange hackle **WING:** Bronze mallard
ORIGINATOR: General Noel Money
IDED USE: Wet fly for summer steelhead
LOCATION: Stamp River

Lemire's Black Irresistible

HOOK: Number 4 to 8 Partridge, Wilson, dry-fly
TAIL: Deer hair, dyed black
BODY: Spun and clipped black-dyed deer hair
HACKLE: Black
WING: Deer hair, dyed black
ORIGINATOR: Harry Lemire
INTENDED USE: Waked fly for summer steelhead
LOCATION: Dean River

were the age of discovery for General Noel Money. After   British Columbia in 1913 to fish Campbell River, he becam   ed with Vancouver Island and in particular Qualicum Beach,   settled. He hooked his first steelhead on March 26, 1914, in   Qualicum River and on April 21 of that same year he took his first trout in British Columbia"—a fine 2 1/2-pound cutthroat. However, shortly after settling in Qualicum Beach, World War I took the General away and upon his return he discovered the "large rainbows" of the Ash, Stamp, and Somass rivers. He fished those rivers for the next 20 years, learning more and more about the river system and the timing of the runs, and developed many fly patterns for those large fish.

However, not only was the General enamored with the large rainbows he pursued, he also enjoyed the natural setting and the wildlife as indicated on this October 5 day: "Great day. 5 grand fish - best 9 1/4 pounds. Saw a cougar, a bear, eagles, deer & ravens."

When the fish arrived above Stamp Falls into the area where he had his "shack" was important to the General and over the years he made earlier and earlier trips looking for fish.

On June 13, 1925, he took a 7 1/2 pound trout from the Stamp and noted in his game book that "this is the earliest date I have ever caught a fish above the falls." With the same entry in the remarks' section, he described the fly as having a "grey wool body, orange hackle, mallard wing" and referred to this as his "Grey Fly, No. 3." On July 30 of that same year he had another good day with five fish to 8 1/2 pounds and all on his "Grey Fly, No. 3."

After 1925, Money didn't record in his game book much about the flies with which he caught fish. The Grey Fly is one of his last creations for which he provided dressing details.

Developed by famed Washingtonian steelhead fly fisher Harry Lemire in 1973, this pattern is an offshoot of the famous eastern American trout fly, the Irresistible, which, according to Harry Darbee in *Catskill Flytier* (1977), was developed "by Joe Messinger of Virginia's Rapidan River" (p. 60).

Harry Lemire has been fishing British Columbia's steelhead streams for over thirty years and is a champion of the skated- or waked-fly technique. This centuries-old British Atlantic salmon fly-fishing technique was introduced and popularized over the last 30 years for Pacific Northwest summer-run steelhead by anglers such as Lemire, Jerry Wintle and Ehor Boyanowsky. About dressing this pattern Harry recommends that you "trim bottom of hackle and body hair flat" as "this allows hackle, body and tail to set flatly on the surface film, giving the fish a good silhouette of the fly." Lemire also says that the fly fishes "best when line, leader and fly are freshly dressed with floatant."

Christened on the Dean River in 1973, this pattern also produced Lemire's and British Columbia's largest-ever dry-fly-caught steelhead. Fishing the fabled Dean River located on British Columbia's central coast, Lemire was starting the last day of his two-week trip and cast into a slick located about fifty feet from shore and, as his Black Irresistible floated downriver, a huge fish rose and intercepted the fly. Later, Lemire slid a 38 1/2-inch long, male steelhead onto the beach. The monster steelhead weighed 23 pounds two ounces.

For only four short years this was the unofficial largest dry-fly-caught fish in British Columbia, being eclipsed in 1977 by Tom Durkop's 25 pound 2 ounce rainbow taken on a #8 Royal Coachman in Kootenay Lake.

Other well-known patterns Lemire uses for waked-fly presentations are the Grease Liner and Fall Caddis. Their dressings can be found in many American steelhead fly-fishing books. In 1986, Lemire introduced his latest pattern, the Thompson River Caddis, to the fly's namesake river. This fly is dressed on Partridge low-water size 2 to 6 hooks and has an insect green dubbed body, black tying thread rib, a wing of green phase ringed-neck pheasant back feather over a small bunch of pheasant rump fibres, and a hackle and head of spun moose hair.

·   For more than a quarter century, British Columbia steelhead have found Lemire's flies to be irresistible and since that 1973 Dean River christening the Black Irresistible has lured fish from the depths on the Bulkley, Campbell, Gold, Kispiox, Morice and Skeena rivers.

Which shall I choose?

Prawn Fly

HOOK: Number 4/0 to 3 **TAG:** Silver tinsel
BODY: Orange wool **RIB:** Silver tinsel
HACKLE: A palmered red hackle
ORIGINATOR: General Noel Money
INTENDED USE: Wet fly for steelhead
LOCATION: Stamp River

Quinsam Hackle

HOOK: Number 2/0 to 8 **TAG:** Yellow silk
BODY: Black wool or seal's fur **RIB:** Oval, gold tinsel
HACKLE: Yellow from mid-point of body
COLLAR: Claret and scarlet hackles
ORIGINATOR: Roderick Haig-Brown
INTENDED USE: Wet fly for winter steelhead
LOCATION: Quinsam River

In the early days of British Columbia's steelhead fishing, fly fishing was considered to be a warm-weather activity and, through the colder days of autumn, winter, and early spring, fly fishers hung up the fly rod and took out the Silex-equipped spinning rod and fished with either a Devon minnow or a prawn. A prawn-user during the colder weather, General Noel Money of Qualicum Beach, about 60 or more years ago, realized that a fly with the red-orange colouration of a cooked prawn may prove an effective steelhead pattern and he devised his Prawn Fly or Red Fly as he sometimes called it.

For years it was one of the staple British Columbian steelhead patterns, but Rogue River steelhead also found it a delectable dish as these 1928 notes from the General's game book attest:

Oct. 22-25 Rogue River 10 fish
3 fish Oct. 25, best fish 9 1/2 pounds
Lost a fish having no gaff—at least 12 pounds
All on prawn fly. No. 1 and 1/0

However, with Bob Taylor's introduction in the 1960s of Colonel Esmond Drury's General Practitioner and its popularization in the 1970s, the Prawn Fly fell into disuse.

It shouldn't have. On the Dean's Camp Run I opened my fly box and examined the patterns all in neat rows. The rain through the night had made the river somewhat coloured and, with the light conditions, I thought I should put on a fairly large, bulky-bodied, bright fly and amongst my favoured and dominating, black-bodied General Practitioners nestled some number 2 and 4/0 Money Prawn flies. I chose a number 2 Prawn Fly.

In the next half hour as I worked my way through the pool with my double-handed 15-foot Orvis Spey rod, 15-foot sink tip, and Prawn Fly, I landed two steelhead, each about eight or nine pounds in weight. Later in the evening, I resorted to the Prawn Fly again after I had a good pull from a fish on another pattern and was unsuccessful in getting the fish to take that pattern again. Sometimes, a change in pattern, backing up a few paces and coming through again works. The Prawn Fly took another female steelhead, a 30-incher this time.

After landing the 30-incher, I headed back to camp content with the day's fishing: six takes, five hooked, four landed, and three on General Money's Prawn Fly. Not a bad day at all.

Having researched and written a book called *The Fly Patterns of Roderick Haig-Brown*, I thought I knew the flies that Haig-Brown developed, but I was wrong. When I started to gather details for this book, Bob Taylor gave me a copy of Roy Patrick's Pacific *Northwest Fly Patterns* (1964) and in the book I noticed a fly called the Quinsam Hackle. Following the dressing Patrick says that "this fly was submitted by Roderick L. Haig-Brown" and that it was "used on Vancouver Island." However, in my extensive delving into Haig-Brown's books and asking those who knew him, none mentioned this fly. And with Trey Combs, in *Steelhead Fly Fishing and Flies* (1976), crediting the fly's development to General Money, I assumed he was correct. Of course, because Haig-Brown and Patrick are both fishing in Valhalla, asking them for verification just isn't possible.

However, from recent research I am confident that this is a Haig-Brown original. In February 1995, I was reviewing Haig-Brown material in the Special Collections section of the University of British Columbia's library and in Box 22 in the outgoing letter file marked 1949 to 1952, I found two letters, one dated May 18, 1949 to Al McClane of *Field & Stream* magazine, the other to a Mr. Irving Kerl of Seattle, Washington, dated January 28, 1951. Haig-Brown in the McClane letter refers to one of his steelhead patterns as just one "of many variations of the prawn fly" and that he prefers "reds and clarets for a bright day, purples, blacks and blues for a dull day." In response to Kerl's request for some Haig-Brown originals, Rod gives dressings for four Haig-Brown flies—three steelhead and one cutthroat—and writes about consistency in dressings. About these flies and their dressings, he says:

I am afraid I am a pretty bad offender myself in the matter of changing fly dressings. I never seem to have the patience to keep on tying a fly in the same way. I think I have been more than usually faithful to the following . . . though:

Quinsam Hackle

Tag:	*Yellow silk.*
Body:	*Black wool or seal's fur, ribbed oval gold tinsel.*
	Yellow hackle wound in about half way up.
Throat:	*Claret and scarlet hackles.*

No. 2/0 to 2 for winter fish, smaller for summer.

One merit these flies have is that they are all easy to tie, which is probably why I use them so much.

Although the Prawn Fly was a Money creation, this variation named after the Quinsam River, a tributary of the Campbell, is Haig-Brown's. With Haig-Brown's comments indicating long use and the date of the letter, I expect that Haig-Brown developed the Quinsam Hackle sometime after the war ended in 1945. Those planted summer-runs in the Campbell and winter-runs in the Quinsam are just waiting for the rebirth of this pattern.

Rainbow

HOOK: 1 or 1 1/4-inch blind-eyed salmon
BODY: Black and fiery brown wool
RIB: Oval, gold tinsel **WING:** Bronze mallard
ORIGINATOR: General Noel Money
INTENDED USE: Wet fly for summer steelhead
LOCATION: Stamp and Ash rivers

Bearing the last name of Captain Edward Stamp, who came to British Columbia from England in 1857 and was the builder of the first sawmill in the Alberni Inlet, the Stamp River supported a large population of summer-run steelhead. They remained undiscovered until, on a typical, rainy, west-coast, Vancouver Island day with the river rising and colouring, General Noel Money took six fish, which he referred to as rainbows. The day was September 15, 1920 and in bold red writing the General made the following notations in his game book:

10 1/2 pounds 9 3/4 pounds 7 3/4 pounds 4. 7 1/2. 6 1/2 pounds 6 Total. Stamp River. Caught them on a 10 ft 6" trout rod & a dusty miller. A grand morning's sport, in heavy water.

That was the only day he managed to fish the Stamp River in 1920, however, that event sparked the "menage a trois" love affair between the General, the Stamp and his "rainbows" which lasted until his death in May, 1941.

The next year the General was back fishing the Stamp and Ash rivers and enjoyed grand sport. In the Ash River on September 11, 1921, he caught six steelhead on a fly that he dressed himself and described as having "shd [shoulder] drake brown wing, black & fiery brown wool body." This trip he stayed on the river for a full week and says that he "took 24 rainbow trout on fly" for a total "weight 187 1/2 pounds" and that the fish averaged "7.8 pounds." "A great week's sport, a splendid river and great fighting fish," were the General's summary comments for this September week's fishing. Later, in subsequent trips he referred to this pattern as his "rainbow" fly.

In those early years up to 1925, he refers to hook sizes in inches which was the designation often used for blind-eyed hooks, rather than numbers such as 1/0 or 4 which became the standard hook designation.

That Money used blind-eyed hooks is supported by hooks and hook packs in Money's stream-side fly-tying wallet.

Although the General described some earlier fly dressings in his game book, this is the first pattern that he admits dressing himself and I believe that it is British Columbia's first locally designed steelhead pattern.

Smith's Illusion

HOOK: Number 2/0
BODY: Wrap with lead then cover with scarlet wool
WING: Polar bear **ORIGINATOR:** Paul Moody Smith
INTENDED USE: Deeply sunk fly for steelhead
LOCATION: Capilano River

Paul Moody Smith, the inventor of "Smith's Illusion," had a long-lasting friendship with the Capilano River. Nearly 50 years after he first fished the river in 1904, Smith recalls:

With another boy I made my first trip to the Capilano River on Dominion Day [July 1] 1904. We crossed the inlet on a small ferry boat that landed, as the ferries have landed through all the years since, at the foot of Lonsdale Avenue.

By what route we reached the river I cannot now remember except that a large part of the way was over skid roads. I retain the impression of slash from fire burns, of tall stumps festooned with wild blackberries, of alder bottoms, of jungles of salmon berry bushes and devil's club, and of but one building—a small church that stood in the Indian reservation.

We first reached the river somewhere very close to where in later years would be the Marine drive bridge and fro[m] this point, during the course of the day, worked down to the mouth.

I was fly fishing and at every cast the river boiled with small trout, most of which were too undersized to keep. They were young steelhead but this I did not know at the time. I caught no fish that day but did hook, on my number eight fly, a beautiful summer run steelhead. This heavy fish made short work of my puny outfit.

When Smith's Illusion was actually developed, Smith's son Brigadier General Paul Dorrien Smith, Retired, was not sure, but in a 9 July 1994 letter to me he says:

I don't know when my father first started to use Smith's Illusion but it could be as early as the '20s. That's when I first started fishing with him. . . . I was too young to wield a fly rod with a heavy weighted fly then. My job was to sit somewhere at the tail of a pool and watch for fish to come up through the shallows, and sing out when I saw one, which was surprisingly often back in those far off halcyon days. It was common too that Dad would hook a fish almost at once when I had seen one come into the pool. Actually, the fish seemed to travel in small groups.

From my earliest memories of those days, I never saw my father use anything but a fly, almost always a weighted one which forced him to tie his own hence the Illusion.

For most of his fly fishing, General Smith's father used the heavily weighted fly with a King Eider floating line and "drifted" the Illusion through the steelhead lies. In the summer months, however, P.M. often used the Capilano-born dry fly—The Whiskey & Soda—detailed later in this section.

Smith's Illusion was named by P.M.'s good friend and fishing companion Frank Darling, master Capilano fly fisher. In the same 9 July letter, General Smith writes:

The name of pattern was given it by Frank Darling who intended it as irony of course. Frank would only use English salmon patterns, summer & winter. Lacking the weight to get down, he didn't catch much in winter but he did get some. No matter how many fish Dad took on the "Illusion" Frank always saw it as a fluke—must have mistaken it for an English pattern he would say.

That the steelhead took P.M.'s fly as an Atlantic salmon pattern replica is doubtful, Paul Moody recognized that, in many instances, the fly must be fished deep to get bottom-dwelling steelhead, and he developed a fly and married it to a fly-fishing technique that permitted just that.

With the building of Cleveland Dam, the upper river—the haven to summer-runs—was lost as was the near fifty years of fly-fishing tradition developed by Capilano fly fishers like Frank Darling and Paul Moody Smith. Smith had many fond memories and experiences fishing with the Illusion on the Capilano, but he lamented about the loss he would experience with the dam's imminence and said, "The Capilano has been my friend—a friend to which I owe a great deal of gratitude."

Smith's Illusion is a pioneer steelhead pattern.

Van Egan with steelhead.

Squamish Poacher

HOOK: Number 2 **TAIL:** Sparse orange bucktail
EYES: Green glass **BODY:** Fluorescent orange chenille
RIB: Silver or copper wire or fluorescent red-orange thread
HACKLE: Orange
WING: Fluorescent orange surveyor's tape carapace
ORIGINATOR: Joe Kambeitz
INTENDED USE: Deeply sunk fly for steelhead
LOCATION: Squamish River

Over the past 20 years, no single steelhead pattern has raised more controversy in British Columbia than this Kambeitz-originated one. I am not exactly sure why so much controversy, but perhaps it was Kambeitz's choice of name. To sport fishermen, poacher has negative connotations associated with it.

Kambeitz is a man of many talents: fisher, painter, wood worker, photographer, to name a few. When he devised his Squamish Poacher creation way back in 1974, and with his catches on the new pattern, he was somewhat taken back by the reactions his unusual pattern received. Perhaps it was Kambeitz's use of non-traditional type materials such as surveyor's tape and glass eyes that raised the ire of local fly dressers and fishers. Controversies similar to this one surrounded the General Practitioner when Colonel Drury introduced it to British streams back in 1953 and other debates have occurred in the fishing community about Atlantic salmon and trout patterns over the years. However, with the passage of time, most patterns receive recognition and acceptance.

Joe is as ardent an angler as you can find and a very skilled one using the locate-and-wait method of fishing. By locate-and-wait I mean: locate a good spot that fish hold in or pass through and spend the prime time working the spot. I remember how well Kambeitz did float fishing the Murray Creek Run on the Thompson River in the early 1970s using this technique. When Joe took up fly fishing for steelhead he adapted this technique quite effectively and it is the reason he developed the Squamish Poacher.

Unlike the majority of steelhead fly fishers who work the runs and use fly patterns with many moving parts to take advantage of the river's flow and steelhead's attraction to moving, life-like things, Kambeitz wanted something that sunk quickly so that he could scour the river bed where bottom-moving-and-dwelling steelhead were found. The compactness he incorporated into the Poacher suited a fast sink and the down-and-across presentation he used.

I remember vividly a conversation Joe and I had on the Dean River in 1984. Kambeitz had just about finished his trip and was spending the last day or two down near the Totem Fly fishers' camp at 4-mile before he left for home. With 75 hook-ups on traditional-type patterns, I had had an exceptionally good trip and had my fill of fishing. Joe and I were watching other Totems fish and talk about flies and steelhead fishing. He said that although he had good catches with the Poacher, it was the complementing technique: 15 feet of size 13 head, short down-and-across casts, working the fly across the bottom that accounted for this success. The secret to success is presentation.

Steelhead Bee

HOOK: Number 2 to 10
TAIL: Fox squirrel, quite bushy
BODY: Equal sections of dark brown, yellow and dark brown wool, silk or seal fur
HACKLE: Natural brown, ginger or honey, sparse
WING: Fox squirrel, quite bushy, set slightly forward and well divided
ORIGINATOR: Roderick Haig-Brown
INTENDED USE: Dry fly for summer steelhead
LOCATION: Campbell River

Developed in the early 1950s by Roderick Haig-Brown for Campbell River summer-run steelhead, Haig-Brown christened the pattern on an early 1951 autumn afternoon on the Campbell River. And what an afternoon it was. He relates the details on pages 70 to 73 in *Fisherman's Summer* (1959) and summarized the day's happenings: "As nearly as I can remember the details, I had risen at least twelve good fish, all to the dry fly, and missed six or seven, been broken by three and killed three."

For years Haig-Brown used this un-named pattern. About the design, the naming of the fly and the desired floating criteria, Haig-Brown in a 7 May 1963 letter to Tom Brayshaw writes:

My point about floss silk bodies is that they don't float as well as fur, and that was why we started looking for something else. Personally, having now used the fur bodies, I don't think the difference is significant.

As to the name of the fly, I suppose one might call it the "B.C. Bee" or the "Steelhead Bee." . . . Fox squirrel is probably the best wing, though I had some moose hair (almost black and a bit speckled) which I thought very good too. I am not sure, but I think the hackle on the fly you have may be too good for best results. I think the fly should float a bit heavy on the water, as did the first ones I made . . . .

Haig-Brown's neighbours and good friends, the Egans, enjoyed good success with the Steelhead Bee. Maxine Egan told me in early 1995 that, for steelhead and most trout, it is the only dry fly she uses. About Maxine's Steelhead Bee exploits, her husband Van writes:

The summer of 1959 saw me attending summer school at U.B.C. It was a hot, sunny summer and one weekend when I returned home Maxine told me a very interesting story. On an

afternoon during the week—it was late July—she had a visit from a film maker from New York who was looking for someone to film steelhead fishing. It was shortly after lunch and the sun was beating down mercilessly. She tried to dissuade him from filming on such a day, saying there no chance of a fish in this weather or at this time of year. He did, however, persuade her to "fish for the camera," saying he had come all the way out here to get some footage and couldn't return with nothing. Maxine yielded.

She took the film maker to the Lower Island Pool where she used a 4-ounce Leonard trout rod and a #8 Steelhead Bee on 4x leader, expecting absolutely nothing. The man set up his tripod and camera, ready to roll. Maxine cast the fly and a 6-lb steelhead grabbed it like it had been waiting the opportunity. It headed off down river, Maxine following, and the cameraman, a short, stocky person, came stumbling along behind. The Campbell's rocks are slippery, but Maxine got the fish and the film maker got his pictures. He was ecstatic.

But now he needed some footage to lead off with, to give the right dimension to the story. So a few casts were made, and suddenly she had another steelhead of about the same size . . . the New Yorker went home happy and Maxine came home rather amazed at her good fortune . . . .

Van Egan assures me that not only is the Steelhead Bee an excellent steelhead dry fly but an excellent dry fly for Vancouver Island trout as well. The Steelhead Bee has become a symbol of Haig-Brown and it is his most recognized and popular steelhead pattern.

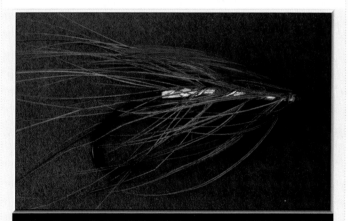

Taylor's Golden Spey

HOOK: Number 5/0 to 4 low-water salmon
BODY: Rear one half of hot orange floss and front half of hot orange seal's fur
RIB: Flat, silver tinsel followed by medium, oval tinsel
HACKLE: Grey heron feather
THROAT: Golden pheasant red-orange breast feather or lemon wood duck flank feather
WING: Two golden pheasant red-orange breast feather, set flat over body
ORIGINATOR: Robert Taylor
INTENDED USE: Wet fly for steelhead
LOCATION: Bella Coola River

Spey flies originated in the River Spey Valley in Scotland, but steelhead fishermen, always in a quest for more effective flies, found the characteristics in Spey flies appealing. Roderick Haig-Brown was the first to recommend a traditional Spey pattern—The Lady Caroline—for West Coast fishing.

Bob Taylor, influenced by some British authors and in particular Eric Tavener's words in his 1931 book *Salmon Fishing* when he wrote about the characteristics of this type of fly with "a long mobile hackle and throat, which give in heavy water of moderate flow an appearance of life unapproached by any other style of fly" (p. 298), was influenced further when in 1965 he saw Syd Glasso's Spey patterns featured in the Inland Empire Fly Fishing Club's *Flies of the Northwest*. The next year after studying the set of Glasso-dressed Spey flies that Sid gave him during a 1968 visit, Taylor started dressing Spey-type patterns.

Often in fly tying the fingers can't get the feathers to do what is needed and innovations happen with the result that the intended fly ends up with a different appearance, often for the better. This happened with Taylor and he says that:

> In 1978 I tied up a Spey fly that was somewhat like Syd's Orange Heron but didn't like the way that the wings set on the hook or the way it swam. I thought about ways to improve the appearance and the swim of this fly and remembered the way that the General Practitioner fly had golden pheasant breast feather tied on flat, cupped over the body. It seemed like an attractive and practical solution to my problem and after tying up a few patterns I knew that this was the solution I had been searching for.
>
> Later, I showed my pattern to Syd during a visit when he was living in Isaquah during 1979 and he told me that he too had the same problems with the orange hackle wing on his Orange Heron and that he liked my flat-wing solution.

In the spring of 1978 during a trip to Bella Coola with fellow Totem Flyfishers Lee Straight and Robin Kendall, Taylor christened his new fly on this steelhead fly-fishing trip; however, he found an unexpected bonus with his catches of cutthroat. He says:

> Although this spring trip was primarily for steelhead we also managed to find some large cutthroats. On one of our drifts I put on a large 3/0 un-named Spey fly and waded in at the top of a run and started casting to a likely looking spot. The fly landed and almost immediately I hooked, played and landed a cutthroat of over 3 pounds. Three more all around the same size followed. During the remainder of our drift I fished many pieces of water and landed several more cutthroats and, in the last pool before takeout, two steelhead, all on this Spey pattern.
>
> Because of my use of golden pheasant feathers in this fly, Straight babtized it Taylor's Golden Spey.

A most attractive pattern, steelhead on the Thompson, Dean and Skeena and other rivers have succumbed to the Golden Spey.

COLLAR: Orange hackle WING: Polar bear
TOPPING: Orange hackle tip
ORIGINATOR: Martin Tolley
INTENDED USE: Wet fly for winter steelhead
LOCATION: Squamish River

Martin Tolley a 1950s immigrant from England arrived in the Lotus Land after a short stay in Eastern Canada. He soon came "face-to-face with a genuine senior fish" as he referred to the king of Pacific Northwest game fish—the steelhead. Tolley, the originator of this version of the Polar Shrimp, was one of the few who promoted the use of flies for winter steelhead through the 1960s.

During Tolley's 1960s Vancouver years, his favourite winter-run stream was the Squamish River, and it was for those fish that he devised his Polar Shrimp. In a 6 July 1995 letter he relates the fly's development:

> It seems I had been working, streamside, on my variant of the Polar Shrimp long before I even knew of the Eel River originals.
>
> My first beginnings on the Squamish—Spring 1960—had been on the noted Wilson's Riffle Run, fishing the cement-coloured May run-off edges with some remnant streamer patterns brought out from Eastern Canada. They scored well, especially the ties with golden tinsels.
>
> In the recess between seasons and whilst cutthroating at Nile Creek, it was Captain Barton who told me of the chenille-style egg-type flies that had hooked fish for him on the Big Qualicum.
>
> By now I had discovered some of the texts with their illustrated fly plates and it was these that prompted my armchair concoctions based on the proven gold tinsel and orange chenille. My use of the hackle tip as a topping was no more than an aimless affectation.
>
> Several frail seasons followed . . . but in the Squamish winter-run seasons of 1965, '66 & '67 the Polar Shrimp was landing near thirty fish per season, thanks to the discovery of the Eagle Run, Brackendale Bar and Judd Road.
>
> However, in our Centennial Year [1967] I was to discover the summer-runs of the Marble, Stilly and Grand Ronde. But during the late '60s I had replaced the orange chenille with dubbed orange polar bear guard hairs which gave the pattern a beautiful fluorescence.

Steelhead, both winter- and summer-runs, from many Pacific Northwest streams have been attracted to Tolley's Polar Shrimp over the past thirty years. Besides his achievements with winter- and summer-run steelhead on the fly, Martin was also one of the founders and the first president of the Totem Flyfishers of British Columbia.

Tolley's Polar Shrimp

HOOK: Number 1/0 to 2 low-water salmon
TAIL: Orange hackle fibres
BODY: Rear half, flat, gold tinsel; front half, orange polar bear underfur

Whiskey & Soda

HOOK: Number 4 to 8
TAIL: A black and a white hackle tip

> **BODY:** Black and white hackles tied in at the hook bend and wound thick and full up the hook shank
> **HEAD:** Black thread, varnished
> **ORIGINATOR:** Austin Spencer
> **INTENDED USE:** Dry fly for summer steelhead
> **LOCATION:** Capilano River

In days long since past, the Whiskey & Soda drifted over summer-run steelhead in once-famous pools with names like Blue Rock, Stovepipe, Blaney's Cribbing, Crown Creek, Upper and Lower Darling, and Snake Ranch (or Whiskey Ranch as some called it). These names are unfamiliar to most present-day steelhead fishermen. All these runs disappeared when the upper Capilano River Valley, behind the Cleveland Dam, was flooded in 1954.

Although the history of this province's steelhead fly-fishing is short, few know that this province's first steelhead dry fly—the Whiskey & Soda—was developed in the 1920s for the Capilano summer-runs by Austin Spencer, the local game warden. However the naming of the fly remained a mystery until I asked Bob Taylor.

He got the story from one of the Capilano's first generation fly fishermen. Bob met Bill Cunliffe in the early 1950s and during one of their many conversations, Cunliffe explained that the Whiskey & Soda got its name from Black and White scotch whiskey, the favoured drink of Capilano fly fishermen. On the label of the dark coloured whiskey bottle were two Scotty dogs, one black and one white. According to Cunliffe, the Black Scotty represented the whiskey, the white represented the soda. The name Whiskey & Soda stems from the fact that it is dressed with only black and white hackle feathers.

To make the fly ride high on its hackle tips, the Capilano fly fishermen treated it with mucilin or cerolene. It's important to remember the Whiskey & Soda was invented for dry fly fishing and that dry-fly fishing—of any kind, never mind the steelhead fishing variety—is a recent innovation. Capilano-anglers-of-the-day, Austin Spencer, Frank Darling, Paul Moody Smith and other dedicated fly fishers found it suited the low, clear, summer water conditions found on the Capilano. One story about the effectiveness of the Whiskey & Soda and Frank Darling, one of the Capilano fly fishing masters, was told me by King White in a letter to me, not too long before White died.

King remembers meeting Frank Darling on the Upper Capilano in 1932. Darling was sitting on a log "resting" the Crown Creek Pool. He had just lost a fish, but had seen another surface in the lower part of the pool, and was getting ready to give it a try. White says this about the fly used and fish caught by Darling that long-ago day:

I invited him to fish the pool while I rested after my long walk. He did and was soon working the pool casting a big gray Whiskey and Soda dry fly. Soon I got up and walked towards the river's edge just above Mr. Darling to watch more closely. I could see his fly sitting up high on the surface riding the waves down to the lower end of the reach. Just then a large fish shouldered through a wave just below the fly, and as it disappeared Mr. Darling's rod lifted to form an arc. The fish fought hard and remained in the pool for about ten minutes. By now I was sure he would land it on the beach, but suddenly the fish tore away and on out of the pool downstream. There was a long steep rapid below, and the river finally rushed against a long cribbing on our side. If the fish stayed on and reached the cribbing it would be gone. I still had my wading staff-gaff over my shoulder, and down along the edge of the rapid I raced over large uneven boulders in my hip waders. Finally I stopped and on looking back up river I soon saw sunlight flashing on part of the flyline at least seventy-five yards below the figure of Mr. Darling. By now he had waded out to the edge of the pool all the while holding his nine foot Payne rod as high as he could. Suddenly I saw the flash of the fish's body behind a big low rock close to my shore and a little above me. In a few moments I made a lucky stroke and gaffed the seventeen pound summer henfish just behind the gill cover.

The fly was still in the corner of her jaw, leader and line intact too, all the way to Mr. Darling who was standing on the shore way above me. Late that afternoon I was chauffeured from the river right to my front gate in Mr. Darling's big black sedan.

The Whiskey & Soda was a Capilano fly and with the death of that river the fly has slipped from use. However, British Columbia's steelhead fly fishers herald its use as a steelheading first for North America.

Wintle's Western Wizard

> **HOOK:** Number 2/0 to 10, heavy wire
> **TAIL:** A clump of deer hair
> **BODY:** Black chenille
> **HACKLE:** Grizzly hackle, fairly soft
> **ORIGINATOR:** Jerry Wintle
> **INTENDED USE:** Wet fly for steelhead
> **LOCATION:** Morice River

Nearly 30 years ago, in a rented cabin at Oso on Washington State's Stilliguamish River, four steelhead fly fishermen, and a wee touch of Scotch whiskey spent the evening developing patterns for the king of Pacific Northwest game-fish, the summer-run steelhead. The anglers were Jerry Wintle of Vancouver, B.C. and three Washingtonians, Jim Lewis, Art Smith, and Bob Arnold.

I am not sure how much liquid libation was partaken that evening in the early 1960s but with minds fogged by liquor and the passage of time, it's no wonder that both Arnold and Wintle have differing versions of what transpired. However, because this is Jerry's story, I shall report his version.

Jerry Wintle doesn't like to tie flies. He would rather inveigle others to dress his creations, and that long-ago evening was no different than any other after-fishing evening with the boys. Jerry didn't tie flies. His task was to keep the liquor flowing and instruct his tiers about what and when to put something on the hook. According to Hoyle (Wintle), he did his job well: he kept their glasses filled, he instructed our main tier, Bob Arnold, and told him to put some of this and that on and, at evening's (liquor's) end, according to Jerry, "Wintle's Western Wizard" was dressed, alias the Spade Fly according to Arnold's version.

Jerry liked the creation. It was a simple pattern—easy to tie, and that suited his tying abilities. He took the pattern home to his native Canada and years later, during a trip to the Morice River, the fly was actually named Wintle's Western Wizard by the late Jack Vincent of Surrey.

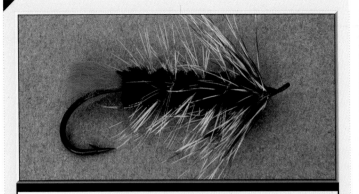

Woolly Worm

HOOK: Number 2/0 to 10 regular salmon
TAIL: A short tuft of red or orange wool
BODY: Black chenille **HACKLE:** Grizzly
ORIGINATORS: Bob Taylor and Jerry Wintle
INTENDED USE: Wet fly for steelhead

I had been into close to four score steelhead on this trip so far and, with only two days remaining, I was starting to feel guilty about the promise I had made to my seven-year-old boy.

Well before I left I was getting my flies ready and my son was tying some flies to sell. Being a helping father, I purchased a dozen of Charles' Woolly Worms, promising I would try them on my trip.

When fishing is good, one is reluctant to change successful patterns, but I had to try my boy's Woolly Worms. On the second-last day of our trip, I started the day with a Woolly Worm, and shortly connected with a good fish. Through the remainder of the day, I managed to hook 11 steelhead and one 16-inch cutthroat. Six steelhead and the cutthroat were hooked on Charles' Woolly Worms. Now I could return home and, when asked, "Dad did you catch any fish on my flies?" I would be able to answer, "Yes, Charles, they really worked well. The steelhead went crazy over them."

This has been a popular North American trout fly for years. Woolly Worms—Palmer-fly or Hackles, as they are called in England—are centuries old. In the fourth edition (1676) of Izaak Walton's *The Compleat Angler*, a section on fly fishing was written by Charles Cotton. For the month of February, Cotton recommends, ". . . a plain hackle, or palmer-fly, made with a rough black body, either of black spaniel's fur, or the whirl of an ostrich feather, and the red hackle of a capon over all, will kill, and, if the weather be right, make very good sport." (p. 353)

The steelhead version of the Woolly Worm was the idea of Jerry Wintle and Bob Taylor and its development took place on a trip down to Washington State's Stilliguamish River in the summer of 1964. Bob Taylor relates the story:

One evening after the day's fishing was done, Jerry Wintle asked me to tie up some flies for the next day. What he wanted were big flies with red tails, black chenille bodies and, when he noticed the grizzly cape in my tying kit, lots of that on. As I was tying this up on a 2/0 hook, I realized that what we were making was that popular trout fly the Woolly Worm.

We ended up with a few to try the next day and the large Woolly Worms were an instant success, but any fly in the hands of Jerry Wintle usually is. After word of the fly's success during that season got around, I noticed, where I had never seen any for sale before, that the Woolly Worm was being sold, at first in Bob's Sporting Goods in Everett and later in other stores, as a steelhead fly. The most popular sizes came to be No. 2, 4 and 6.

Wintle and Taylor have used the Woolly Worm in most steelhead rivers they have fished and, after 30-years use, it is a staple Northwest steelhead pattern.

Yonge's Firefly

HOOK: Number 2 Eagle Claw 1197G
TAIL: Hot orange hackle fibres, half as long as the body
BODY: Fluorescent orange chenille
RIB: Medium, oval, silver tinsel
THROAT: Hot orange (long and full)
WING: Medium-sized clump of white marabou fibres over medium-sized clump of white polar bear hair (Take several turns of thread around base of polar bear hair and pull forward so hair is cocked slightly from body.)
SIDES: Jungle cock **ORIGINATOR:** Bill Yonge
INTENDED USE: Wet fly for winter steelhead
LOCATION: Squamish River

This next pattern was developed by the late Bill Yonge for Squamish River steelhead in the late 1960s. Yonge provided the details in Issue Number 59, November 1980, of the Totem Flyfishers' newsletter the *Totem Topics*. He writes:

This pattern is really a composite of several other patterns and ideas. About 1969, after a couple of years flyfishing for winter steelhead, there seemed to be no single pattern that consistently outfished others.

Most flyfishers like to develop fly patterns that work well for them and can be fished with confidence. I am no different. Most of the standard bright patterns I used caught fish but no one seemed to have a pattern that was the killer. I had been fishing with patterns that were similar to the Firefly, but without the marabou and the jungle cock eyes, and they worked well enough.

One day while fishing the Squamish, I ran into Dorsey Cunliffe and he showed me the flies that had been working well for him. They were tied with a fluorescent yarn body and a marabou wing. Impressed with the action of the marabou wing, I tried his style of flies and they also caught fish. They did, however, have two drawbacks. The soft marabou wing had an annoying habit of wrapping around the body and, aesthetically, they didn't appeal to me as they weren't tied with conventional materials. I then went back to my original pattern, and substituted the polar bear hair wing for the marabou. I was still plagued with the problem of the marabou wrapping under the hook shank. Putting polar bear hair under the marabou solved this problem, and adding the jungle cock was for appearance's sake. Whether it adds to the effectiveness of the fly, I can't say. I am sure the reason the fly works well for me is that I have confidence in it and use it almost exclusively for winter fish. My backup fly is the General Practitioner.

Yonge's Firefly was a staple Squamish River pattern. Unfortunately, this river has fallen on bad times and few steelhead remain of the once strong runs that fly fishers enticed with Bill's creation.

HAIG-BROWN
QUINSAM
HACKLE

STEEL HEAD

Hook : No. 2/0 – 8

TAG : YELLOW SILK

BODY : BLACK WOOL OR SEAL'S FUR

Rib : OVAL, GOLD TINSEL

HACKLE : YELLOW FROM MID-POINT
OF BODY

COLLAR : CLARET AND SCARLET
HACKLES

PREFERS REDS AND CLARET

FOR BRIGHT DAYS

PURPLES, BLACKS AND BLUES
FOR DULL DAYS

Fly Patterns or B/C

Interior Trout

* Doe Spratley
  Black & Dk Olive G
Black O'l Lindsay
Egg 'N' I
 Brayshaw's Fancy
Carers Special
Edwards Sedge
* Lioness
Little Rivers #2   *
Nations Silver Tip
Nation Silver Tip Sedge
Travelling Sedge
Vincent Sedge
* Werner Shrimp
X Williams Green Bodied Sedge
X Williams Gray Bodied Sedge

* LIONESS

Very Good For Cutts, Rainbows May Sept.
Steelhead and Salmon.
Exceptional for Cutts

*American Coachman

Asellus

Black Caterpillar

Broughham's Clowholm Lake

Brougham's Nicomekl

Brown Caterpillar

Bullhead

Cedar Borer

Cowichan Coachman

Cumming's Fancy

Dark Caddis

Fiery Brown Caterpillar

*Fry Fly

Gammarus

General Fry

Humpback Fry

Local Silver Doctor

Mysid

Dressed by the originator

Section Three:

Coastal Trout Patterns

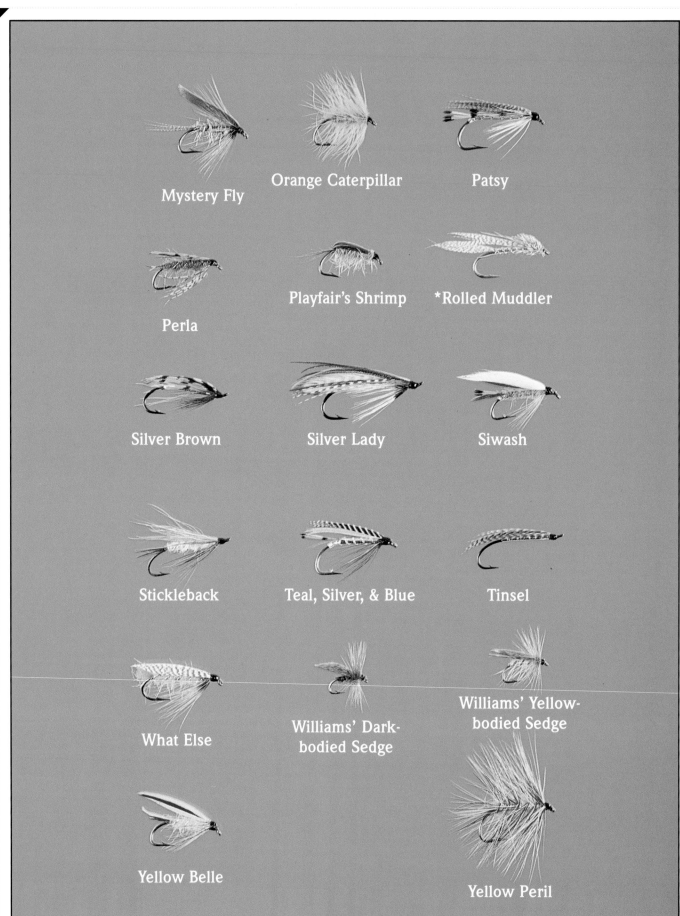

Mystery Fly

Orange Caterpillar

Patsy

Perla

Playfair's Shrimp

*Rolled Muddler

Silver Brown

Silver Lady

Siwash

Stickleback

Teal, Silver, & Blue

Tinsel

What Else

Williams' Dark-bodied Sedge

Williams' Yellow-bodied Sedge

Yellow Belle

Yellow Peril

Coastal Trout Patterns

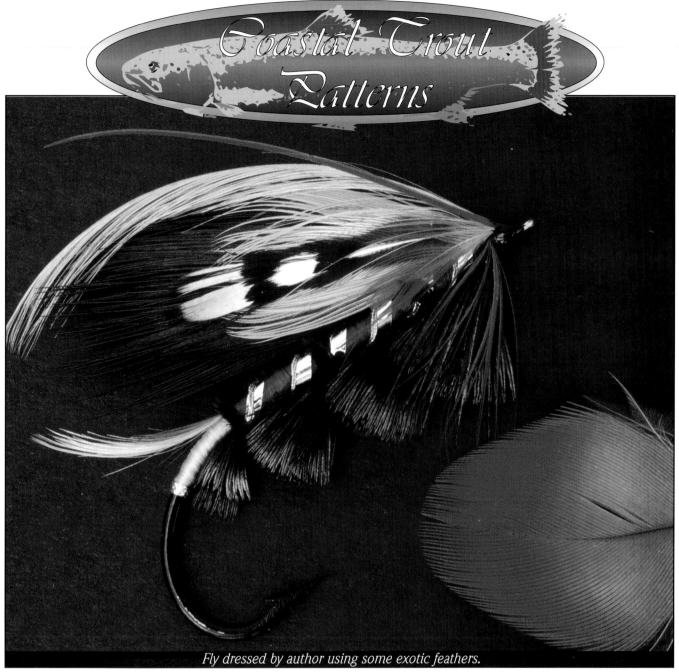

Fly dressed by author using some exotic feathers.

One of the fish colonists found in abundance during the early days of British Columbia that came readily to the fly was the cutthroat. John Keast Lord in his 1866 book, *The Naturalist in British Columbia*, tells us that this fish lives everywhere and "is to be met with in the lakes and rivers in Vancouver Island . . . and away up the western sides of the Cascades" (Vol. I, p 78). Lord designed British Columbia's first fly for the cutthroat.

Over the next 75 years, many others recorded the abundance of the cutthroat and the sport it offered. J. W. Boddam-Wetham in his 1874 book, *Western Wandering*, mentions the "capital trout and salmon fishing" around Victoria. Sir C. Phillips-Woolley in his *The Trotting of A Tenderfoot* (1884), besides writing about the good salmon fishing off Cape Mudge, tells of a canoe trip to the Salmon River where he caught salmon-trout (cutthroat) to 4 1/2 pound. The cutts, he says, "preferred bright flies."

F. G. Aflalo, in *Sunset Playgrounds* (1909), revels about the sea-run cutthroat fishing in Victoria and says that the chance of catching a sea-trout in salt water was a "chance surely all but unique in all the eleven-and-a-half million square miles of the British Empire" (p. 188). Fishing in other Vancouver Island jewels such the Cowichan and Oyster rivers and those waters of the Lower Mainland such as the Fraser

sloughs, Stave River, Harrison River and Lake and the small Nicomekl provided testimonials to the abundance of the cutthroat and the sport it provided.

The flies, however, that predominated through the last half of the 19th and the first quarter of the 20th centuries originated in Great Britain with a few out of Eastern North America. Of the 30 flies recommended for use in British Columbia by A. Bryan Williams in *Rod & Creel in British Columbia* (1919), only one, the Cowichan Coachman, owed its roots to a local river and British Columbian fly dresser. However, as increasingly more local fly fishers ventured out after the cutthroat, more and more local patterns were developed.

Anglers such as Geoffrey Playfair, Roderick Haig-Brown, Wilfred Francis Brougham, A. Bryan Williams as well as other unknown fly developers realized that the cutthroat deserved locally designed flies. These anglers laid the foundation for anglers such as Earl Anderson, Van Egan and Tom Murray and others who followed and also developed a love affair for the coastal trout and too developed flies for their preferred fish.

Fly fishing is based on tradition and all those fly fishers—Playfair, Haig-Brown, Brougham, Williams, Anderson, Egan, and Murray—provide roots for present and future generations of fly fishers to build on.

American Coachman

HOOK: Number 6
TAIL: A slender strip of red swan
BODY: Lemon-yellow wool
RIB: Flat, silver tinsel—three turns
COLLAR: Brown hen hackle
WING: White bucktail
ORIGINATOR OF NAME: Jim Kilburn
INTENDED USE: Wet fly for sea-run cutthroat trout
LOCATION: Beaches and estuaries

Asellus

HOOK: Number 8
BODY: Olive seal's fur
BACK: Peacock herl
RIB: Fine, gold wire
COLLAR: Badger hackle
ORIGINATOR: Roderick Haig-Brown
INTENDED USE: Cutthroat trout
LOCATION: Mohun Creek

In an article titled "Tidewater Trout: Part 2" which appeared in the July 1968 issue of *Western Fish & Game* magazine, Jim Kilburn mentioned that for sea-run cutthroat beach fishing his "first choice is the American Coachman streamer" and that this "streamer has a lemon-yellow wool body ribbed with silver, a white polar bear wing, a tail of either red polar-hair or red wool, and a full brown hackle."

In response to my inquiry about the fly's origin, Kilburn wrote back said that he "first came across the pattern in a sporting goods store in Courtenay in the late 1950s." "It was labeled 'California Coachman,' but because it bore no resemblance to that particular pattern," Kilburn re-named it. The California Coachman was developed by a San Franciscan, Mr. J. W. Fricke, in the first quarter of this century and was originally called the Yellow Royal Coachman and, according to A. Courtney Williams in his book, *Trout Flies* (1932), was exact in detail to the Royal Coachman "but with a yellow silk body" (p. 123). The only resemblance between Kilburn's Courtenay-found pattern, which he named the American Coachman, and the California Coachman is its white wing, yellow in the body and brown hackle.

Later in Kilburn's October 20, 1994 letter response, he says:

Meanwhile, the fly is probably destined to remain the American Coachman. Without question, the fly is the most consistent pattern for sea-run and freshwater cutthroat that I have ever used, both in its original and modified form . . . .

The modified American Coachman now preferred by Kilburn is dressed on number 8 or 10 three extra-long hook and has a red polar bear fur or hackle fibre tail, lemon-yellow body with silver rib, a wing of polar bear fur with a couple of stands of Krystal Flash, and no hackle.

Just north of Campbell River, flowing into Menzies Bay, is a little creek referred to by the locals as Trout Creek and Haig-Brown in his writings as Cedar Creek. Mohun Creek, its real name, had good populations of sea-run cutthroat trout. It was during his visits to Mohum estuary that Haig-Brown encountered many of his frustrations such as taking short, following and swirling without taking the fly that many other anglers experienced when fishing sea-runs. Convinced that the solution to his sea-run cutthroat problems rested with the development of a good asellus imitation, Haig Brown, in "Part Three, Estuary Fishing, Chapter 2., Patterns and Problems" in *Fisherman's Fall* (1964) writes:

The solution, I decided, was not in mysid, but asellus. . . . a close aquatic relative to the terrestrial sow bug or wood louse that one finds nearly everywhere in rotting wood. Like the wood louse, it crawls many-footed and clings to slivers of wood and bark; threatened, it rolls itself into a defensive ball. Unlike the wood louse, it swims underwater, quite swiftly and effectively, on its back, and this presumably is when the cutthroats find it, though they may also pick it off rocks and waterlogged wood, as they do snails and caddis larvae. Its colour is usually a dull olive, though this may vary to slate-blue or orange. (p. 119)

Haig-Brown's imitation had a bulky olive seal's fur body, fine gold wire rib, with a back tied in at the hook bend and again at the eye. And to give that-ever-so-critical-to-success life and movement, Haig-Brown wound on, just behind the hook eye a large, soft, badger hackle. With the enthusiasm that fly tiers who fly fish often have for their creations, this pattern showed great initial promise, but it too just like his Mysid "tapered off from the dramatic to the normal" (p. 119). But it proved effective enough. Moreover, he had successes with the Asellus miles away from estuaries in freshwater. Because of the freshwater successes, he wondered if sea-run cutthroat and salmon took creations like his Asellus and Mysid for what the fly tier intended or because they appeared in front of them and looked like something good to eat.

However, Haig-Brown recommends the Asellus as a good, solid, effective pattern that takes cutthroat, coho and pink salmon well enough in estuaries to be included in a sea-run trouter's fly box.

Brougham's Clowholm

HOOK: Number 6 or 8
TAG: Oval, gold tinsel
TAIL: Teal flank fibres
BODY: Burgundy wool or seal's fur
RIB: Oval, gold tinsel
THROAT: Burgundy hackle
WING: Off-white swan
ORIGINATOR: Wilfred Francis Brougham
INTENDED USE: Wet fly for cutthroat trout
LOCATION: Clowholm Lake

Brougham's Nicomekl or Cohoe

HOOK: Number 6 or 8
TAIL: A few fibres from a golden pheasant tippet feather with a small segment of red swan
BODY: Rear half of yellow floss; front half of burgundy dyed polar bear underfur or wool
RIB: Oval, gold tinsel
THROAT: Burgundy hackle
WING: Bronze mallard
ORIGINATOR: Wilfred Francis Brougham
INTENDED USE: Wet fly for cutthroat and coho
LOCATION: Nicomekl River

The dressing for this fly I gleaned from a sample shown in the frontispiece of W. F. Pochin's *Angling and Hunting in British Columbia* (1946). Wilfred Brougham, the fly's inventor, was a British barrister who immigrated from England in 1897. In order to practice law in British Columbia, Mr. Brougham had to supply affidavits on his character and it is a coincidence that one of his references was Dr. T. W. Lambert who wrote *Fishing in British Columbia* (1907). Dr. Lambert's book is a jewel and contains a significant amount of Thompson River and other British Columbia fly fishing information. Dr. Lambert in his 1897 affidavit says that he has been acquainted with Mr. Brougham for the past twelve years and knows "him to be of good moral character & integrity."

Brougham lived and worked at his profession in British Columbia for almost four decades. An ardent fly fisher, he pursued British Columbia's trout of lake and stream until his death in January 1938. Frequently, he fished Harrison Lake with George Reifel and enjoyed the excellent fishing that the Harrison and other places offered. For example, on March 26 and 27, 1927, George Reifel says that they "caught 85 fish" many at the mouth of Silver Creek" on a small fly, no. 12." In those by gone days, the rivers and lakes of the province offered big catches to the fly fisher who ventured forth, often to difficult-to-get-to places. This fly's namesake is one such place.

Located north of Vancouver, the Clowholm River runs into the head of Salmon Arm, a branch of Sechelt Inlet. About the river and the best fishing opportunities, A. Bryan Williams in *Rod & Creel in British Columbia* (1919) says that "this stream has the advantage of always being clear" and that "the best months for fly fishing are July and August" (p. 99).

In Williams' later fishing book, *Fish & Game in British Columbia* (1935), he says that "a few good Cut-throats can often be taken in salt water at low tide" but that "the best fishing is at the end of the second lake where the stream comes in" (p. 83).

Brougham's Clowholm was dressed and sold locally by Harkley & Haywood of Vancouver; however, it is another feather-winged pattern that in the last 30 or more years has lost favour with fly fishers.

Flowing into Mud Bay just north of the Canada-USA border in Surrey can be found this fly's namesake, the Nicomekl River. Once a prolific coho and cutthroat producer, the Nicomekl drew anglers from all over the Lower Mainland to her banks. Wilfred Francis Brougham, the inventor of the Nicomekl fly, fished the "Nic," as it was often affectionately referred to, in the 1920s and '30s and possibly earlier.

This pattern appears to have been referred to by two names, Brougham's Nicomekl or Cohoe. The frontispiece in Pochin's 1946 book is the earliest record of Brougham's patterns and he showed the Nicomekl and Clowholm and no Cohoe. Brougham's Nicomekl or Cohoe, however, was a standard for many years. Ray Bergman in his 1932 book, *Just Fishing*, included Brougham's pattern in his list of wet flies "which have proved indispensable to me." In the *** footnote, Bergman says that Brougham's Cohoe is:

A fly very effective in British Columbia. Mr. Ernest W. Summers of Vancouver sent me one to try out and it was so good that I felt compelled to add it to my list of northern patterns. (p. 74)

In 1950, when J. Edson Leonard's book, *Flies*, was published, the Nicomekl was included as one of the 2,200 dressings. Later, in 1958, when Roy Patrick of Patrick's Fly Shop in Seattle, Washington put out his third edition of *Pacific Northwest Fly Patterns*, after the dressing for Nicomekl, he says that it is "a very good Canadian coastal fly for Steelhead and Sea-run Cutthroat."

The Umpqua sports a similar colour combination to the Nicomekl and is a popular coho pattern in British Columbia. Brougham's Nicomekl predates the Umpqua's use in British Columbia by years and traditionalists should supplant the USA-developed Umpqua with this pattern. The Nicomekl's pleasing colour combination and style is one that should be relied on when cutthroat or coho conditions demand a dark pattern.

Bullhead

HOOK: Number 4 or 6 low-water salmon
TAIL: A few fibres of light mallard flank feather
BODY: Flat, silver tinsel
HACKLE: Dark red, claret, blue or badger
WING: Strips of light mallard flank enclosing four bronze peacock herls and sometimes a few strands of polar bear fur
ORIGINATOR: Roderick Haig-Brown
INTENDED USE: Wet fly for cutthroat trout
LOCATION: Campbell River

Cedar Borer

HOOK: Number 6 or 8
BODY: Mixed blue and emerald green seal fur
RIB: Fine, oval gold tinsel and bronze peacock herl
COLLAR: Light blue hackle
WING: Peacock sword
ORIGINATOR: Roderick Haig-Brown
INTENDED USE: Wet fly for cutthroat and rainbow trout
LOCATION: Campbell River

The bullhead (sculpin), considered by many to be an ugly little fish, frequents most of British Columbia's lakes and streams. In Volume 1 of *A Naturalist in British Columbia* (1866), John Keast Lord says that the bullhead's name is ". . . nearly as ugly as the owner . . . With such a name, we are the less disappointed to find the entire family of our friends ill-favoured, prickly, hard-skinned, and as uncomfortable to handle as to look at . . ." (p. 130).

Every boy who has ever dunked a worm into one of our streams knows about this "little pest." In *The Western Angler* (1939), when discussing the lake-fishing opportunities of Vancouver Island, Haig-Brown states there have been some very large fish taken from lakes such as Nimpkish, Upper and Lower Campbell, Buttle, Sproat, Great Central and Cowichan. Haig-Brown witnessed a 11 1/2-pound, troll-caught cutthroat from the Nimpkish, and he personally has taken cutthroat as large as 5 1/2 pounds on the fly from that system. Why fish grew that big in lakes of coastal watersheds was pondered by Haig-Brown and he mused about their distinctness, individuality, and feeding habits:

An important question is whether these large fish are of a distinct type or are simply individuals that have adapted themselves early in life to predatory feeding. I think there can be little doubt that they are all primarily predators or that sculpins are their chief diet; one rarely catches a fish over 1 1/4 pounds in any of the lakes without finding one or more sculpins. (Vol. I, p. 187)

With the listing of the bullhead pattern in *The Western Angler*, Haig-Brown became the first British Columbian fly tier to attempt to imitate (somewhat impressionistically) the fish that Lord recorded 75 years earlier; and because he witnessed the bullhead enough times during the cleaning of many fish, one that demanded an imitation.

British Columbia's coastal streams are not prolific bearers of trout food and that is one of the reasons, wherever possible, trout migrated and became big in the bountiful sea. However, there are some rivers such as Haig-Brown's home river, the Campbell, and the Cowichan where there is a mix of anadromous and resident trout. Sea-run cutthroat and resident rainbows in the Campbell and Cowichan are not that particular and will take advantage of whatever food comes their way, even food of a terrestrial sort.

The coastal forests of British Columbia abound in insect life and every now and then some accidentally find their way into the water. Haig-Brown knew this and knew that the large terrestrial beetle was often found in the stomachs of fish and that fly fishers could profit by an imitation.

About the Cedar Borer, in his *The Western Angler* notebook, after listing the fly's ingredients he admitted his fly "maybe not a good imitation but fish take it well enough." However, Haig-Brown realized that many flies work some of the time and that no fly works all the time. Having a broad-based experience fishing from youth in England, spending some time fishing in Washington State when he first came to North America, and with close to ten years fishing in British Columbia, he knew what types of flies catch fish. In the same notebook, about some of his patterns such as the Brown and Black caterpillars and the Cedar Borer, he says:

none of these flies are "sure killers" Is there such a thing? But in the right hands they catch all the fish one needs. Plenty of others just as good, but I haven't found any much better.

In a note following his listing of the Cedar Borer ingredients in *The Western Angler* (1939), Haig-Brown says that "this is a freak-looking fly" but trout in coastal streams take this beetle whenever they happen to appear in the water and that "it is rather comforting to have even the roughest imitation" (Vol. II, p. 175). As a closing note, he says that his "dressing takes fish well under these conditions."

Cowichan Coachman

HOOK: Number 8 & 10 **BODY:** Claret floss
RIB: Oval, gold tinsel **THROAT:** Claret hackle
WING: White swan **ORIGINATOR:** Unknown
INTENDED USE: Wet fly for cutthroat and rainbow trout
LOCATION: Cowichan River

Jewel, precious gem, and magnificent river are some of the words that have been used to describe this fly's namesake, the Cowichan. Unlike most coastal streams that contain small amounts of insect life, the Cowichan River is rich. The geological feature that produces this richness was recorded in a 22 March 1860 report from the Colonial Secretary's office. The author of that report noted that "the soils throughout the Cowichan Valley is Calcareous, seemingly formed by the decomposition of Limestone rock" (p. 2). Water seeping through soils of this nature are rich in calcium and the amount of calcium dissolved in water affects the insect-bearing capacity of rivers, within limits. With prolific insect life, fish thrive and it was this thriving fish population that drew sportsmen from all over the world to fish the Cowichan's cutthroats, rainbows and, later, the introduced brown. To accommodate the visiting anglers, the Cowichan's first fishing lodge was constructed in 1880.

About the river and its prospect for fishing, A. Bryan Williams in *Rod & Creel in British Columbia* (1919) writes:

> Of all the magnificent rivers of this province none have attained greater fame, and justly so, than the Cowichan. It has been fished by white men of all degree, including Royalty. It has been fished with the fly . . . for the past thirty years, and yet to-day in spite of all, it is still a splendid river for a good fisherman. (p. 67)

Williams recommended the Cowichan Coachman in sizes 8, 9, and 10 as one of the best flies for Cowichan rainbows and for other Vancouver Island streams.

However, Williams gives no indication about the origins of the Cowichan Coachman. There is no doubt in my mind that the Cowichan Coachman owes its pedigree to the Royal Coachman but when the Cowichan Coachman was first dressed and by whom is vague. John Haily, a New York fly tier, introduced the Royal Coachman to eastern streams in 1878. The Royal Coachman is one of the patterns recommended by Horace Annesley Vachell in *Life and Sport on the Pacific Slope* (1900) for the Cowichan River and, with that recommendation, we know that the Royal Coachman's use had spread to the west coast and into British Columbia before the turn of the century. Whether the Cowichan Coachman was invented before or after the turn of the century, I have not been able to determine.

With the passage of time and no good records, sources I explored indicate three different patterns; however, the dressing given here is for the earliest source and gleaned from the colour plate in A. Bryan Williams' 1919 book *Rod & Creel in British Columbia*.

Negley Farson in his 1942 book *Going Fishing* says that the Cowichan Coachman was "invented and tied by an English lady down on the coast" (p. 58). Farson describes, however, a plum-bodied, plum and white married-winged fly similar in style to the Yellow Belle, described elsewhere in this book.

In the fall of 1994 I contacted Charlie Stroulger, long-time guide and Cowichan River fisherman, and he provided the third version of this fly. Stroulger claims that the fly was invented in the late 1920s by a Mr. Vidal and dressed by a Mrs. Leather, both of Cowichan Lake, however, the dressing is not close to either of the first two.

With few written references to go by during the first century of fishing in British Columbia and commercial tiers guarding their secrets, word of mouth was the principle means of passing on fly dressings. With the passage of time it's understandable that different versions of the Cowichan Coachman evolved. Be that as it may, the Cowichan Coachman as deduced from Williams' sample is Vancouver Island's first locally designed fly pattern.

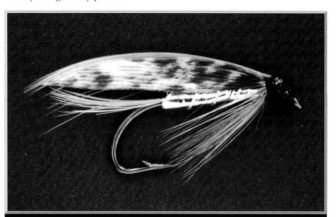

Cumming's Fancy

HOOK: Number 6 or 8
TAIL: A golden pheasant crest feather
BODY: Flat, silver tinsel
RIB: Fine oval, silver tinsel
THROAT: Brown hackle
WING: Lightly mottled turkey with golden pheasant
crest feather overall
ORIGINATOR: Walter Burgess
INTENDED USE: Wet fly for cutthroat trout
LOCATION: Harrison River

W.F. Pochin in *Angling and Hunting in British Columbia* (1946) wrote about one of British Columbia's less celebrated fish, the cutthroat, and says:

> The Harrison Cutthroat, while not one of the largest of game fishes, is one of the sportiest. Three pounders have been taken, but he rarely obtains that weight. However, a good day's catch will include fish up to and over two pounds. Best of all he rises freely to flies and on the table is unsurpassed. . . .
>
> The Harrison Cutthroat is ever in search of salmon fry, upon which he feeds, and the best flies are silver bodied. Cumming's Fancy has always been a favourite . . . . (pp. 41-42)

This British sea-trout pattern, sold by the firm of Cumming's & Co., was introduced in the late 1920s to British Columbia's Harrison River cutthroat by the firm's Vancouver representative Walter Burgess. According to Martin Tolley in his article on the Cumming's Fancy in the April, 1968 issue of *Northwest Sportsman* magazine:

After the Harrison successes Burgess scored again when he used the fly in salt water for the first time. That event took place at the mouth of the Capilano and thereafter his Fancy was firmly established in local favour.

That the fly remained in use till this day is a testimonial to its effectiveness, but keeping a fly's use alive is often the result of certain individual fly fishermen and, in the Fancy's case, John Massey deserves some of the credit. About Massey's use, Tolley's says:

Still a winner for use off the beaches, its most assiduous fan is definitely John Massely [Massey]. John hooked fish after fish with the Cummings one day, and two other anglers closed in for a share of the fun. Though fishing shoulder to shoulder the others never had a touch and John kept right on catching cutthroat, calmly indifferent to the competition. It has been Massey's Fancy ever since.

Lee Richardson was another Fancy fancier and in his book, *Lee Richardson's B.C.* (1978), says:

We found the trout schooled up in a sheltered cove near Reifel's cabin and immediately began taking fish. It was the first time I had ever used the Cumming's Fancy, though later I was to use nothing else. The trout came up out of deep water, often three or four at a time . . . and the Indian was hard pressed to net one before another was bought alongside. (p. 23)

Although the Cumming's Fancy originated in Great Britain, in examining the many British Angling books in my collection, I have not found any reference to a fly by this name or that matches its description. With its adoption by British Columbian cutthroat fishers and its near three-quarter-century use here, the fly has earned a place in British Columbia's fly fisher's boxes and is rooted here to stay.

Dark Caddis

HOOK: Number 6 **TAIL:** Dark mallard wing quill sections
BODY: Very dark green seal's fur **RIB:** Oval, gold tinsel
THROAT: Furnace or dark olive hackle
WING: Dark mallard wing quill sections
ORIGINATOR: Roderick Haig-Brown
INTENDED USE: Wet fly for cutthroat trout
LOCATION: Campbell River

Caddisflies are one of the world's most abundant aquatic insects. In the western USA and British Columbia, there are over 300 species and they outnumber western mayflies and stoneflies combined. Every fisherman has encountered some of these case-builders which, incidentally, make their homes from a variety of materials—stones, twigs, or evergreen needles. For many species of caddisflies, these homes are "mobile"—that is, they are dragged around by the insects which make them; and, when they are dragged across the mud of still or slow-moving water, they leave tell-tale trails behind them. Trout will eat homes and all. But not all caddis build homes and, anyway, it is the pupa and free-living forms that are more sought after by Mr. Trout.

Some popular caddis—called sedges in Britain—imitations were developed well before Haig-Brown wrote *The Western Angler* (1939), by British immigrants, Bryan Williams and Tom Brayshaw. Williams' Dark-Bodied, Grey-Bodied, Green-Bodied, and Yellow-Bodied sedges and Brayshaw's Travelling and Olive sedges are detailed elsewhere in this book. All are dry flies. A. Bryan Williams' sedges were the first dry flies developed for British Columbia's lakes and streams, and Haig-Brown rates Williams' Grey-Bodied Sedge as "the deadliest dry fly, and the deadliest fly of any sort, wet or dry, in the mountain streams . . ." (Vol. I, p. 194).

Because the coastal streams of his adopted land offered rare opportunities for dry-fly fishing, Haig-Brown, schooled in Britain during his youth in the wet-fly technique, realized the potential of a good wet-fly caddis imitation and devised his Dark Caddis.

About his Dark Caddis, he says his pattern is quite similar to the famous British trout fly, Greenwell's Glory, and is "a good summer fly in many cutthroat streams" (Vol. II, p. 174).

Fry Fly

HOOK: Number 6 or 8 low-water **THREAD:** Grey
TAIL: A golden pheasant crest feather
BODY: Flat, silver tinsel
RIB: Fine, oval, silver tinsel if the less durable mylar is substituted for tinsel
THROAT: Pale blue dun or grizzly
WING: Narrow, married strips of green and blue goose veiled with light mallard flank, and with slender strips of dark mallard or teal overall
ORIGINATOR: Van Egan
INTENDED USE: Wet fly for cutthroat trout
LOCATION: Campbell River

Van Egan's long-time friend, Roderick Haig-Brown, admired the cutthroat trout and says that, "The cutthroat is at his best in a river that is open to the sea. . . . Such a fish will come nobly to wet fly or dry. . . and when you set the hook he will run as boldly as any fish of his size" (*A River Never Sleeps*, pp. 128-129). Egan, a traditional fly tier, combined tinsel, swan and the natural barred marking of light and dark mallard into this eye-catching and fish-pleasing pattern to catch those fish that are at their best in rivers open to the sea.

Haig-Brown wrote many times about the bold-fighting cutthroat of Vancouver Island streams and, in particular, those of his home river, the Campbell. After Egan moved to Campbell River in 1955, he too became enamored with the cutthroat and to take advantage of the spring's salmon-fry migrations, devised his Fry Fly.

Because of the heavy metal pollution in the 1970s and the elimination of virtually all living things in the Campbell proper, Van has bittersweet memories of those cutthroating years on the Campbell with Ted Pengelley and the Fry Fly. When the tide was right and the salmon fry were hatching in the spring, Van and Ted would get up in the early hours of the morning, head down and fish the water just below the highway bridge. To keep this fishing from being over exploited, they would leave the river before the town's people crowded the bridge and highway on their way to work in the morning. Sweet it was to catch those beautiful fish and bitter it was to see them destroyed by preventable industrial pollution.

Van was and still is an admirer and user of Haig-Brown patterns, but when he compared his catches using Haig-Brown's Silver Brown with those of his Fry Fly, he found the Fry Fly a far more consistent cutthroat catcher.

Gammarus

HOOK: Number 6 to 14
TAIL: A golden pheasant crest feather
BODY: Olive seal's fur **RIB:** Oval, gold tinsel
HACKLE: Brown **THROAT:** Blue jay
WING: Hen pheasant
ORIGINATOR: Roderick Haig-Brown
INTENDED USE: Wet fly for cutthroat and rainbow trout
LOCATION: Vancouver Island lakes

Developed by Roderick Haig-Brown in the 1930s for Vancouver Island migratory and non-migratory trout, Haig-Brown in volume one of *The Western Angler* says the Gammarus "is a good shrimp imitation and useful for any trout in any water" (p. 174).

Haig-Brown was one of the first British Columbian anglers to realize the value of having a freshwater scud imitation in his fly box. Even the legendary Bill Nation, who based his operation out of Echo Lodge located on Paul Lake, didn't specifically target the freshwater scud and develop a pattern for this insect that proliferated in Paul Lake and, according to autopsies performed on Paul Lake trout, represented over 55 percent of the trouts' food. Haig-Brown's pattern was one of the first.

In his chapter called "Some Fauna of Interior Lakes" about the fresh-water shrimps and their imitations, Haig-Brown says:

The common fresh-water "shrimps," abundant at all depths in Paul Lake and an extremely important fish food, particularly during the winter. . . . Colour varies from pale yellow to steel blue. Size up to 1 inch.

I do not think sufficient attention has been paid to the imitation of fresh-water shrimps. (Vol. I, p. 109)

In place of that really good imitation, Haig-Brown suggested his Gammarus fly, but says that better imitations could be produced. On page 178 of that same volume, he says that migratory cutthroat trout:

in tidal water are usually feeding either on amphipods or on fry, and on the good days an imitation of one or other will nearly always do well. It is not at all easy to find good shrimp imitations . . . generally, I prefer the fly I have called Gammarus . . . .

On page 193 when discussing tackle and flies for non-migratory cutthroat and rainbows, he says that the Gammarus is a worthwhile pattern and "can be fished on sizes down to 13 or 14 with effect."

Haig-Brown claims that the Gammarus is just a simplification of the Golden Olive salmon fly and that it is not altogether different from the English trout fly, the Invicta. An examination by the author of both these patterns' dressings, however, reveals the Gammarus to be a combination of both with some Haig-Brown thrown in. Haig-Brown is more than justified in claiming it as his own creation.

General Fry Imitation

HOOK: Number 4 or 6 low-water salmon
TAIL: Small, pale, red or orange feather
BODY: Flat, silver tinsel
THROAT: A small red hackle
WING: Mixed, not layered, strands of dyed yellow, orange, blue, green and some natural polar bear fur
ORIGINATOR: Roderick Haig-Brown
INTENDED USE: Wet fly for cutthroat trout
LOCATION: Campbell River

Just like in ancient times where Jason and the Argonauts searched for the golden fleece, generations of fly fishers in all areas of the world have quested for the ultimate fly. A search in vain probably, but as successes with variations on a theme mount, thoughts about the ultimate fly are conceived and flies dressed. Haig-Brown had many successes in salmon fry pattern design during his first 20 years in British Columbia. The Silver Brown, an imitation of the cutthroat or coho; the Silver Lady, an imitation of the spring or chum salmon; the Humpback, an imitation of the pink salmon; and two other baitfish patterns, the Bullhead and Stickleback, are examples of those successes.

For his all-purpose fry imitation Haig-Brown recommends a pale red or orange tail which both the Silver Lady and Silver Brown sport. All of his fry and baitfish patterns, except the stickleback, had silver bodies, his preference for the all-purpose fry fly. A red hackle for the throat because it added brightness and red seemed to attract fish. A hairwing rather than the conventional feather-strip wing, because hairwings had more movement; polar bear rather than bucktail because it was more translucent and flexible; and a variety of colours: orange, yellow, blue, green and white perhaps to cover the many different light conditions encountered in a day's fishing.

Haig-Brown by his own admission was not a very enthusiastic fly tier and preferred simplicity in fly design. In a January 28, 1951 letter to Tom Kerl of the Washington Fly Fishing Club, about some sample fry and baitfish patterns he sent the club, Haig-Brown says that "one merit these flies have is they are all easy to tie, which is probably why I use them so much."

In *Fisherman's Spring* (1951), he mentions that if he could vary the quantity of material in the wing and the size of hook upon which the fly is dressed, he wouldn't mind being limited to a single fry imitation. The General Fry Imitation was his choice.

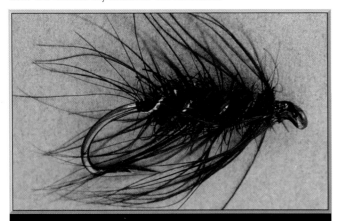

The Haig-Brown Caterpillars

Black

HOOK: Number 6 or 8 **BODY:** Black seal's fur
RIB: Fine, oval gold with **HACKLE:** Black

Brown

HOOK: Number 4 or 6 **BODY:** Olive seal's fur
RIB: Oval, silver tinsel **HACKLE:** Natural red-brown,
long and soft

Orange

HOOK: Number 6 or 8 **BODY:** Orange seal's fur
HACKLE: Orange

Fiery Brown

HOOK: Number 6 or 8 **BODY:** Fiery brown seal's fur
HACKLE: Fiery Brown

ORIGINATOR: Roderick Haig-Brown
INTENDED USE: Wet fly for cutthroat and rainbow trout
LOCATION: Campbell River

During the writing of The Western Angler, Haig-Brown jotted down his thoughts of things that he wanted to include in his book. In his notes on stream cutthroat patterns, he gave some rules for tying:

1. Impression rather than imitation.
2. Seal's fur body or silver body.
3. Palmerwise hackle lightly veiling all except sil[ver] body.
4. Imitation: amusement rather than anything else.

Simple flies such as brown & black caterpillar as good as any. Can be tied simply or with complication—Simple just as good. "Secrets" all nonsense.

In a margin note he says that his Black Caterpillar "on No. 6-8 hook, with ragged black or metallic green feather wound over [is] an A 1 ant imitation." During his research he learned that places like Harkley & Haywood in Vancouver considered the make-up of many local fly patterns to be trade secrets and wouldn't give him pattern listings. He pondered if he should release the secret ingredients for his Black Caterpillar. However, in his cutthroat notes he put an asterisk beside his Black Caterpillar in two different locations and noted at the bottom on his notebook page "to hell with 'secrets'" and that the asterisk referred to "secret materials."

Although he listed hook sizes of 4 to 8 in *The Western Angler* (1939) for his Black and Brown caterpillars, he says that they are "both good, No's 2/0—10" and that the Brown Caterpillar was "also good [for] summer steelhead." I can attest that Thompson River rainbows and whitefish also find the Brown Caterpillar appealing. Vancouver Island rainbows also like the Black Caterpillar.

In 1994, Van Egan and I made a spring trip up into Haig-Brown country and fished the Nimpkish River system. We encountered poor fishing conditions and fish were hard to find. I decided that I would search the water with the only Black Caterpillar I had in my fly box. Five out the ten rainbows I managed to find, with 16 inches the largest, came to the Black Caterpillar. And of course when you have a single sample of a fly that is working well something usually happens to it and eventually the body hackle was severed by a fish's teeth.

Why the Black Caterpillar was so effective that day, I can't answer; although, under trying fishing conditions, I often put on a black fly and get results. However, I believe like Haig-Brown that "there are no 'sure-killer' flies" and that "there are plenty of adequate flies & that's all a decent fisherman needs."

Haig-Brown, after he noted the dressings for the Black and Brown caterpillars, recommended "other caterpillars [of] different seal's fur [with] matching hackles" and says that "Orange good, Fiery brown good, etc. etc."

All palmer-type fly patterns are simple in nature and are often good producers. Tie some, you'll like them.

Humpback Fry

HOOK: Number 8 low-water salmon
TAIL: Yellow hackle fibres or other suitable yellow material
such as a golden pheasant crest feather
BODY: Flat, silver tinsel **THROAT:** Yellow hackle
WING: Mixed, dyed green and blue polar bear with a few
strands of peacock sword feather overall
ORIGINATOR: Roderick Haig-Brown
INTENDED USE: Wet fly for cutthroat trout
LOCATION: Campbell River

Pink, humpback or hun-num, the ancient Fraser River native Indian name for the pink salmon, are common names for Oncorhynchus gorbuscha, the smallest of the Pacific salmons. Like all anadromous salmonids, the pink matures in the sea and most pinks return after two years of sea-feeding to spawn. They often return in the tens of thousands to smaller streams and in the millions to some our larger streams such as the Skeena, Fraser and Harrison rivers. They are late summer and fall spawners with the eggs incubating over winter and hatching in the spring. The fry immediately start their seaward migration and are the feast of spring when, in the millions, they emerge from the gravel into the jaws of opportunistic trout.

Also waiting for the spring hatch are opportunistic fly fishers who for generations have relied on silver-bodied patterns such as Mallard & Silver, Tinsel, Local Silver Doctor, and Teal, Silver & Blue. However, Haig-Brown thought that the fly dresser should strive to reproduce the characteristic silver-blue-green of the humpback fry. His Humpback fly was his attempt and about this pattern, in *Fisherman's Spring* (1951), he asserts that it "is an effective fly when the humpback fry are going down in good numbers" and that "it has also caught fish, including steelhead and coho salmon, . . . much later in the season" (p. 33).

With those successes, the Humpback Fry is a must for the spring trouter.

I am sure costly for the fishermen to purchase. When local tiers started to dress the standard of the day salmon patterns and in this case the Silver Doctor, either because of lack of materials, fly-tying skill or just plain expediency, they reduced the number of materials from 24 to 8.

The pattern that I was fortunate enough to examine and from which I derived the dressing was loaned to me by Mr. George Reifel of Vancouver and taken from a collection that his grandfather acquired when he fished local streams in the 1920s and '30s. It was dressed on a number 9 hook.

Bryan Williams in his 1935 book, *Fish and Game in British Columbia*, says that when he mentions the Silver Doctor in the text that "the fly here referred to is the local one and not the regular salmon fly." He also mentions that "it is a very useful fly, particularly on coastal waters in the spring" (p. 46).

In 1972, the now late Jack Vincent included the Local Silver Doctor in a set of flies he dressed for Jim Railton's *B.C.'s Fresh Water Fishing Guide*. The pattern has changed little when I compare Vincent's with the circa 1930 sample owned by George Reifel. Reifel's had a teal overwing with tippet tail; Vincent's overwing was light mallard with a golden pheasant crest feather tail.

For those traditionalists that prefer to catch fish on classy flies that work, although much simpler than its progeny, the Local Silver Doctor still fits the bill.

Local Silver Doctor

HOOK: Number 6 to 10 **TIP:** Fine oval, silver tinsel
TAIL: A few fibres from a golden pheasant tippet feather
BUTT: Polar bear underfur or seal's fur dyed red
BODY: Flat, silver tinsel **RIB:** Fine oval, silver tinsel
THROAT: Silver Doctor blue hackle
WING: Underwing of red swan with mallard or
teal breast over
ORIGINATOR: Unknown
INTENDED USE: Wet fly for cutthroat trout
LOCATION: Lower mainland

Mysid

HOOK: Number 10 to 14 **TAG:** Orange tying silk
TAIL: Five strands from a golden pheasant
neck tippet feather
BODY: Flat, silver tinsel **THROAT:** Natural blue hackle
WING: Barred wood duck flank feather
ORIGINATOR: Roderick Haig-Brown
INTENDED USE: Wet fly for sea-run cutthroat
LOCATION: Vancouver Island estuaries

When describing the sport available on Vancouver Island, Horace Annesley Vachell in his book, *Life and Sport on the Pacific Slope* (1900), recommends many flies for the "turbulent northern rivers" of the Pacific Coast. Vachell's list of patterns is one of the first I have managed to locate where actual names are given. The Silver Doctor is high on his list.

A. Bryan Williams in *Rod & Creel in British Columbia* (1919) also recommends the Silver Doctor and says it is "to be tied on No. 6 and 8 hook" and that it "is a very killing fly, especially with a bit of colour in the water, but should be fished extra deep" (p. 42). In the frontispiece of Williams' book he shows a fully dressed number 6 Silver Doctor. Consisting of compound tails, body, throat, and multiple wings and with about 24 different materials, tinsels, and feathers, the Silver Doctor is a very complicated and time consuming pattern to dress. In the first part of this century most British Columbian-used flies were British-made and

Along the edges of the Cedar Creek [Mohun Creek] estuary there are great numbers of small, transparent mysid shrimps throughout the summer months. Most of them are about half an inch long or less, slightly humped and with regular black speckling along the back. The little cutthroats often came into the shallows at the edge of the flooding tide where these tiny shrimps were massed in thousands . . . . (Fisherman's Fall, p. 118)

Seeing these as easy pickings for the sea-runs, Haig-Brown concluded he must have an imitation of this tiny crustacean for his estuary fishing and set to work. About his attempt at a Mysid imitation and its successes, he writes:

The first attempt I made at imitating these little creatures was the most successful, and since the fly has proved effective for other

types of fish under quite varying conditions, it seems worth giving the dressing . . . . The body was rather short for the hook size, and I hoped that its silver, with the lightly barred wing feathers, might give some illusion of transparency. On its first trial this fly securely hooked three of the small fish in quick succession, and I felt that the problem was solved; within an hour it had also taken a sixteen-inch coho jack and a cutthroat of about the same size and I was inclined to believe I had solved all estuary problems for all time. I named the fly the Mysid and tied some more like it. . . . (p. 118)

The Mysid was not the sure-fire, catch-all imitation he had hoped for. But knowing that the mysid shrimp abounds in great numbers and is a readily available trout food, Haig-Brown pondered why they are not under constant attack. "They seem totally defenseless and should be a most attractive type of feed," he writes on page 120. However, he learned when he captured some for his aquarium that the small "coho were enthusiastic, but totally ineffective" (p.121) in catching the tiny shrimp. And he thought that that may have been the reason the estuary trout displayed uncertain response to his Mysid imitation.

Hence, he decided that he had not found the ultimate estuary pattern. The Mysid, however, proved to be an effective and a worthy fly for sea-run cutthroat and it took coho and pink as well. What more can a fisherman expect?

The Mystery Fly
(Puntledge River)

HOOK: Number 6 to 10
TAIL: Mallard flank or bronze shoulder
BODY: South American kid fur **RIB:** Fine, oval, gold tinsel
HACKLE: Barred rock or brown rooster feather
WING: Strips from a wild goose secondary flight feather
ORIGINATOR: Jack Hames
INTENDED USE: Wet fly for cutthroat trout
LOCATION: Puntledge River

Another Vancouver Island river system which was home to huge Chinooks, coho, summer- and winter-run steelhead and cutthroat trout and would have been the envy of most North American communities had it not been destroyed by development and habitat destruction, is the Courtenay system, near Comox.

The Puntledge River, the Courtenay's main tributary, ·was a favoured haunt of the Hames family who have lived in the Comox Valley since 1914. Born in 1913, Jack Hames fished the Puntledge and other local rivers from boyhood. For 20 years, starting in 1958, he wrote newspaper articles about life, the fauna, hunting and fishing in his community. In 1990, Jack's wife, Gertrude, reprinted some of his articles in *Field Notes: An Environmental History*, and among the many fishing stories is one called "The Mystery Fly."

In the early 1930s when fly-less and with little or no money to spend on flies, Hames was searching through his father's flybook and found what he would describe later as the mystery fly. Jack intended to only borrow his father's fly and return it later that day but it worked so well he kept it and eventually lost it when he snapped it off his gut leader. He searched in vain but couldn't find a replacement. With the dressing implanted in his brain, years elapsed before he learned how to fix fur, feather and tinsel to a hook. However, skills obtained, he was determined to replace the mystery fly and searched for the materials. The wild goose secondary flight feathers used for the wing, the drake mallard flank or bronze shoulder for the tail, and the barred rock or brown rooster feather for the hackle posed no difficulty as they were readily available. The grey material for the body, however, proved more challenging. But he did find some un-named grey fur amongst his mother-in-laws' dressmaking materials. With all the materials in his possession, his mystery fly was reborn and it produced as well as the original lost many years ago.

However, as his supply of the un-named grey fur that he raided from his mother-in-law's sewing kit became depleted, he searched in vain for this magical silver-tipped fur that held its firmness and lively glisten when wet. After discussing this with fly fisher, Bob Taylor, of Vancouver, Taylor offered to take the remnants of Hames' small patch to a furrier for identification. Reluctantly, Hames let Taylor take the fur away, and was ecstatic when Taylor returned with a large swatch of the magical South American kid.

With his supply worries abated, Hames tied up a good stock in different sizes and because it provided him with a visual link to the river he fished and loved for so many years named the fly, Puntledge River.

Patsy

HOOK: Number 6 to 10 **TAG:** Silver tinsel
TAIL: A few strands from a golden pheasant tippet feather
BODY: Green floss **RIB:** Flat, silver tinsel
THROAT: Badger hackle
WING: A few fibres from a golden pheasant tippet feather enclosed by bronze mallard
ORIGINATOR: Unknown
INTENDED USE: Wet fly for cutthroat trout
LOCATION: Lower mainland

This 1930s vintage cutthroat pattern incorporates the black-barred and black-tipped orange neck feather—tippet—of the colourful golden pheasant that was ever so popular in many of the British sea-trout patterns such as the Teal & Green, Teal & Red, Teal & Silver which so many British Columbian fishermen relied upon in the early days of cutthroat fishing.

I am confident in saying that the Patsy owes its pedigree to the British Teal & Green trout fly, but with bronze mallard replacing the teal wing. However, instead of just using tippet for the tail the designer incorporated it also into the winging. Rumour or superstition, I am not sure what it was, but tippet in the pioneer fly fishers' days was thought to be an item that British Columbia's coastal and interior trout found appealing. Tippet used in patterns of early anglers such as Bill Nation, Tom Brayshaw, Rod Haig-Brown and others attest to the popularity of that feather. Perhaps the fly's originator thought, why not make the fly doubly appealing to the trout and incorporate it in the winging also.

The Patsy was included in the list of standard coast patterns supplied by Harkley & Haywood to Roderick Haig-Brown in 1939 and was also listed in *The Western Angler*. In my extensive research I have not found another reference to this pattern, but green-bodied coho and cutthroat patterns with similar type wings are still in use today. Perhaps the progeny of the Patsy?

Perla

HOOK: Number 8
TAIL: A section from a golden pheasant tail feather
BODY: Olive, primrose yellow, or bleached green to match local fauna
RIB: Oval, gold tinsel
THROAT: Badger hackle or brown partridge
WING: A section of golden pheasant tail feather, set to lie flat over body
ORIGINATOR: Roderick Haig-Brown
INTENDED USE: Wet fly for cutthroat trout

Stoneflies were long ago recognized as an important trout food. A. Bryan Williams in *Fish and Game in British Columbia* (1935), about the spring Adams River fishing, says:

the spring months are usually the best, when a hatch of Stone Flies occurs. Excellent sport is always to be had when the hatch is on if you use a Stone Fly Nymph (p. 111).

In the "Trout Flies" section of the same book Williams says that Stone Fly Nymphs. . .

When fished very deep and slowly, they are very killing when the Stone Fly is hatching out. In some waters they are very deadly, usually about May or late April (p. 47).

Unfortunately, Williams, who was not a fly dresser, didn't give a dressing for the Stone Fly Nymph. In his earlier book, *Rod & Creel in British Columbia* (1919), he says that the Stone Fly is killing and in the frontispiece shows a standard wet-fly construction for this pattern.

Tom Brayshaw in his diary entry for April 11, 1933, recorded a partial dressing for a stonefly nymph. About that day's fishing at the Adams and the stonefly nymph Brayshaw says:

At 3 I got a 4 pound "kelt"—very red, put it back. At 3.30 I got one at the small East mouth of the river—a "dolly" of 6 pounds on fly! At 4 another trout from the main stream of 1 3/4 pounds all three fish on stonefly nymph dressed of deerhair with a yellow mohair body ribbed with black thread.

Unfortunately, without a better description I would only be guessing at the construction. Moreover, in searching through the Brayshaw diaries to the end of his fishing days, he never again made reference to the use of a stonefly nymph.

Although other stonefly nymph dressings were developed, mostly American, none received much attention from British Columbian fly fishers. Haig-Brown in *Fisherman's Spring* (1951) recognized that stoneflies are common to most British Columbian streams and that our fly fishers should be fashioning local imitations. The Perla was one that he contrived for Vancouver Island streams' stonefly nymphs such as those found in the Campbell and Nimpkish rivers.

However, Haig-Brown knew that the fisherman to be truly effective must have faith in what was at the end of the line. But equally important, he knew that the wet-fly presentation must complement the pattern. Perla, like imitations of other bottom-crawling nymphs, needs to be fished deep and slow.

Playfair's Shrimp

HOOK: Not stated but probably a number 6 to 10
TAIL: Brown polar bear fur **BODY:** Hare's ear
SHELLBACK: Brown polar bear
ORIGINATOR: Geoffrey Playfair
INTENDED USE: Wet fly for sea-run cutthroat trout
LOCATION: Vancouver Island

If you asked any British Columbian fly fisher well versed in lake and stream fishing where they would rely on a shrimp pattern, most would say the rich lakes in the interior of the province such as Tunkwa, Peterhope, Roche, Paul, Pinantan, Dragon and so on. Not too many anglers, if any, would suggest fishing sea-run cutthroat in estuaries. Yet, the mixing of coast stream's acidic water with that of the sea provides a nutrient-rich environment ideal for small crustaceans and baitfish. It is easy picking, thus prime sea-run cutthroat habitat. Yet, most fly tossers almost exclusively rely on silver-bodied baitfish imitations, not crustacean patterns. It is often a mistake.

Searching through many angling books written during the first 35 years of this century, none of the writers prescribes a tied-down wing like that in Mr. Playfair's recipe and it may be the first in British Columbia, North America and possibly the world. The great angler G. E. M. Skues developed one of the first British shrimp patterns in 1935 which is about the time that Mr. Playfair must have developed his. Evidence to support that Playfair developed his pattern in the mid-to-late 1930s are three-fold: first, Roderick Haig-Brown's book *The Western*

Angler which lists Playfair's Shrimp was published in 1939; second, polar bear fur became popular with fly tiers in the mid-1930s; and third, earlier British Columbian books like A. Bryan Williams' *Fish & Game in British Columbia* (1935) didn't list this pattern.

Although he personally had not used Playfair's Shrimp, about its usefulness Haig-Brown in *The Western Angler* says that "it is an excellent and simple pattern," and that Mr. Playfair ensured him "that it kills very well in estuarial waters" (Vol. II, p. 176).

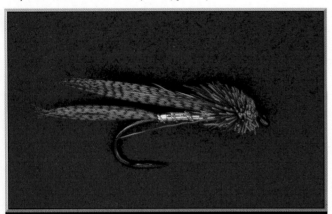

Rolled Muddler

HOOK: Number 12, Mustad 9671 (2X long)
TAIL: Light mallard **BODY:** Silver mylar
RIB: Oval tinsel, wound reverse to mylar
WING: Rolled or slender strips of light mallard flank feather
HEAD: Deer hair, spun and clipped with a few strands of deer hair extending down along the body. Use red tying thread and tie deer hair in so that there is some red thread showing behind and in front of head
ORIGINATOR: Tom Murray
INTENDED USE: Wet fly for sea-run cutthroat
LOCATION: Sunshine Coast beaches

Desirous for an imitation of the one-and-a-half inch long, local, salt-water, beach stickleback, Tom Murray developed the Rolled Muddler in the early 1970s for Sunshine Coast sea-run cutthroats. The Rolled Muddler is an offshoot of the ever popular Muddler Minnow, developed years earlier by Don Gapen for Ontario brook trout. Details about Murray's new cutthroat fly appeared in the Totem Flyfishers' newsletter, *Totem Topics*, Issue 32, October, 1974. Tom writes to then club president Jack Vincent:

As you know, Jack, I have had an exceptional year for cutthroat trout. My biggest to date has been 2 1/2 pounds and 18" long, with a number in the 1- to 1 1/2-pound class.

Through all of this fishing has evolved a sort of Muddler. I call it my "Rolled Muddler" because of the rolled mallard wing and tail. I have been using small sizes—#12, 3x long hooks—because they hold and hook better than the larger hooks. The tail is rolled, medium-long, light mallard ([Jack Vincent] Editor's note: grey barred mallard). Body is silver tinsel. Wing is rolled mallard as long as the tail. No underlay or ribbing. The head, as with all muddler types is, of course, deer hair. But—and this seems to make the big difference—the heads are clipped to a definite arrow-head shape. The head shape is like that of the sculpin with only four or five, if any, of the longer hair shafts left alongside the hook shank. It is most important to have these flies very sparse.

I fish very close to the shore and have hooked most of my fish within five or six feet of the water's edge. I have found a fast, jerky retrieve most successful, but combinations of a long, slow pull seem to work too.

Years later in the *Gilly*, published in 1985, Murray writes about one of his more memorable cutthroat days:

It was a day in late October; a beautiful B.C. fall day; a cutthroat day. My fishing partner and I decided to work the rising tide as our first choice.

As we approached the water, we saw a fish move about thirty feet out. The tide has just turned. After two quick false casts used with a quick jerking retrieve, my partner was into the first fish of the day. I don't know how many searuns we hooked and released that day but we had never had a day like it before . . . almost a fish a cast. They ranged in size from twelve to perhaps twenty-six inches. (pp. 136-137)

The Rolled Muddler's success is witnessed by its popularity throughout the province in river, stream, and along the cutthroat beaches, wherever searuns are found.

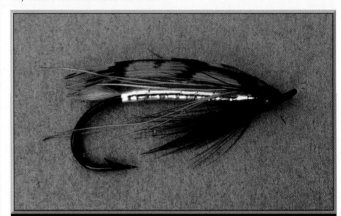

Silver Brown

HOOK: Number 6 or 8 low-water salmon
TAIL: A small, whole, Indian crow feather
BODY: Flat, silver tinsel
THROAT: A natural red-brown hackle
WING: Slender strips of golden pheasant centre tail feather enclosing a few strands of orange polar bear fur
ORIGINATOR: Roderick Haig-Brown
INTENDED USE: Wet fly for cutthroat trout
LOCATION: Campbell River

Developed in the 1930s as an imitation of a cutthroat trout or coho salmon fry, Haig-Brown claims that the Silver Brown is an effective cutthroat pattern "for maturing fish in August and September" and that it also "takes summer steelhead and coho in fresh water" (*The Western Angler*, Vol. II, p. 174). On September 4, 1936, the Brayshaws and Haig-Browns went on a picnic to the Campbell's Canyon Pool, Brayshaw recorded in his diary the events of the day and a partial dressing for the fly that his friend used on that long-ago day. Brayshaw writes:

Sept. 4th Boats out with high hopes but nothing doing only two small tyee being caught yet the water was alive with fish.

Made up lunch & went with the H[aig]-B[rown]s and Mary Ellmore to the Canyon Poll for trout & a picnic. I couldn't fish it as I had no waders. Roddy in half an hour got three of 3 3/4, 1 3/4 & 1 1/4 on a slim silver bodied fly: #6 L[ow] W[ater] hook, brown hackle & G[olden] P[heasant] tail wing.

Haig-Brown's original dressing didn't include the orange polar bear hair. That came later and the full dressing is given on page 32 of *Fisherman's Spring* (1951).

The Silver Brown remains an effective fly to this day as the following account attests. In an August 1990 trip to the Skeena River water-shed, fellow Haig-Brown admirer Bob Taylor and I decided to drive over ~~~~roat trout. We ~~~~t—Bob with a

~~~~and finding fish ~~~~r for the return ~~~~his first choice. ~~~~his last ten fish

~~~~) years. He has-~~~~e Silver Brown, ~~~~neck feather for

~~~~n's accounts of ~~~~nately, the cut-~~~~venties and the ~~~~so many others ~~~~bring it back. I ~~~~y first cutthroat

~~~~salmon
~~~~et feather
~~~~ger hackle
~~~~ender strips
~~~~a golden

~~~~ubstitute
~~~~wn
~~~~t trout

~~~~rown-1930s-origi-
~~~~lesigned by Haig-
~~~~e of its attractive-
~~~~nen as well as fish.
~~~~summer-run steel-
~~~~fry are running.
~~~~me fly for late win-
~~~~-run Dollies and

I remember the first fish I ever caught with the Silver Lady. Fishing the Squamish River on March 16, 1980, I took two fine sea-run Dolly Varden char of 16 and 21 inches. Two weeks later from that same river, a 7-pound steelhead was lured to this fly. However, there is one steelhead taken on a Silver Lady that has stuck in my mind for the past dozen years.

Often in the spring I make sojourns to some of Vancouver Island's steelhead streams, and in early April 1982 I made my usual trip and fished some of the Upper Island streams. There were few fish around and the trip unrewarding fish-wise. On my way back home, I stopped to visit relatives in Nanaimo and the day I was to return to Vancouver, I decided to make the 1 1/2-hour trip and try the Cowichan River above Skutz Falls. In the late morning, just below Bear Creek as I dangled my #4 Silver Lady over the lip of the pool's drop-off, it was taken by nice 8-pound male steelhead. This put some icing on what was an otherwise poor fishing trip.

The Silver Lady has saved the day on other occasions. On April 25, 1993, I snuck the afternoon from work, drove the 70-odd miles to the Harrison River, and fished into the spring evening. Cutthroat sometimes target a fry of a certain size or colouration and can be very difficult to catch. Harrison River cuts in particular. I can remember times fishing the darkening evening knee-deep in water and having cuts almost at my legs taking fry and having a difficult time enticing them to my fly. However, on this particular day, I did find some fry-feeding fish and chose a #8 Silver Lady as my weapon. I managed to hook one short of a dozen fish up to 20-inches that afternoon and all but one came to the Silver Lady.

I highly recommend it.

Siwash

HOOK: Number 4 to 14 **TIP:** Fine oval, gold tinsel
TAIL: A few fibres from the golden pheasant tippet feather and two slender strips of red goose
BODY: Yellow mohair or seal's fur
RIB: Fine oval, gold tinsel **THROAT:** Brown hackle
WING: Paired strips of red swan for underwing and paired strips of white swan for overwing
ORIGINATOR: Unknown
INTENDED USE: Wet fly for cutthroat trout
LOCATION: Lower Mainland streams

Although the Siwash's originator is unknown, evidence shows that its development dates back into the early 1920s or before and for almost one-half century was a favoured cutthroat fly of lower mainland fly fishers. A. Bryan Williams, in *Fish and Game in British Columbia* (1935), says that the Siwash . . .

is a very useful fly on the coast. You can use it in all sizes from a No. 14 up to a No. 6 for trout. On a No. 4 it is useful for Cohoe

Buck Tozi — white — Red — Brown — Coho
Beach fly — wet fly Coho
Coho Blue & CohoGolden
Coho Red for Coho
Wet fly for Coho
Mallard, Silver & Peacock

[sic] and Jack salmon fishing in such streams as the Nicomekl, Harrison and Vedder (p. 46).

One of the Lower Mainland's most productive cutthroat river systems even today is the Harrison just east of Mission in the Fraser Valley. However, in the early days, because of the accommodation, facilities, and fishing, the lake was the destination of most fly fishers. George C. Reifel visited the Harrison Lake regularly through the 1920s and '30s and recorded the sport in his diary. For March 8, 1925 he recorded that he and his friend Brougham visited Harrison Lake and at "Carrys caught 40 fish weighing 48#, all on fly using Siwash and Silver & Teal," and that they were "all large fish."

The limit at 25 fish a day was very generous during the 1920 and '30s. With fish averaging just over a pound, the 40-fish day for two anglers described by Mr. Reifel was still 10 fish short of their daily limit. Anglers were few and sport was plentiful and flies such as the Siwash and Teal & Silver produced well not just on the Harrison but on other Lower Mainland streams. In August 1925, Reifel describes a fishing trip to the Nicomekl River in Surrey:

August 10 - 1925 caught 3 fish with No. 9 fly -Siwash - one hour before dusk. Next day caught limit [25 fish] by 3 o'clock (small fish) with Silver & Teal also Siwash & small Professor #9 between Paterson's and bend close to Cloverdale bridge.

The Siwash with its colour scheme of red, white, gold, brown, and yellow, I believe, owes its lineage to the Parmachene Belle, developed in the early 1880s for brook trout in Maine's Rangley District on the United States' Eastern seaboard.

Stickleback

HOOK: Low-water salmon, sized to suit
TAIL: Claret hackle fibres
BODY: Silk or wool. Very light green or a good blue
RIB: Oval, silver tinsel **THROAT:** Claret hackle
WING: Sparse polar bear fur—mixed orange, blue, green, yellow or olive
ORIGINATOR: Roderick Haig-Brown
INTENDED USE: Wet fly for cutthroat trout
LOCATION: Campbell River

John Keast Lord in volume one of *The Naturalist in British Columbia* (1866) talks about the abundance of this little fish and says that:

In the months of July and August it would be difficult to find a stream, large or small, swift or slow, lake, pool, or muddy estuary, east and west of the Cascade Mountains, that has not in it immense shoals of that most irritable and pugnacious little fish the stickleback . . . . (Vol. I, p. 121)

Later Lord talks about the colouration of the stickleback and says that the fish's "colours decking his scaly armour . . . flash with a kind of phosphorescent brightness . . ." (Vol. 1, p. 122).

To get the kind of body colouration that Lord describes has always been difficult for fly tiers. Traditionally baitfish imitations incorporated a silver body, however, Roderick Haig-Brown was the first to recognize that possibly body materials other than tinsel may be better. "There is also green in his general colouration and a fair brightness of belly and lower sides," he wrote in *Fisherman's Spring* (1951), and he said that "silk or wool of very light green and a good blue seem better" (p. 29). Even then that phosphorescent or, I think, pearlescent stickleback body colour, described by Lord 130 years ago and recognized by Haig-Brown as important, has not been successfully duplicated by fly dressers. However, there are other factors such as shape, size and movement that fly dressers rely on to fool the wily trout. Haig-Brown, about imitation and fish responding to juicy items that come into their environment says that:

No fish, not even an erudite and objectively-minded old brown trout, is going to analyze all this. But every fish has been comfortably rewarded many times by responding promptly to the general impression of it all. The least the hopeful angler can do is attempt to reproduce this impression. (Fisherman's Spring, p. 29.)

Summer and fall cutthroat trout fishing with a good stickleback imitation can be a rewarding experience. In the late summer of 1994 I had my most-memorable-to-date, Lower Mainland cutthroating experience. With a real storm howling outside my office window, it was one of those days that I wondered if I should venture out of my comfortable surroundings. However, I braved the elements, took the afternoon off and went fishing. It seemed that the storm moved up the Fraser Valley as quick as I drove the highway and we arrived at the Harrison River together.

As I readied myself, I tied on my newly devised stickleback imitation, incorporating a lemon wood duck tail and wing and pearlescent body colouration copied from a sample stickleback that popped out of a gorged cutthroat's gullet a couple of weeks before. Usually I have to do some searching for Harrison cutts, but today the first fish took when I cast my line onto the water just to get it away from me so that I could zip my coat and put on my hood and protect myself from the rain and wind. I didn't look back; my first pass through the run yielded 12 trout to the rod with nine landed. I more than doubled that during the rest of the day and left the river quite satisfied with the day's events. I mused as I returned home: a good stickleback imitation is a must for summer and fall cutthroating.

A 20-inch Dolly Varden.

Teal, Silver & Blue

HOOK: Number 6 to 10
TIP: Fine oval, silver tinsel
TAIL: A few fibres from both a golden pheasant tippet
feather and a blue hackle feather
BODY: Flat, silver tinsel
RIB: Fine oval, silver tinsel
THROAT: A blue dun hackle feather
WING: Paired strips of blue swan underwing with
strips of teal for overwing
ORIGINATOR: British trout fly
INTENDED USE: Wet fly for cutthroat trout
LOCATION: Harrison System

Tinsel

HOOK: Number 8 low-water salmon
BODY: Flat, silver tinsel
WING: Slender, brown with black bars strips from the
breast feather of a male hooded merganser
ORIGINATOR: Unknown
INTENDED USE: Wet fly for cutthroat trout
LOCATION: Vancouver Island streams

Two days Harrison Lake, caught lots of fish, judge weight 80#, all fly, using Silver & Teal . . . fished 15-mile, Silver Creek & 20 mile . . . Brougham & I. 65 fish

That was what George Reifel recorded in his diary for March 17th, 1925. Almost 70 years later when I contacted Reifel's grandson, also named George, he said that he had some of his grandfather's fishing things. Among the paraphernalia there was a fly pattern which he had hundreds of and that fly pattern was the Teal, Silver & Blue.

It is noteworthy that the habit of incorporating a specific material, to better represent the colouration of salmon fry, dates back so many years.

Undoubtedly, this pattern is an offshoot of the British trout fly Teal & Silver which was introduced to British Columbia around the time of colonization. A. Bryan Williams in *Rod & Creel in British Columbia* (1919) says that the Teal & Silver "is to be tied on No. 6, 7 and 8" and is a very good fly "for fishing at the estuaries of streams such as Campbell River, Pender Harbour and in any stream at all coloured" (p. 43). In *Fish and Game in British Columbia*, A. Bryan Williams' 1935 book, he gives high marks to the Teal & Silver when he says "for wet fly fishing for Cutthroat trout on the mainland coast waters in the spring the Teal & Silver heads the list . . ." (p. 48).

In this reference he also suggests that the fly may be dressed "occasionally a size or two smaller" (p. 46). With that recommendation this changed the span of hook sizes on which the Teal, Silver & Blue was dressed from 6 to 10.

It is one of the oldies that the new generation of fly fishers would find useful if they took the time to dress a few and slip them into their fly boxes for when the cutthroat are slashing and surface feeding on salmon fry.

In the fall of the year the salmon return to their natal streams and bury their eggs in the stream bed and through the winter and early spring the life-giving, well-oxygenated water flows over the eggs and they mature. Sometime in the spring, after months of incubation, the young fish emerge from their rocky nursery into the free-flowing stream and in some coastal streams the cutthroat trout are there waiting.

And so are the fly-fishers. The province at one time had a closed season for trout. The opening, however, often coincided with the spring, salmon fry emergence. For years the phrase, "The fry are out, let's go 'Tinsel' fishing," marked the start of the fly-fishing season. The word "Tinsel," referring to the fly pattern of that name.

When the Tinsel was developed and by whom is uncertain; it was not listed in A. Bryan Williams' 1935 book *Fish and Game in British Columbia*, however, Roderick Haig-Brown listed it and gave its dressing in *The Western Angler* (1939). Haig-Brown gave the fly a very high recommendation when he mentioned that, "On the start of the humpback [pink salmon] hatch a silver-bodied fly is almost essential, and the Tinsel is the deadliest of them all . . ." (Vol. 1, p. 179).

Haig-Brown has influenced my fly-fishing thinking for most of my 30-year fishing career and because of his Tinsel recommendation I dressed some on number 8 hooks and put them in my cutthroat box, ready for my next trip to the Harrison.

It was a work day but I needed a break and decided to make the 70-mile trip to the Harrison, arriving there late in the afternoon, even though I expected to find difficult fishing conditions because of a very high river. And high the river was. It confined me to fishing few spots and some only from my boat, a tedious procedure consisting of anchoring in the current and making many moves to fish a piece of water. However, I tied on a Tinsel and over the next four hours I managed to hook eight cutthroat, landing four. Considering the difficulties, a most rewarding afternoon.

The Tinsel is one of the simplest of flies, easily dressed, and a fly worthy of a place in any cutthroat fly fisher's box. For fly tiers wanting to dress the Tinsel, the hooded merganser's breast feathers recommended by Haig-Brown for the wing are hard to obtain but a drake mallard's bronze shoulder feathers make a suitable substitute.

What Else

HOOK: Number 8 and 6, 2 or 3 extra long
TAIL: A tuft of fluorescent red wool
BODY: Medium yellow dyed polar bear underfur
THROAT: Brown cock, soft, neck feather
WING: Light mallard flank feather **RIB:** Oval gold tinsel
ORIGINATOR: Earl Anderson **LOCATION:** Harrison River

Williams' Dark-bodied Sedge

HOOK: Number 14 **BODY:** Very dark green seal's fur
RIB: Black floss **HACKLE:** Dark brown
WING: Hen pheasant centre tail
ORIGINATOR: A. Bryan Williams
INTENDED USE: Dry fly for rainbow and cutthroat trout
LOCATION: Vancouver Island streams

Evolution is the word that best describes the development of the What Else. Well over 100 years ago, the Professor, developed by famed British author Christopher North, was introduced to British Columbia's trout by British fly-fishing colonials.

The Professor, a long time popular pattern for cutthroat, went through many small changes, mostly at the hands of Vancouver-born, commercial fly tier and fisherman, Earl Anderson. Many years ago, he replaced the original North-specified red ibis tail with a tuft of red wool. Whether this made the fly more appealing to the cutthroat is debatable.

However, most Professor fishers claim Earl's remaining changes made the fly a much better fish catcher. He went to work on the body and substituted first a body of medium yellow mohair which in turn was replaced by a teased-out one of medium yellow, dyed, polar bear underfur.

To improve the appearance and make the fly more streamlined for river fishing, Earl revised the wing's angle from a steeply cocked one to one that lies flat, enveloping the top of the bear underfur body.

He also insisted that the throat hackle be of a softer feather so that there is more movement as the current or stripping action works on the fly during fishing.

The last change, and one that some claim is of significant importance, was suggested by Anderson's brother Arne. He thought that the ordinary red wool tail should be replaced by a tuft of fluorescent red wool.

Jack Vincent was the one who gave Earl's creation its new name. Jack had used the Professor since his early fly-fishing days and being in the same business as Earl followed the fly's transformation and made good use of Anderson's alterations. Jack found Earl's revised Professor was "not only primarily a trout fly, but it also belonged in the fly box of coho fly fishers." Later in Vincent's article on "The 'What Else' Fly" in the May 1972 issue of *Western Fish and Game magazine*, he says:

> *Nor is the usefulness of this fly restricted to the Lower Mainland only. Both trout and coho go for it on Vancouver Island, and I should imagine, in some of our other coastal rivers as well. It is second to none for the beach cutthroat in the areas I fish for them.*

Jack had the fly on so frequently and found it so productive that when asked what fly he had just caught his fish on would respond, "a wool-bodied Professor, what else." Eventually his response was shortened to just "What Else."

Unable to find a sample or a pattern listing, I found that gleaning a dressing for Williams' Dark-bodied Sedge difficult. The pattern's listing was determined by examining a picture of a dark-bodied, Harkley & Haywood-dressed fly, mistakenly called Williams' Brown Sedge in W.F. Pochin's 1946 *Angling and Hunting in British Columbia*. The fly in question is a very dark green-bodied fly with dark rib, dark brown hackle, and a mottled brown wing. However, even under 8x magnification, the dark-bodied fly's construction was hard to determine. Nevertheless, Williams did say on page 41 of *Fish & Game in British Columbia* that "On the coast there are a number of different species, one so dark coloured as to appear black . . . ." The fly in Pochin's book is very dark bodied and does appear to be black to the naked eye.

Later in his book, where he describes trout flies and suggests sizes, Williams says that for dry-fly fishing "the Sedges are most important" and recommends that fly fishers "for coastal waters" supplement the Yellow-bodied Sedge with a "small, dark-bodied on No. 14" (p. 47).

Dry fly opportunities on coastal streams are rare; however, having a few of Williams' Dark-Bodied Sedges for those rare instances is probably wise.

The introduced brown provides good sport on the Cowichan.

Williams' Yellow-bodied Sedge

HOOK: Number 12 **BODY:** Yellow wool
RIB: Brown floss followed by a palmered yellow hackle
HACKLE: Light brown **WING:** Hen pheasant centre tail
ORIGINATOR: A. Bryan Williams
INTENDED USE: Dry fly for rainbow and cutthroat trout
LOCATION: Cowichan River

When Haig-Brown wrote *The Western Angler* (1939), he commented on the degree of variation in dressing and naming of standard patterns found among fly tiers from the various locations in the province. Because of those things, he was reluctant to provide his readers with pattern listings for the standard-of-the-day, British Columbia-developed patterns. He recommended that amateur tiers order samples from reputable tackle dealers and from those samples deduce accurate dressings. Haig-Brown listed about a half dozen tackle shops in Vancouver, Victoria and Kelowna, but none of Haig-Brown's recommended sources exists today and determining the dressings of old patterns is sometimes puzzling.

This dressing, like its companion Williams' Dark-Bodied Sedge, was deduced by examining a Harkley & Haywood-dressed sample featured in the frontispiece of W. F. Pochin's 1946 book *Angling and Hunting in British Columbia.*

Most of the coastal streams are acidic and produce small quantities of insects and that is the prime reason most of the fish that frequent coastal rivers are anadromous. Dry-fly fishing opportunities are not that common in our fast-flowing, insect-barren, coastal streams. Some streams though do support sedge populations and A. Bryan Williams in *Fish & Game in British Columbia*, says that there is one "with very light yellowish-brown wings and a bright yellow body that has several black bars. This particular species is eagerly taken by the trout" (p. 40).

However rare the opportunities for coastal dry fly fishing are, one jewel, the Cowichan River on Vancouver Island, does provide good dry-fly sport and Williams, about the Cowichan dry-fly opportunities, says that "There are in the spring two hatches of sedges, one yellow-bodied and one very small and dark. The yellow sedge fished dry is very killing at times" (p. 88).

Not long ago, Joe Saysell, whose family has lived, fished, and guided on the Cowichan for almost 50 years, sent me a yellow-bodied wet fly thought up by his father in the mid-1950s. The consistent similarities between Saysell's and Williams' patterns, led me to believe that perhaps Joe's father's fly's ancestor is Williams' Yellow-bodied sedge.

Williams' Yellow-Bodied Sedge

Type: Dry **Body:** Yellow wool
Rib: Yellow hackle stem **Hackle:** Brown
Wing: Brown hen pheasant **Hook:** Size 12

Saysell's Little Yellow Bucktail

Type: Wet **Body:** Yellow wool
Rib: Oval gold tinsel **Hackle:** Brown with black bars
Wing: Brown bucktail **Hook:** Size 12 to 6

Saysell's father's fly had a brown tail, Williams' fly none and the Saysells found that steelhead took the fly when dressed on the larger sized 6 hooks, while Williams recommended his fly for trout fishing only.

Yellow Belle

HOOK: Number 6 and 8
TAIL: Married strips of yellow and red swan
BODY: Yellow wool or seal's fur
RIB: Oval, silver tinsel
THROAT: Mixed yellow and red hackles
WING: Married yellow, red, yellow strips of swan
ORIGINATOR: Unknown
INTENDED USE: Wet fly for cutthroat trout
LOCATION: Lower Mainland

This pattern is another that owes its pedigree to H. P. Wells' Parmachene Belle, developed in 1878 for brook trout in Maine's Rangely region. During the early part of this century and into the 1960s the belief persisted that, later in the year when the salmon fry had left the river and silver-bodied flies had lost their appeal, cutthroat appeared to prefer flies with some yellow in their make-up.

A. Bryan Williams reinforced that theory and recommends that when the cutts do not respond to the silver-bodied fry imitations "it is advisable to use such flies as the Siwash, Parmachene Belle . . ." (*Fish & Game in British Columbia*, 1935, p. 48).

This belief that cutthroat preferred yellow-bodied flies such as the Professor, Siwash, the Yellow Belle, which incorporated a yellow/red theme throughout their make-up, and the yellow/red hackle, the Yellow Peril, dominated the fall cutthroat fishery.

I can remember Earl Anderson, a local tackle salesman for Woodward's, telling me in the mid- to late-1960s about the cutthroat's preference for yellow. Being new to fly fishing, I can't recall if I bit or not and bought some yellow-bodied patterns. Many of these superstitions are exploited by salespeople and guides solely to get you to buy more flies.

However, in the 1990s most yellow-bodied cutthroat flies attract more fly-eating moths than fish. About the only yellow-bodied fly that has survived the passage of time is the Professor. But even that 175-year-old pattern has gone through a transformation which is described in this book under the title of What Else.

Yellow Peril

HOOK: Number 6 and 8
TAIL: Red and yellow hackle fibres
BODY: Yellow seal's fur or wool
RIB: Medium, gold tinsel
HACKLE: Red and yellow **ORIGINATOR:** Unknown
INTENDED USE: Wet fly for cutthroat trout
LOCATION: Nicomekl and Serpentine rivers

Nestled in the countryside in the drainage basin tributary to Boundary Bay are two streams, the Nicomekl and Serpentine rivers, that in their hey day were jam-packed full of cutthroat trout and coho salmon. In the first half of this century, because of the lack of roads and cars, they were considered remote to most Lower Mainland fly fishers, and those streams produced a fishery all to themselves. In the 1920, '30s, 40s, & '50s the British Columbia Electric Company ran its fishermen's special to get anglers out into the valley to fish them.

Because the fishing areas of these slow-moving, meandering, tidal streams ran through the fertile lowlands, the river water appeared coloured at most times and a large full-bodied fly seemed to work better. The Yellow Peril was the choice of many Nicomekl fly fishers.

Francis Whitehouse, about the Nicomekl River, its cutthroat and the Yellow Peril, in his 1945 book, *Sport Fishes of Western Canada*, has this to say:

> But the Nicomekl deserves discussion for two reasons: (1) Since more Cut-throat are taken there in a year than any other piece of water in the Province, and (2) The Fly-fishing technique employed is somewhat unique.
>
> Of several flies in favour on the Nicomekl, that most commonly used is tied on a No. 6 hook: a hackle admixture of yellow and red; and bearing the name of "Yellow Peril". The line is cast well across to the reeds on the other side, permitted to sink, and recovered slowly by twisting it back and forth over the thumb and little finger of the non-rod hand. . . . The fly, near the bottom, is moving along in short jerks, the hackle, as it should, closing and opening to simulate life. . . . Instead of winding the line as described, I find that recovering it with the non-rod hand in short jerks to a loop, or loops, serves much the same purpose. I have gone to some length as to this Nicomekl fly-fishing method, since the principle involved holds good not only with hackle flies imitating insects, but with silver-bodied bucktails posing as fry and minnows. The darting progress, coupled with the closing and opening of the hairs, constitute their attraction to fish. (pp. 34-35)

Unfortunately, the Nicomekl River fishing that Whitehouse described is a thing of the past and, with urban development and sprawl, the Nicomekl is struggling to survive just like the Yellow Peril. It is not found in many present-day cutthroaters' fly boxes.

Ron Schiefke swimming the What Else through Harrison runs for cutts and coho.

Saltwater Salmon Patterns

Section Four:

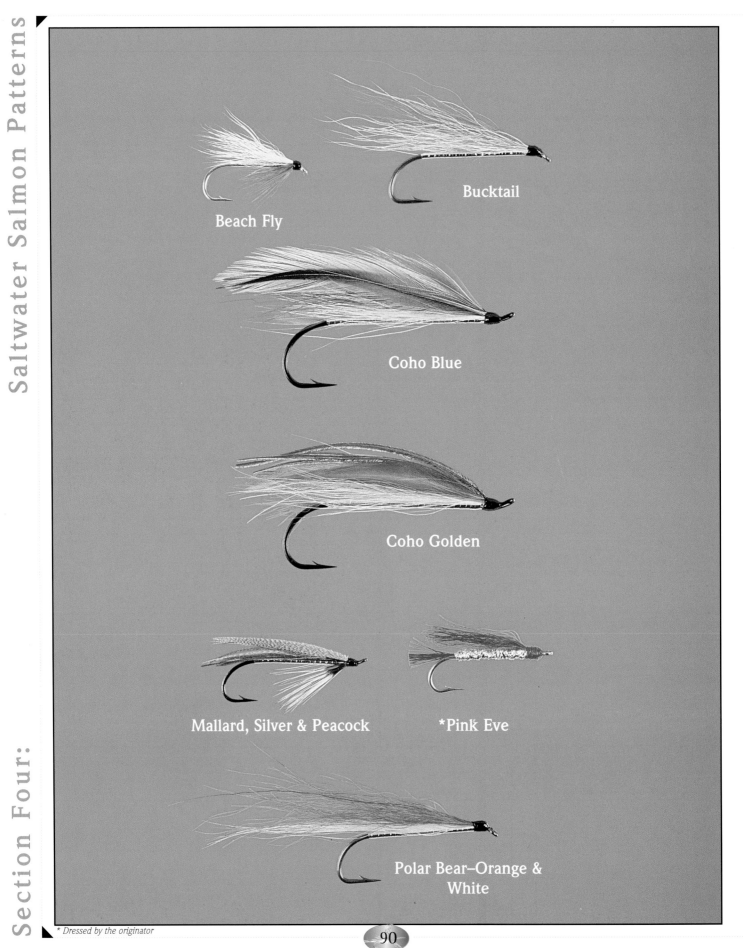

Beach Fly

Bucktail

Coho Blue

Coho Golden

Mallard, Silver & Peacock

*Pink Eve

Polar Bear–Orange & White

Saltwater Salmon Patterns

Charles Lingren and Randel Mindell with pinks on the Pink Eve, QCI, 1990.

In ancient times it was recorded by the poet Homer that it was the face of Helen of Troy that launched a thousand ships. More recently in Northwest history, it has also been recorded that salmon was the fish the decided the boundary of two countries.

In the mid 1800s, it was commonly believed that Pacific salmon would not take the fly. Indeed, it was also rumoured that England's Foreign Secretary in the 1840s, Lord Aberdeen (on the advice of his brother-in-law, Captain John Gordon, who had actually fished for Pacific Coast salmon), suggested giving Washington and Oregon to the Americans to avoid war. The territory was evidently not considered worth fighting for simply because the Pacific salmon would not take the fly. That story—a favourite along the Pacific Coast—circulated for many years. Clearly, Captain Gordon was not impressed with the country he saw or with the methods used for catching Pacific salmon. He concluded that he would not give "'the most barren hills in the Highlands of Scotland'" for all he saw on the Pacific Coast (Akrigg, British Columbia Chronicle: 1778-1846, p. 378).

Just think—had Captain Gordon seen with different eyes, and had he caught some Pacific salmon on the fly, the B.C.-U.S.A. border might today be much farther south.

What Captain Gordon reported didn't deter fly fishers from trying and succeeding. John Pease Babcock in his 1908 book, *The Game Fishes of British Columbia*, says that he had caught both spring and coho with a fly and recommends the Harrison River as "the most accessible and productive water for those who desire to take salmon with a fly."

Moreover, the Harrison is still a favoured river for many Lower Mainland fly fishers seeking salmon with the fly. Fly fishing for salmon in the saltwater, however, become a preferred method for many after the introduction of the bucktail fly sometime in the mid-1920s. Haig-Brown recorded that history in *The Western Angler* (1939), gave us the dressings for his two coho flies, and recorded that the substitution of polar bear fur for bucktail revolutionized the sport.

Most saltwater salmon fishers are, however, out for meat and not sport and therefore bait or lures are their favoured poisons. Because of that, we have had little fly development over the past 60 years, and the polar bear flies developed in the 1930s are still the preferred lures of saltwater fly fishers. However, Vancouver Island fly fisher, Barry Thornton, has spent the last 20 or so years plying the waters of Georgia Straight with his creations and a couple of his patterns grace the pages of this section. Recently, Thornton's book, *Saltwater Fly Fishing for Pacific Salmon* (1995), was released followed by *Salmon to a Fly* by Jim Crawford. Works like those penned by Thornton and Crawford will spark the interest of many and, as others take up the sport, they will explore and develop new patterns and contribute to the fly-tying heritage of this under-used, fly-fishing opportunity.

Beach Fly

HOOK: Number 6 or 8 long-shanked stainless steel
BODY: Flat, silver tinsel
THROAT: Green, red, purple or black hackle
WING: Polar bear **ORIGINATOR:** Barry Thornton
INTENDED USE: Wet fly for coho salmon
LOCATION: East Coast of Vancouver Island

Bucktails

HOOK: Number 2/0 to 8
BODY: Flat silver tinsel
WING: Brown, red and white, blue and white, or
green and white hair from a deer's tail
ORIGINATOR: Unknown
INTENDED USE: Wet fly for coho salmon
LOCATION: Duncan and Cowichan bays

When polar bear replaced bucktail in the mid-thirties, a multitude of colour combinations were developed. In the ensuing years flies were dressed in a multitude of sizes, varying from huge number 5/0s to small number 8s. Haig-Brown suggested in *The Western Angler* (1939) that fly fishers should experiment with combinations of fur, feather and tinsel so that fly development would grow from season to season. Many things were tried and new things are still being tried as new synthetic materials become available. In the 1930s some anglers even painted eyes on the head of their bucktails in the hope of making their flies more authentic and duping the fish. However, most anglers realized that the eyed-patterns were none the more effective and were abandoned by most fly dressers. Every now and then one of these old ideas is reborn and packaged as something new.

However, after nearly 60 years of history and development little is new and the majority of standard saltwater patterns are dressed with a silver body and a polar bear wing, often with some other material thrown in such as a Flashabou or Krystal Flash.

When beach fly fishing became more popular in the 1970s, '80s and '90s, the beach tinsel tosser found that the 2/0 to 5/0 standards used by the open-water saltwater boat fishers were difficult to cast and they dressed smaller sizes. Barry Thornton's Salmon Beach Fly, a variation on the early polar bear streamers, is dressed on size 6 and 8 hooks and it incorporates a throat hackle. Haig-Brown suggested in *The Western Angler* that a hackle throat may be a valuable addition to saltwater patterns.

Thornton says that this pattern evolved "after much discussion and experimentation" in the early 1980s and has proved successful for "homing coho in estuary/beach situations."

It is not known who introduced the Bucktail to coastal waters or if it was first introduced to interior trout streams. We do know though, that fly fishing for coho developed around the turn-of-the-century. John Pease Babcock, Deputy Commissioner of Fisheries for British Columbia, in Provincial Bulletin 25, *The Game Fishes of British Columbia* (1908), says that he has "caught both the Spring and Coho salmon in the Province with a fly." Earlier exploits by visiting British sportsmen also attest to the fact that salmon were caught with the fly. However, most of those early fly fishers used silver-bodied Atlantic salmon or sea-trout flies. The Bucktail came later, probably sometime in the mid-to-late twenties.

Bucktail fly fishing for coho is uniquely British Columbian and, according to Roderick Haig-Brown in *The Western Angler* (1939), there were some "keen fishermen who can claim an eight- or ten-year-old habit of spending September and October with a fly rod in some bay where the cohoes school and feed, it is only since 1935 that the sport has become widely known and really popular" (Vol. II, p. 46).

In the mid-1930s, the standard-of-the-day Bucktail was dressed with a "silver body and white, red and brown bucktail hairs about 2 inches long on a 2/0 hook" (Vol. II, p 49), wrote Haig-Brown. However, in 1935, it was found that flies dressed with longer hairs, up to three or more inches in length, and with green hairs often replacing red, were often more productive.

The trolled fly was favoured by many anglers because it produced better than the cast, but there were, however, anglers who insisted on taking their fish with a cast fly. In October 1932, Mrs. E. S. Tait was fishing off Vancouver Island casting for cohoes. After landing several fish, she cast again and was into a large fish. After a lengthy battle she was surprised with the 43-pound tyee lying in the bottom of her boat. Mrs. Tait used a Hardy trout fishing outfit, 70 yards of line and a 1/0 Campbell River bucktail fly.

Charlie Stroulger of Duncan, a teenager during the late '20s and early '30s, in a November 1994 letter, remembers Frank Darling of Capilano River fame casting for Cowichan Bay cohoes. Stroulger writes:

As far as bucktailing in Cowichan Bay I can only remember a trolled fly with a large Victoria spinner. These flies were quite bushy and were brown and white. In those days the Bay was teeming with fish [1920s and '30s].

The 1st man that did fly casting for cohoes was a Mr. Darling

A coho jack taken in the tidal section of the Tlell River on a silver-bodied fly.

from Vancouver. He used to rent a rowboat from Ordanos and had a man row him. [He] had a Hardy 3 piece cane rod . . . and was an excellent caster.

Furthermore, Darling was dressing his bucktails with polar bear as early as 1933.

Bucktails are also effective trout flies. A. Bryan *Williams in Fish and Game in British Columbia* (1935), about bucktails, says:

> *These flies, which have only come into use in recent years, are unquestionably of great importance. They are tied in several different patterns, but the ordinary brown, red and white, with a silver body is preferable. The blue and white is favored on Vancouver Island. You require them in a number of sizes from as small as No. 8 for trout to as high as No. 2/0 for Cohoes. (p. 46)*

Tom Brayshaw recorded the first usage of the Bucktail for interior trout with a diary entry for June 4, 1933 in which all his Little River fish taken that day were "on bucktail and silver."

Bucktails are as popular today as they were in the 1930s, but most are now dressed with polar bear.

Coho Blue

HOOK: 2 1/2-inch Long Dee or 7/0 low-water salmon
TAIL: A large, blue hackle tip **BODY:** Flat, silver tinsel
WING: White under blue polar bear fur, with blue, then badger hackles laid alongside, and some heron hackle sprigs overall
ORIGINATOR: Roderick Haig-Brown
INTENDED USE: Wet fly for coho salmon
LOCATION: Duncan Bay

Fly fishing for coho salmon flourished along the east coast of Vancouver Island in the late twenties and thirties, as is attested by this short August 4, 1929, note in General Noel Money's game book which says that he went to Duncan Bay just north of Campbell River with the Deacons and caught nine coho "all on the fly." Another affirmation of this grand sport was provided by Roderick Haig-Brown, when he responded to Captain Brayshaw's letter on 6th October 1934:

> *The coho season here has been truly wonderful—& still is for that matter; Ann & I caught ten in four hours yesterday, all on fly. And it has been possible to get anywhere from 10-20 or more a day ever since September 1st. Why don't you try them next year? They present a first-rate problem to a keen flyfisherman for this reason: though a trolled fly is deadly, a cast fly is definitely not so. Most fishermen use two rods, trolling a fly on one while casting with the other; & I very much doubt if many more than two fish are caught on the cast fly to ten on the trolled fly. As far as I can make out this is because the fish follow a fly for so long before finally taking it.*

The problem therefore is to turn out a fly that the fish will snap at more readily, & a good fly-tier should be able to do it.

Although Haig-Brown never considered himself to be a good fly tier, he said that he tied flies "mainly because I cannot buy what I want" in a February 1956 press release to Earl Burton of *Sports Illustrated* magazine. However, the Coho Blue is one of the patterns he developed for coho salmon because he wanted something specific in a fly and couldn't buy what he wanted.

Coho Golden

HOOK: 2 1/2-inch Long Dee or 7/0 low-water salmon
TAIL: A few fibres of orange polar bear fur
BODY: Flat, silver tinsel
WING: White under olive polar bear fur, with red jungle cock or natural red hackles laid alongside, and a few strands of peacock herl and a golden pheasant crest feather over all
ORIGINATOR: Roderick Haig-Brown
INTENDED USE: Wet fly for coho salmon
LOCATION: Duncan Bay

In *The Western Angler* (1939), Haig-Brown says:

> *The art of catching cohoes by attractive and sporting means is very far from fully developed, and there are many waters that have been little explored by the angler. In Duncan Bay and most of the waters south of Seymour Narrows a seventeen- or eighteen-pound cohoe is a very big fish. . . . I have caught them up to twenty-four pounds of the mouth of a small creek just south of the Nimpkish and I have seen a twenty-nine pounder caught in Baronet Pass. Perhaps larger cohoes are not altogether needed . . . but the crash of a twenty-pounder jumping clear of the water in his first run has a memorable savagery . . . . There seems a ruthlessness, a momentary surge of overwhelming power, in the strike of a twenty-pounder to a fly that is lacking in the strike of a fish much smaller. (Vol. II, pp. 55, 56)*

Haig-Brown, although fascinated by the sport, was not too sure that fly fishers had considered or taken advantage of other materials besides the multi-coloured combinations of bucktail and polar bear fur streamers. He thought that other materials may prove to be more effective and about the winging, he thought that perhaps "whole saddle feathers, both dyed and natural, mixed with the hair" would make an excellent wing. In addition he says that "peacock herl is valuable," along with a score of other materials: turkey or golden pheasant tail, and the light and dark saddle feather of the red jungle cock are all good. He recommended that a myriad of combinations be tied and tested and that the development of effective flies "must grow and develop from season to season" (Vol. II, p. 50).

The Coho Golden was developed from those thought processes that he put down on paper in *The Western Angler*. It is a fly that incorporated the standard-of-the-day silver body, but instead of the all-fur wing, Haig-Brown combined feather and fur to make an extremely attractive pattern.

Mallard, Silver & Peacock

HOOK: Number 2 low-water salmon
BODY: Flat silver tinsel **THROAT:** Badger hackle
WING: Peacock and mallard flank
ORIGINATOR: Tom Brayshaw
INTENDED USE: Wet fly for coho salmon
LOCATION: Duncan Bay

This Brayshaw fly is a variation of the very successful and simply dressed Silver & Mallard trout pattern. Brayshaw first used it during a 1936 trip to Vancouver Island when he decided to give coho fly fishing at Duncan Bay, just north of Campbell River, a try. After rowing the mile or so up to Duncan Bay with his wife, Becky, they both had a successful day tossing feather and hair-winged lures to salmon. Starting at 10:30 and finishing at just after 4 they caught a total of 10 salmon and one seagull.

In his diary he gives the dressing for the fly he used: "#2 low water hook, silver body, badger hackle & grey mallard & peacock wing."

He also gives a brief account of the fish and bird that he caught.

Charles Lingren and Toby Rogers with QCI-caught pinks.

After landing his first coho, Brayshaw records:

I got a 5 1/4 cohoe & two four-pound humpbacks besides putting back 3 grilse. Left the Bay at 4 & rowing home had a big strike off the kelp & got a 10 1/2 pound cohoe—I also caught & released a seagull in the Bay.

A few days later Brayshaw was again out casting to salmon in Duncan Bay and, early in the afternoon on the ebb tide, he took a 7 1/4 pound spring and a 9 1/2 pound coho on his Mallard, Silver & Peacock pattern. In just a few hours salmon fishing with his new fly, Brayshaw took cohoes, pinks and springs. With such catches, indeed, a most worthwhile pattern for the tinsel-tosser to have in his fly box.

Pink Eve

HOOK: Number 2 to 6 Mustad 34011 stainless steel
TAIL: Pink FisHair or polar bear fur
BODY: Oval, silver tinsel
WING: Pink FisHair or polar bear fur
ORIGINATOR: Barry Thornton
INTENDED USE: Wet fly for pink salmon
LOCATION: Eve River

Considered the sportsman's fishes, the coho and Chinook have attracted most of the attention from the saltwater angling community in the last century. However, the pink salmon, when it returns to its natal stream on its cycle year, provides good sport for the fly fisher.

The Pink Eve fly pattern, developed by veteran Vancouver Island fly fisher, Barry Thornton, in about 1980, has been luring pinks to the rods of many beach fishers since its inception.

Barry says that "this pattern was initially used at the estuaries of the Eve, Keogh, and Cluxewe rivers" and that with the reintroduction "of pink salmon to other rivers like the Oyster and Puntledge it has become a standard for these estuaries and beach areas." Besides its attractiveness to estuary pinks, Thornton has also found that "this is an effective pattern for 'blueback,' pinks and coho during April, May and June" when he is open-water saltwater fly fishing.

I remember the first time that I witnessed the successes of the Pink Eve. I had taken my son Charles to the Queen Charlotte Islands for a late summer fishing vacation and I had remembered the axiom "pink for pinks" as I attached the fly to his line. My son had a grand day's sport hooking about 30 fish in three hours and killing his first limit of fly-caught salmon.

Postulations abound in the fishing community and "pink for pinks" is a classic example. The Pink Eve produced regularly for my son during the remainder of the trip, but I found it no more killing than my silver-bodied, mallard-winged standard. What was more critical for success was fishing at the correct depth and for those conditions we encountered the critical depth was just under the surface.

Polar Bear Hairwings

HOOK: Number 2/0 to 8 **BODY:** Flat silver tinsel
WING: Polar bear: white under followed by yellow,
red, blue, purple, mauve, or green
ORIGINATOR: Unknown **INTENDED USE:** Coho salmon
LOCATION: Cowichan and Duncan bays

According to Roderick Haig-Brown, 1935 was a consequential year for saltwater salmon fly fishing. Previous to 1935, fishermen used the standard bucktails, dressed on 2/0 hooks with bucktail wings about 2 inches long, but in 1935 they realized that longer winged flies better represented the cohoes' quarry, the needlefish. Also in the '30s, flies of more brilliant lustre dressed with the more translucent and flexible polar bear hair replaced the dull and brittle bucktail hair.

Tommy Brayshaw didn't fish Duncan Bay in 1935; however, he did with his wife Becky in 1936, and recorded in his diary usage of polar bear hairwing flies. He writes:

Sept. 1st. Did not go out early. Took Mr., B. down to the bus at 9 then called on R. H[aig]-B[rown] & decided to go to Duncan Bay. . . . A few boats there [but] all blank, nothing doing till after lunch when at 1.45 Becky got a cohoe 6 1/4 pounds on white & orange polar bear. I followed with a 4 1/2 pounder . . . Becky got another of 6 pounds . . . .

Later, in 1938, Brayshaw recorded the first that I have managed to locate, documented-in-writing usage of polar-bear winged flies for trout on the Adams River.

For the saltwater salmon fly fisher, the switch to polar bear hair and longer winged flies that resulted in larger catches is undoubtedly true, but with the longer winged, single-hooked flies, fishermen started to complain about short-taking fish.

Charlie Stroulger, long-time Duncan guide and sportfisher, in a November 1994 letter, remembers those short-taking fish and says:

Polar bear started to come alive in the late 1930s and early 1940s. . . . In those days we only had single hooks and the hair was too long so the fish were taking short.

I went to a friend of mine that tied flies and asked him if he could [put on] a trailer hook . . . . He tied the trailer hook on with copper wire and I believe this was the start of the double hooks. It really made a difference in catching cohoes.

In the '30s as it is today, throwing with a fly rod a two-inch-long bucktail or polar-bear hair-wing fly dressed on a 2/0 hook was possible, but unless fish were milling fly casting to cohoes in the ocean was a chancy proposition. When the fly length was increased to three inches and longer and with the addition of the trailer hook, casting was almost impossible and trolling the big flies became ever more popular. The sport that developed around trolling flies for cohoes—whether the flies were constructed of deer hair or polar bear hair—became known as bucktailing and that name has stuck to this day.

A 15 lb. chinook taken on a fly. Smaller than Mrs. Tait's, nonetheless a nice catch.

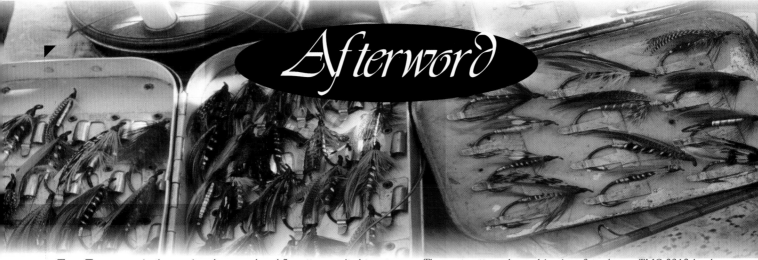

Afterword

Many areas in the province have produced fly patterns suited to their areas and fish, and space doesn't permit me to list the many local patterns from the geographic regions in the province. However, the Skeena Specials described in Terrace angler Robert Brown's letter are representative of the ingenuity and creativity of local anglers. Rob writes:

Dear Art,   *4 December 1995*

Belatedly, here are some Skeena Specials.

The oversized marabou contraption is Doug Webb's patent, dubbed the "Trick or Treat," for its Halloween colours, by me. This was the fly that attracted those 3 Thompson steelhead on that afternoon of disasters on the Graveyard.

My theory is that the two or three strands of copper tinsel tied under the wing reflect enticingly off the mirror adding allure to an already alluring leech dressed on Tiemco 3/0 or 1/0 salmon hook, with a tail and overwing of orange polar bear underfur, body of black wool, black marabou collar with two or three strands of copper tinsel under the polar bear over wing.

The dark fly tied on the Diachi "Bob Johns" hook is called "A Touch of Blue" for the tag & dyed blue grizzly body hackle. This fellow is relatively new. You'll notice that your style of dressing has a strong influence on this pattern dressed on size 6 to 2 ring eye TMC 200R or Diachi equivalent, with a gold tinsel tip and rib, blue floss tag, red dyed golden pheasant topping tail, black wool and seal fur body, blue body hackle, orange beard with a wing of black bear fur.

The "Skinny Skunk" is Finlay's variation. The body is tying thread. The Partridge & Orange hybrid is also a "Fin Ferguson Favourite." I armoured it with vinyl and set it on a heavy scud hook for purposes of penetration. In this size we use it for summer steelhead. When stalking cutthroat we dress it on 16s and 18s.

The simple pink streamer, with tail and throat: hot pink hackle; body: salmon wool; rib: oval silver tinsel; wing: polar bear fur; head: hot orange thread, is Doug Webb's "Pink Dynk," the flagship of his armada of steelhead flies for years.

The "Muddler" is my spin on Gapen's great dressing. Note, I use an orange beard hackle, a wing of deer hair instead of a collar and an underwing of orange polar bear. I fish this bug lazily, on the end of long leader and a floating line. It's caught me many summer fish.

The silvery blue contraption dressed with a blue tail, silver body, dark blue throat, blue polar bear wing with a few strands of peacock herl over is "Shirley's Fancy," originally tied by Roy Chapplow at Shirley Culp's suggestion.

The blue fly is mine. "Something Blue" is its working title, but I'm thinking of calling it "Miles Davis" for the great jazz trumpeter.

I've used this dressing off and on for 4 years, and I've hooked winter steelhead with it when they were resistant to other patterns. The dressing consists of a body of blue braid followed by blue seal fur (lately blue Flashabou dubbing) and a hackle of blue grizzly behind blue pheasant.

The next pattern dressed in sizes 8 to 4 on a TMC 2312 hook with a tip of copper tinsel, tail of orange dyed tippet, body of purple "poppin yarn," purple body hackle (front third), pink throat, wing of orange dyed golden pheasant breast feather, and brown head, is called "Crepescule." I tied it for dark bottomed rivers, the Lakelse, specifically.

The Burlap-bodied, Carey-hackled, Muddler-headed combo is the "Mud Flap." Usually I wrap lots of lead on this one so I can roll it nymph-like, along the bottom.

The yellow-bodied, silver-ribbed fly is the "Lakelse Locomotive." The wing is a tuft of raccoon, while the tail and hackle are owl. The fly was invented by Dan Gledhill of Thornhill.

The odd looking USD [upside down fly] fly is "Skinny Side Up" a killing sockeye fly based on a pattern invented by Laurie Parr and popularized by Ed Chapplow. Laurie's pattern was named the "Ferry Island Fancy" by me. The dressing consisted of a body of silver braid, blue Krystal Flash wing and hot orange chenille head. Webb dressed this fly upside down to avoid the hangups that attend sockeye fishing.

The orange-dyed tippet-tailed, dark blue-bodied, grizzly-hackled wizard fly is, well, a "Blue Wizard."

The red-tailed, maroon-bodied with gold rib, claret-hackled orange-dyed squirrel is called the "Dynamite Stick." I don't know if it's a regional pattern; a young guy I met on the Lakelse 15 years ago told me it is, and that his uncle had invented it.

Finally, I must own up to creating the pink wiggler with the tail of pink rubber strips, body of pink tinsel chenille with a heavy pink marabou collar. It's called "Seafood" and was the subject of an article I wrote for Fly Rod & Reel *some years back.*

So that's it.

Merry Humbug, Rob

Brown's Skeena Specials attest to the diversity in the fly tying community throughout the province. Local anglers are developing new or altering existing patterns to suit local conditions or anglers' fancy. And with a continuing array of synthetic materials being developed to entice the imagination of fly fishermen, fly tiers, as they have since fur, feather and tinsel were used to dress the first flies hundreds of years ago, will continue to experiment and develop new and uniquely named creations.

Bibliography

Adams, Joseph. *Ten Thousand Miles Through Canada*. London: Methuen & Co. Ltd., 1912.

Aflalo, F. G. *Sunset Playgrounds*. London: Witherby & Co., 1909.

Aikins, Mary S., ed. *A Cutthroat Collection*. Vancouver: Maclean Hunter Ltd., 1984.

Akrigg, G. P. V. and Helen B. Akrigg. *1001 British Columbia Place Names*. Vancouver: Discovery Press, 1970.

——. *British Columbia Chronicle: 1778 - 1846*. Vancouver: Discovery Press, 1975.

Ashley-Cooper, John. *A Salmon Fisher's Odyssey*. London: H. F. & G. Witherby Ltd., 1982.

Babcock, John Pease. *The Game Fishes of British Columbia*. Victoria: Bureau of Provincial Information, Bulletin No. 25, second printing, 1910.

Bergman, Ray. *Just Fishing*. New York: Alfred A. Knopf, Inc., 14th printing, 1961.

Chan, Brian M. *Flyfishing Strategies for Stillwaters*. Kamloops: Privately printed, 1991.

Combs, Trey. *Steelhead Fly Fishing and Flies*. Portland: Frank Amato Publications, Inc., second printing, 1978.

Darbee, Harry and Austin M. Francis. *Catskill Flytier*. New York: J. B. Lippincott, 1977.

Davy, Alfred G., ed. *"The Gilly": A Flyfisher's Guide to British Columbia*. Kelowna: British Columbia Federation of Fly fishers, 1985.

Edson, J. Leonard. *Flies*. New York: A. S. Barnes and Co., 1950.

Farson, Negley. *Going Fishing*. London: Clive Holloway Books, second edition, 1981.

Grantham, Ron., ed. *Totem Topics: 25th Anniversary Edition*. Vancouver: Totem Flyfishers, 1993.

Haig-Brown, Roderick. L. *The Western Angler*. Vol. I & II. New York: The Derrydale Press, 1939.

——. *A River Never Sleeps*. New York: William Morrow & Co., 1946.

——. *Fisherman's Spring*. New York: William Morrow & Co., 1951.

——. *Fisherman's Summer*. New York: William Morrow & Co., 1959.

——. *Fisherman's Fall*. New York: William Morrow & Co., 1964.

Hames, Jack. *Field Notes: An Environmental History*. Courtenay: Privately printed by Gertrude Hames, 1990.

Hutchison, Bruce. *The Fraser*. Toronto: Clark, Irwin & Co., 1950.

Kelson, Geo. M., *The Salmon Fly*. Goshen: The Angler's and Shooter's Press, 1979 reprint.

Loewen, Gen. Sir Charles F. *Fly Fishing Flies*. Toronto: Pagurian Press Limited, 1978.

Lord, John Keast. *The Naturalist in Vancouver Island and British Columbia*. Vol. 1. London: Richard Bentley, 1866.

Lingren, Arthur J. *My Steelhead Flies*. Vancouver: Privately printed, 1989.

——. *Fly Patterns of Roderick Haig-Brown*. Portland: Frank Amato Publications, 1993.

Luard, G. D. *Fishing Adventures in Canada and U.S.A.* London: Faber and Faber Ltd., 1950

MacFie, Matthew. *Vancouver Island and British Columbia*. Toronto: Coles Publishing Co., 1972 reprint.

Murray, Allan, ed. *Our Wildlife Heritage*. Victoria: The Centennial Wildlife Society of British Columbia, 1987.

Oglesby, Arthur. *Salmon*. London: Macdonald and Company Ltd., 1971.

Orvis, Charles F. & A. Nelson Cheney. *Fishing with the Fly*. 1st Tuttle. Rutland & Tokyo: Charles E. Tuttle Co., 1968.

Paterson, Wilma & Peter Behan. *Salmon & Women*. London: H.F. & G. Witherby Ltd., 1990.

Patrick, Roy A. *Pacific Northwest Fly Patterns*. Seattle: Patrick's Fly Shop, 1958; 1964.

Pochin, W. F. *Angling and Hunting in British Columbia*. Vancouver: Sun Directories Ltd., 1946.

Raymond, Steve. *Kamloops*. New York: Winchester Press, 1971.

——. *Kamloops*. Portland: Frank Amato Publications, revised edition, 1980.

——. *Kamloops*. Portland: Frank Amato Publications, third edition, 1994.

Read, Stanley E. *Tommy Brayshaw: The Ardent Angler-Artist*. Vancouver: University of British Columbia Press, 1977.

Richardson, Lee. *Lee Richardson's BC*. Forest Grove: Champoeg Press, 1978.

Righyni, R. V. *Advanced Salmon Fishing*. London: Macdonald & Co. Ltd., 1973.

Rogers, Sir John. *Sport in Vancouver and Newfoundland*. London: Chapman and Hall, Ltd., 1912

Roskelley, Fenton, ed. *Flies of the Northwest*. Portland: Frank Amato Publications, 1986.

Shaw, Jack. *Fly Fish the Trout Lakes*. Canada: Mitchell Press Ltd., 1976.

——. *Tying Flies for Trophy Trout*. Surrey: Heritage House Publishing Ltd., 1991.

Seton-Karr, H. W. *Bear-Hunting in the White Mountains or Alaska and British Columbia Revisited*. London: Chapman and Hall, Limited, 1891.

Surette, Dick. *Trout and Salmon Fly Index*. Rev. ed. Harrisburg: Stackpole Books, 1978.

Tavener, Eric. *Salmon Fishing*. London: Seeley, Service & Co. Limited, 1948 reprint.

Vachell, Horace A. *Life and Sport on the Pacific Slope*. London: Hodder and Stoughton, 1900.

Van Fleet, Clark C. *Steelhead to a Fly*. Boston or Toronto: Little Brown & Company, 1951.

Walton, Izaak and Charles Cotton. *The Compleat Angler*. London: J.S. Dove, 1676 edition, Sir John Hawkins' reprint, 1825.

Wells, Oliver. *General Report on the Cowichan Valley*. Victoria: Colonial Secretary's Office, 1860.

Whitehouse, Francis C. *Sport Fishes of Western Canada and Some Others*. Toronto: McClelland & Stewart Ltd., third printing, 1946.

Williams, A. Bryan. *Rod & Creel in British Columbia*. Vancouver: Progress Publishing Company, 1919.

——. *Game Trails in British Columbia*. New York: Charles Scribner's Sons, 1925.

——. *Fish and Game in British Columbia*. Vancouver: Sun Directories Ltd., 1935.

Williams, A. Courtenay. *Trout Flies*. London: A. & C. Black, Ltd., 1932.

Periodicals

Egan, Van. "The Black & Blue." *Totem Topics*, 80 (1987): 5.

Chan, Brian. "Confessions of a . . . Chironomid Addict." *Fly Lines*, 47 (1991): 9-10.

Lingren, Art. "Of Anglers & Angles... A Portrait of People, Places & Things: Earl Anderson." *Fly Lines*, 54 (1993): 7-9.

——. "Of Anglers & Angles... A Portrait of People, Places & Things: Denny Boulton." *Fly Lines*, 55 (1993): 11-13.

——. "Of Anglers & Angles... A Portrait of People, Places & Things: Capilano River...Then & Now." *Fly Lines*, 56 (1993): 10-11.

——. "Of Anglers & Angles... A Portrait of People, Places & Things: Wintle's Western Wizard." *Fly Lines*, 57 (1994): 15.

——. "Woolly Worm." *British Columbia Sport Fishing*, 9, 1, (1990): 68.

——. "British Columbia's First Dry Fly and the Capilano River." *British Columbia Sport Fishing*, 10, 2, (1991): 4-6, 32.

——. "Flies, Flies, Flies." *BC Fishing Directory & Atlas*. Port Coquitlam: Art Belhumeur, 1992.

Kilburn, Jim. "The Cowichan Brown." *Northwest Sportsman*, 25, 1, (1968): 4

——. "Tidewater Trout: Part 2." *Western Fish & Game*, 3, 4, (1968): 20-21, 53-59.

——. "The Lake: From Top to Bottom." *Western Fish & Game*, 4, 2, (1969): 10-11, 26, 44-47.

——. "Mayflies and the Armchair Angler." *Western Fish & Game*, 4, 3, (1969): 20-21, 50.

——. "The Way of the Sedge." *Western Fish & Game*, 4, 4, (1969): 12, 36-40.

——. "PKCK." *Western Fish & Game*, 6 , 1, (1971): 17, 46-47.

——. "Anderson Stone Nymph." *Western Fish & Game*, 6, 3, (1971): 8, 46-47.

——. "The British Columbia Flyfisher." *Western Fish & Wildlife*, 6, 6, (1971): 18, 45.

——. "The Caverhill Nymph." *Western Fish & Wildlife*, 10, 2, (1975): 12, 13.

Massey, John. "British Columbia Trout Have World-Wide Taste . . . But Like B.C. Flies Best!" *Northwest Sportsman*, 21, 7, (1966): 5-7.

Murray, Tom. "Popular Flies: The Tunkwanamid and the Cumming's Fancy." *Northwest Sportsman*, 32, 6, (1977): 6, 7.

——. "Popular Flies: Professor and the American Coachman." *Northwest Sportsman*, 32, 5, (1976): 6.

Railton, Jim. *B.C.'s Fresh Water Fishing Guide*, *Northwest Sportsman*, 27, 7, (1972)

Raptis, Loucus. "The Gomphus That is Not." *The Steelhead Bee*, 13, 4, (1994): 2-7

Tolley, Martin H. "Popular Flies: Cumming's Fancy." *Northwest Sportsman*, 23, 6, (1968): 8

——. "Popular Flies: Tom Thumb." *Northwest Sportsman*, 23, 7, (1968): 5

——. "Popular Flies: Black O' Lindsay." *Northwest Sportsman*, 24, 10, (1968): 6

——. "Popular Flies: Colonel Carey." *Northwest Sportsman*, 24, 12, (1968): 7

Vincent, Jack. "The 'What Else' Fly." *Western Fish & Game*, 4 , 4, (1969): 24, 25, 53.